I want to acknowledge that many recipes in this book would not have existed or would have evolved differently if not for sugar and spice imports that were made possible due to brutality and slavery by companies like the Dutch East India Company (VOC) and private individuals. Sugar and spices had a cost, and that cost was paid by those held in bondage.

These recipes help tell this story and the social and political history of our world, and the desire people had, and continue to have, for spices and sweetness. Belgium, the Netherlands and Germany switched their primary sugar production to domestic beet sugar in the 19th century, which was an economic decision.

Dark Rye AND Honey Cake

Words and photography

Regula Ysewijn

Illustrations by
Bruno Vergauwen

weldon**owen**

Foreword

This is a gorgeous book. It's a book full of recipes I want to cook, foods I want to eat, and pictures I want to lose myself in for hours on end. It is also a fascinating read, a love letter to the culinary heritage and rich social history of the Low Countries, and an at times intimate glimpse into the personal journey Regula has undertaken over the past several years.

What do I, a British historian, know of the history of Belgium and the Low Countries? Bits and pieces. I studied the wars of the 17th and 18th centuries in school and know a great deal about the highly specific topic of Vauban's barrier fortresses. I read about European political history at university and have a superficial knowledge about how the areas now contained within northern France, Belgium and the Netherlands were torn apart and apportioned to different countries regardless of the desires and identities of the populations living there. And I fell in love with the incredible artistic outpourings from mainly Flemish artists of the early modern era, so unique in style and subject, and so useful to the food historian. Many of the paintings illustrated in this book are like old friends to me, from Bruegel to Peeters, from *banketletter* to *peperkoek*.

The joy of this book is that now I know more. Regula's writing, as lyrical as always, has opened my eyes to the ways in which language and politics are so intertwined in the culture of the Low Countries, and how this feeds directly into its baking heritage. She's enriched my knowledge of everyday bakes and also explained what I'm seeing when I drool over long-gone tarts and cookies in the paintings I thought I knew so well.

Then there are the photographs, which avid readers of Regula's books have come to expect to be beautiful. She's always had an Old Masterish touch, and the pictures here are like Rembrandts come to life. We walk with her through the history of baking, and through the towns and villages of her native country. The fact that her love of Belgian bakes has grown so gradually is reflected throughout, and each word, each recipe, and each picture unfolds like a story being told.

Reading Regula's introduction I am struck by how much we have all lost in the last few years, and yet how loss may also turn to gain. Between Brexit and Covid, the easy, open relationship between Britain and its continental neighbors has been redrawn. Those who, like myself and Regula, lived happily with a small part of ourselves wedded to a different country have had to turn inward, and question what makes us who we are. So while this book is a history book, and a recipe book, and a book of beautiful pictures, it is also a statement of hope. For in letting go, just a little, of her love for England, Regula has shone a powerful light on Belgium. If just a little of what comes from the current turmoil is as glorious as this, then the future may be bright indeed.

Dr Annie Gray, historian

CONTENTS

RECIPES

"Be gracious and good to the whole world"

These words begin a 17th-century cookery manuscript (known as the *Brabants kookboek*) that is held in the Hendrik Conscience Heritage Library in Antwerp, where I spent many hours working on this book.

They are unusual for a cookbook, more akin to words of wisdom shared by a grandmother. Maybe this is exactly what this is. Handwritten cookery notebooks are usually family heirlooms: many are started by one person and passed on to be continued by subsequent generations of cooks.

The discovery of this manuscript was memorable because of its age and that nearly all of it was in Dutch. That it comes from the region where I was born gave me a connection to it. Reading through the fragile pages, studying the handwriting, it made me think about the women who owned this manuscript. I imagined sometimes that they were my ancestors, filling a gap in my own history, because I do not have recipes that have been passed down through generations. I was born into a family where food was there to cook and eat but not to discover, savor, and note down.

I often wonder what would have happened if my mother had been a keen cook or baker. Would I have had cookbooks to play with and guide me when I first started to take an interest in food? Or would I have taken cooking for granted because it was right there and not missed and wondered about? Perhaps everything that happened and didn't happen – the books, spices, cake tins, and guidance I didn't have – was exactly as it should have been for me to become the person I am today.

By contrast, all my early childhood memories are connected one way or another to the food on our travels. I assumed that culinary revelry was something for holidays abroad. The greatest gift my parents ever gave me was to take me on travels around Hungary, the Czech Republic, Switzerland, Austria, and later England, Wales, and Scotland. At home in Belgium, the food was dull, the vegetables boiled to death eighties-style, stripped of flavor and texture, no pepper, no salt, just thyme from a jar that probably still isn't empty today, twenty years

on. Food was never embellished. It was there to sustain you without filling you with joy. Puritan. Like Victorian nursery food.

Crossing the border on our trips in summer therefore felt like switching from black and white to technicolor. It was a revelation of flavors and scents.

My previous books came from a childhood fascination with Britain, its history and its food culture, which turned into a lifelong passion. My infatuation with everything British provided me with an escape route from Belgium. Not only from the unimaginative food I associated with it, but also because in looking at your own country, you also see its faults.

In Belgium you can never escape the issues of Flanders versus Wallonia and our language divide (see page 15), which caused, and still causes, so much upheaval. I didn't understand our complicated history and politics, as so very few people here do. I fled into the world of Jane Austen and Charlotte Brontë and fed my Anglophilia by the ladleful, unblemished by political and social issues that could cloud my view of perfect little Britain. To embrace my own country I needed to become a stranger looking in, just as I had been a stranger looking at British food and culture, unspoiled by the realities.

My book *Belgian Café Culture*, written after getting my Belgian beer sommelier degree in 2016, helped build the foundations for a pathway home. In a box of books from the late Alan Davidson's library, I found a Dutch-language cookbook from the 18th century. It persuaded me to look. From then on I started to collect and read centuries-old Dutch-language cookbooks, just as I had collected English cookbooks for the previous ten years.

Every cookbook and manuscript I read took a little part of the heart I had locked away from my country. As a writer you need to absolutely adore the subject or characters you are writing about. They need to take over your life, your dreams, every waking moment of your thoughts. In order to write the book and make it the best it can be, your heart not only needs to be in it – you need obsession.

'm noch ander

en peertaerte te maecken

n een criecktaerte te

uee taert te maecken

een taert van eÿeren

INTRODUCTION

I gave the culinary history and also the history of my country a place in my life, and gave it time to grow. It was like a seed I always had stored away in a box but never wanted to plant. And now that I had planted it, I wanted it to grow slowly and form deep and strong roots. That way the flower that would grow out of the seed would grow a tall stem that could take the gusts of wind. The flower is this book, and the stem is the years of finding my way home and the research that followed once the publisher who said no to this book in 2016, because she sensed I wasn't ready, said yes in 2020.

Before I could even start to write the book, I had to learn how our borders came to be, and how they have changed over the past eight hundred years. Because when looking at the history of this region, you cannot look solely at Belgium, a country that was only created in 1830 in an act of geopolitical cleverness.

A better way to look at the history of this region is to look at the Low Countries. Because when it comes to politics and also culinary customs, we share this history, these stories, and many traditions.

To write an overview of Low Country cuisine I'd need four times the number of pages I was granted, so this book focuses on the heart of the Low Countries where I was born and the influence it had on the wider Low Countries, who in their turn influenced this region.

Baking really shows the heart of a food culture. Towns proudly baking their *vlaai*, their *peperkoek*, or their regional *gebildbrot* – figurative-shaped bread for festive occasions. Baking traditions are the traditions that survive hard times, and manage to remain relevant in a modern day and age.

Be it Carnival or Saint Nicholas, Saint Martin, Christmas, or New Year's Eve, the people from the Low Countries made a fire and heated their ovens, waffle irons, and pans to bake their favorite festive treats.

PIETER BRUEGEL II (1564–1638): *The Battle between Carnival and Lent*, KMSK Brussels. This is a copy of a painting by his father, Pieter Bruegel the Elder.

A recipe for a feast

The first printed cookbook in the Dutch language, *Een notabel boecxken van cokeryen*, was published in Brussels in the early days of printing, around 1510. The whole book is dedicated to recipes for weddings, banquets, and other festivities.

That is why this book is arranged loosely by feast and festival, starting from the Twelve Days of Christmas, with waffles and winter breads; pancakes for Candlemas and Carnival; pretzels for Lent; *vlaai* and fried dough for *kermis* (fairs); and all the special sweet treats of Saint Nicholas and Saint Martin. A whole year of festival baking.

The importance of food in Flemish and Dutch art

For my research I didn't just look at six centuries of cookery texts; I also turned to art. Flemish and Dutch art of the 16th and 17th centuries places food in a central and allegorical place, which created a window into the past. With Pieter Bruegel the Elder as our guide, we witness *The Battle between Carnival and Lent*, showing the contrasting aspects of the celebrations.

Carnival is the period of self-indulgence that falls the week before the start of the forty-day period of abstinence (Lent) preceding Easter. It culminates on a day known in Dutch as Vastenavond, in German Fastnacht, Mardi Gras in French, and Shrove Tuesday in English.

In the painting shown opposite, coming from the left, the procession is headed by the personification of Carnival: a man crowned with a pie that is missing a piece, riding a wine barrel with a ham attached to its front by a knife. The fellow has clearly enjoyed many rich dinners and is wielding a spit with a hog's head, a large and smaller fowl, and sausages. Behind him walk masked and unmasked characters with candles, cooking utensils, or musical instruments. A nun is carrying a table on her head bearing a plate of pancakes, fine white bread buns, and waffles, and running at the back is a masked character with a plate of waffles and a child holding a *vollaard* (see page 72) under her arm and another type of cake in the other hand. The more you look at the painting, the more bizarre it becomes. In the foreground two men play dice next to a waffle, while one of the men has three waffles attached to his head. Immediately behind, in the background of the Carnival parade, a woman is baking waffles using a large black

waffle iron over an open fire with a tub of batter beside her.

By contrast, Lent is represented by an emaciated character – possibly a woman – seated on a chair on a cart, wearing a beehive (a symbol of divinity) as a hat and holding a bunch of twigs used for disciplining. Her spear in this jousting scene is a large baking paddle with two herring; behind her is a bowl of mussels, unleavened bread, and pretzels (which are associated with Lent). The main character is followed by people carrying flatbread on sticks: one has a plate with a herring on his head; another carries a sack of unleavened bread; and, in front of him, a woman carries a basket with bread and pretzels. While the other parade is surrounded by eggshells, meat bones, and a couple of playing cards, here there are only a few scattered mussel shells.

What Bruegel painted was never just a window into the lives of common people or religion. More than simply décor, it was a conversation starter when it was displayed prominently in people's homes, though we mainly see his works in museums today. In the matter of food, it might have served as a reminder of what was "traditional." Waffles and pancakes for Carnival; herring and pretzels during Lent. *Vlaai* as a sign of plenty in his *Netherlandish Proverbs* painting (see page 144). Golden rice pudding at weddings in his *Peasant Wedding* piece. A bit like seeing someone's Christmas cake on social media and being reminded to make your own.

In Belgium, a feast with a traditional banquet serving cured meats, sausages, fruit, vlaai, and rice pudding is still called a "Bruegel table" in honor of the artist's work.

Bruegel lived and worked and was most likely also born in my home town of Antwerp (though he also lived and worked in other places). Antwerp is significant not only in the life and work of Bruegel but also culturally and economically: it was the place to be in the Low Countries from the mid-14th century, when many of the baking traditions we still cherish today were starting to develop. Bruegel was surrounded by great minds and innovators of 16th-century Antwerp, such as humanist cartographer Abraham Ortelius, the influential printer Christoffel Plantijn, and art collector Nicolaes Jonghelinck, to name a few. In his incredible world atlas published in 1570, Ortelius called Antwerp not just the capital of this land but of the whole of Europe.

THE HEART OF THE LOW COUNTRIES

The Low Countries is a North Sea coastal region in northwestern Europe, forming the lower basin of the Rhine–Meuse–Scheldt river delta. Historically, the area includes current Belgium, the Netherlands, Luxembourg, French Flanders (now part of France), and the German border region. This is why we share parts of our food culture.

Much of the land for some distance inland is either below sea level or just slightly above it, hence the "low" in Low Countries, but also the name Flanders. "Flemish" and "Flanders" come from the Low German *Flauma*, for "flooded land," because the area is a landscape of polders and moors. This influences the growing of hardier crops, such as rye, barley, and buckwheat, which in turn influences the development of the baking culture.

In medieval times, the Low Countries were divided into numerous semi-independent duchies, which eventually – after a lot of wars and revolts – turned into the countries we know today. Because of its geographical location and access to the sea, the region saw very early economical development.

In this book I'm focusing on the heart of the Low Countries – the region of current Belgium – with expeditions into French Flanders, Germany, and the Netherlands, because baking doesn't know any borders and borders have shifted while culture has remained in place. You can change the name and ownership of a region, but you cannot change its customs. Hence we share *vlaai* in Dutch and Flemish Limburg and filled waffles in West Flanders and French Flanders, to name just two examples.

■ 15TH CENTURY
■ PRESENT DAY

LANGUAGE BORDERS

I grew up in Flanders (formerly called Brabant), the Dutch-speaking part of Belgium. Despite the common language, Dutch and Flemish people tend to use different words for things and have different meanings for words, too, which can lead to confusion and hilarity. We also have different accents. This means that while we share the same language we have two *natiolects*: Netherlandic Dutch and Flemish Dutch.

The Germanic Frankish language is the origin of the Dutch language, but it also left its imprint on French, which is Romanic with a lot of Germanic influences.

While a lot of Dutch people claim, in a form of linguistic nationalism, that Netherlandic Dutch is the main language and Flemish Dutch is merely a dialect, the Dutch language was in reality born in medieval Flanders. The earliest surviving complete text in Dutch was found in the Flemish city of Gent (Ghent) and dates to 1236 (*In der sieker dienste: de Statuten van de Leprozerie van Gent*). Nearly all of the 13th-century texts in Dutch came from Bruges, which, together with Ghent, was one of the most important cities in the Low Countries at that time.[1] The contemporary name for the language was not "Dutch" nor "Flemish," but "Diets." While in Dutch the name of the modern language is "Nederlands," the English name "Dutch" has far more linguistic relation to "Diets." It was a printer from Ghent, Joos Lambrecht, who first used the term "Nederlandsch" for the language in his *Nederlandsche Spellijnghe*, printed in 1550.

When abroad I'm often addressed in French when I tell people I'm Belgian. When I tell them I speak Dutch, they cannot understand because then they assume I am Dutch. Belgium actually has three official languages: apart from Dutch and French there is also a German-speaking minority in eastern Wallonia. This region is Ostbelgien and was annexed after the First World War. Our rather confusing government consists of the Flemish, Walloon, and Brussels governments, who each has its parliament too. Then there are the county commissions: the Flemish, the Walloon–French, and the Walloon–German. This is so confusing that most Belgians do not understand how it works. There is also a constant power play between the French and Flemish politicians.

From 1430, French became the language of the Flemish court with the arrival of the dukes of Burgundy. Frenchification of the high bourgeoisie in the cities of the Southern Netherlands did happen, especially with the Austrian acquisition of the former Spanish Netherlands in 1714. From the 18th century, French had become the language of the elite all over Europe.

Even though French was the upper-class lingo, early cookery books and manuscripts of Flanders, Brabant, and the Netherlands were in Dutch. This shows that however posh it was to speak French, it did not replace the local language or dialects.

When Napoleon annexed the Southern Netherlands, he forbade the use of any language other than French in official institutions, such as the law. After his defeat at Waterloo in 1815, the current territories of Belgium, the Netherlands, and Luxembourg became again unified as the United Kingdom of the Netherlands under King Willem I. He enacted a law in 1819 that all official institutions were to use the Dutch language, which of course annoyed the French-speaking elite. Willem I founded the universities of Ghent and Liège and invested in education in Dutch to improve the intellectual development of the Dutch-speaking people in the south of the kingdom, an area which later became Belgium.[1]

There were not only precarious religious issues, as the south had remained Catholic while the north was Protestant, but also an economic divide between the north and the Southern Netherlands. Even the government swapped locations every six months, between Brussels in the south and Den Haag (The Hague) in the north, to keep everyone happy or "keep the church in the middle," as we say in Dutch.

I'll write in more detail about this later when I get into the rise and fall of prosperous Antwerp that led to the "golden century" of Amsterdam (see pages 22–27).

The focus in the northern Netherlands was on its long stretch of sea, allowing shipping and bringing the riches and trade connected to colonization. The south had more crafts, cottage industries, and agriculture. Willem I provided funds to develop an industry in the Southern Netherlands.

The birth of Belgium

The bourgeoisie of the Southern Netherlands (what is currently Belgium), Catholic and French-speaking, were looking at the French revolutions when the Republic was overthrown and replaced by a constitutional monarchy with Louis XVIII. The bourgeoisie wanted to break away from the Dutch Willem I and become independent. In 1830 an uprising broke out during a performance of *La muette de Portici*, an opera about a revolt in Napoli (Naples) against an unlawful (Spanish) king.

The working class in the Southern Netherlands was struggling, and they blamed those in charge, so this was just a match to light the bonfire that had been sitting there waiting to be lit. This political strife is what ended the United Kingdom of the Netherlands: even though most of the people shared a language and much of a food culture, there were too many other differences – especially according to the French-speaking bourgeoisie – to unify us into one single nation.

In 1831, the German Leopold of Saxe-Coburg and Gotha, who had British nationality by his marriage to the crown princess of England, was elected head of state at the National Congress. On 21 July, he took the oath as the first king of the Belgians. The new King Leopold of Belgium was everyone's friend and spoke German, English, French, and some Russian, but not the language most of his people spoke: Dutch.

The language border

Systematic discrimination against working-class people by the French-speaking elite had led to great social inequality. The freedom of language in Belgium was used by the government as the right to use French, as Dutch was not regarded as a proper language. Flemish people who did not speak French – the majority of people in Belgium – were treated as second-class citizens.

The most extreme way to belittle people is to use language as intellectual warfare. Flemish people spoke only Dutch, which kept them from being able to understand their rights under the rule of law and raise their social status, as education too was only in French.

The Flemish movement was initially a cultural movement, with many French-speaking elite connected to it, but from 1840 onwards, a number of Flemish supporters also started formulating political demands.

When in 1860 two innocent Flemish men were convicted for murder because they could not defend themselves as they were unable to speak or understand French, they were decapitated on the Grote Markt (Grand Place) in Charleroi. This gave the Flemish movement something very important: martyrs for the cause. It was proof of the disregard the French-speaking elite had for common working-class people, especially those who spoke Dutch.

The politician Edward Coremans was one of the people who condemned the inequalities and discrimination against Flemish people. He submitted a bill to have the communication and publication of laws in both French and Dutch in 1895. In 1896, he stated in a speech in parliament that the Flemish people, which then numbered 2,700,000 individuals understanding exclusively Dutch, find themselves in the unjust and tyrannical situation of having to obey laws that they cannot read or understand! The equality law bill was passed on 19 November 1896. The Belgian Constitution, however, would not receive an official Dutch translation until as recently as 1967.

In the past the language border delineated social status, differentiating the upper class who spoke French from the working class who spoke Dutch or Walloon. Today the border runs geographically through Belgium and it no longer forms a barrier between upper and lower class, but between Dutch- and French-speaking people of largely the same social standard. This is misleading, because the working-class people of Wallonia were equally discriminated against by the French-speaking elite. It was never about Wallonia against Flanders; it was the centuries-old disdain of the rich for the poor.

But because the Flemish had to defend their language and beg for basic human rights, which is something French-speaking Walloons did not experience, this epoch weighs much more heavily in Flemish history. And it is much more politically and culturally loaded. If the difference were not language but skin color, it would have a name.

Wallonia, the region where French-speaking Belgians live, used to have a thriving economy during the Industrial Revolution, second only to the United Kingdom. Its extensive deposits of coal and iron allowed Wallonia to build an industry and, for just over a century after Belgium was created, Wallonia was the prosperous side of Belgium, while in Flanders people starved. Many Flemish moved away from "Poor Flanders" to regions with factories, such as Wallonia or northern France.

The heavy industry collapsed after the Second World War, and Wallonia declined economically. The closing of the precious coal mines was another blow. Since then, Wallonia has had a very high rate of unemployment; in fact, Alain Gerlache, journalist for the French-language Belgian communications group RTBF, has stated that in Wallonia there are people being born into families where the parents have never done a day's work, creating a cycle of unemployment and a *situation désespérée* with no prospects.[2] Meanwhile Flanders has managed to better itself, and wealth has shifted from Wallonia to Flanders. Not bad for a people who just decades before had been fighting for their language and enough money for their next meal.

Today common Flemish and Walloons divide themselves by stereotyping each other. Because Wallonia can't seem to get out of its economic hardship, some Flemish people think Walloons just don't want to work. Equally, some Walloons think Flemish people hate them, possibly because they are worried Flemish people think of Wallonia when they think about the French-speaking elite that kept them down. Some Walloons also think all Flemish people collaborated with the enemy during the Second World War, though there were also people in Wallonia who collaborated. It is true that the resistance in Wallonia was strong, but it also existed in Flanders. This could easily be solved by bringing us together around a table to see that we aren't so different when it comes to our food customs, which could be a unifier.

Instead we each have our own newspapers, magazines, TV channels – heck, we even have a separate *Bake Off*. This division is our greatest tragedy, but suits the political landscape perfectly. To use the words of a revered Belgian author, Tom Lanoye:

"Belgium consists of two separate countries: the Belgians on the one side, and their politicians on the other."

The fact that each language community has its own parliament strengthens the idea that Belgium is not united. Many German-speaking Belgians do not feel as though they are Walloon; Andreas Kockartz, journalist for the Flemish broadcaster VRT has stated: *"Wir sind Belgen aber keine Walloonen* [We are Belgians but not Walloons]."[3]

The creation of a national identity and cuisine

To legitimize Belgium's independence from the Netherlands, but especially from France, Belgium needed a collective past.

The greatest common memory is the "Battle of the Golden Spurs," which happened in 1302: also known as "that time we beat the French oppressor." The reality is that it wasn't history that taught me about this, it was literature. Even my school used the story created in literature and not the history books to teach us about our history. Tricky business.

Hendrik Conscience wrote *The Lion of Flanders*, a romanticized tale about the Battle of the Golden Spurs. He wrote it in 1838 at a time when newly founded Belgium was looking for its identity. An identity, cultural or culinary, is something we as humans seem to need as much as the air we breathe.

While the Belgian government wanted to make it all about Belgian patriotism, what Conscience unknowingly did was take this battle and make it all about the struggle for Flemish power and the power of the people. In his story, the battle was about getting rid of the French (which can be interpreted as all people who speak French, rather than those from France). Yet one of his protagonists, Guy of Namur, was from Namur, which is in present-day Wallonia. French-speaking people fought with the Flemish rebels against the French occupier.

Conscience, as part of the Belgian Romantic movement, took a large artistic license to make the story more epic and based his story not on the early sources in Latin, which he could not read, but on the already romanticized chronicles from the 15th century, when the battle was already mythical. Without it being the author's intent per se, the book has contributed strongly to the growth of the Flemish movement in the 19th century, even though the book was used as an example of Belgian strength, rather than Flemish, at the time it was published. Belgium needed a PR campaign; it needed to convince its people that they had an identity and that started with the name Belgium, which is, like Conscience's story, also partly based on reality. "Belgium" comes from "Belgae," a group of tribes living in northern Gaul during Roman times. And we get taught in school that Julius Caesar once spoke the words, "the Belgae are the bravest of all Gauls." So we have a good story to justify the name.

In reality Caesar's comment did not stop there. In the *Bellum Gallicum* it reads further:

> because they are the furthest removed from the culture and finer civilisation of the provincia, fewer merchants travel to them and thus by their import (of goods) incite sluggish spirits, and they are close by the Germanic tribes who live across the Rhine, with whom they are constantly at war.

This puts the great compliment on which the name Belgium is founded into perspective, and I can conclude with the words of Caesar himself on this:

> *Fere libenter homines id quod volunt credunt.*
> (People like to believe what they want to believe.)

And people are also selective in their memory – how they want to remember things, or want other people to remember them.

Ambiorix, our Belgae hero, supposedly slaughtered a Roman legion, although there is actually no archaeological proof of the battle. It isn't even certain that Ambiorix existed at all. Caesar's words about the brave Belgae, the hero Ambiorix, and the Battle of the Golden Spurs were used after 1830 to create an alternative history and a sense of Belgian identity. Belgian, not Flemish, and that's important to note.

This new Belgian history was being forged in other ways as well. In 1831 Gérard Le Grelle became the only directly elected mayor of Antwerp. In 1840 he founded the Rubens festival in the town, in memory of the famous painter, to stimulate the growth of a Belgian identity, which was at that time nonexistent. Belgium had been founded just ten years earlier.

The French-speaking elite of Brussels were copying Paris: French restaurants were opened, headed by French chefs, and the menus and dishes were all French. The luxury French restaurant was the new trend. There is a saying in Belgium: "If it rains in Paris, it drizzles in Brussels."

Nineteenth-century travel guides about Belgium write about French cuisine and its wines, and also mention German and English beers. Belgian beer, our national pride, was absent, and Belgian cuisine was nonexistent.

A travel guide from 1888 mentioned that in addition to luxury restaurants, there were also common restaurants in the alleys to the north of the Grote Markt in Brussels that were mainly visited by Belgians. The restaurants were good, according to the guide, serving oysters (not an exclusive luxury food at the time), steak, and mutton chops. Simple food, in contrast to the lavish dishes prepared *à la française* or *à la parisienne* in the high-society restaurants around the Stock Exchange. But simple food well prepared is worth its weight in gold, and that is also understood by the many new visitors to the city, with the rise of tourism.

The Brussels International Exposition of 1910 accelerated the trend for local restaurants, and more and more information was given in the press about Belgian cuisine, especially in France. Dishes were renamed with a regional flavor: *poussin Malines*, *waterzooi gantoise*, *truites de la Semois*. Travelers could now enjoy "local" cuisine as part of the experience. The culinary began to be part of the cultural.

Even French visitors, who previously enjoyed the posh restaurant scene, enjoyed the more common restaurants on Rue des Bouchers. Historian Peter Scholliers mentions in his book a magazine from 1930 which reports that the French love this lively area of the city, with its folk food houses where you can feast on mussels and chips for a fair price at marble tables covered with paper tablecloths and napkins. Thus our national dish was born.

Belgium took this newly created culinary culture to heart: after all, there is no better way to build identity than through culinary delights.

ANTWERP: SUGAR CAPITAL OF EUROPE

The name Antwerpen **came from a medieval legend that told how the Roman soldier Silvius Brabo saved the city from the terror of the giant Antigoon, who demanded a toll from people who wanted to pass the river Scheldt. When someone couldn't pay, the giant cut off their hand and threw it into the river. When Brabo defeated the giant, he chopped off Antigoon's hand and threw it into the river. "Throwing a hand" in Dutch is** *hand werpen*, **which became Antwerpen in the local dialect, where the H at the start of a word is silent. Or so the legend goes.**

Antwerp, built on a Gallo-Roman settlement, always had the ambition to become a great city, a metropolis of trade and arts and crafts. The city was strategically placed by the river Scheldt, which connected Antwerp to the sea. After the Zwin – a waterway formed by a storm in 1134, connecting inland Bruges to the sea – silted up, Bruges and nearby Damme declined and Antwerp grew in importance.

The spices and sugar that were an integral part of the further development of a baking culture were being traded on the Antwerp market from the end of the 15th century on. The earliest account of a sugar refinery in Antwerp can be found in 1508, with the name Jan de la Flie *suyckersierdere*.[4] By the 16th century, Antwerp had become the principal artery of the whole European economy,[5] and the city overtook Venice as the capital of sugar refining in Europe.[4]

In the 15th and 16th centuries, a shift came in the production areas of sugarcane. Up until the end of the Middle Ages, sugar plantations were situated in Sicily, the Levant, the east coast of the Mediterranean Sea, and Morocco, which was convenient to Venice. Promoted by Portugal and Spain, plantations grew in the Atlantic: the Canary Islands, Madeira, the Azores, Paraguay, Cape Verde, Sao Tomé, and later the Antilles, New Spain, and, most importantly, Brazil. Portugal chose Antwerp as its port of trade and processing.

By 1560 Antwerp counted at least twenty-five sugar refineries, but there could have been many more. A petition dated 1575 includes the names of twenty-eight sugar refiners.[4] At this time, the refineries were all situated in the center of the city, close to the river, in domestic buildings large enough to house an entire enterprise and with warehouse space to pack and dry the sugar loaves before they were ready for sale.

This is where the Suikerrui, or Sugar Canal, gets its name. The Sugar Canal stretches from the wharf to the city hall. Initially, it was just the first part that was called the Sugar Canal, while the other parts were called Salt Canal and Butter Canal, depending on the businesses nearby.

The harbor of Antwerp provided employment and allowed the import and export of luxury goods and cloth. Numerous skilled textile workers in Antwerp processed imported English cloth: nearly two-thirds of all cloth shipped from England went to Antwerp, often even more. This brought great traffic of well-taxed luxury goods back to England with the returning ships. Export was thriving; sugar and spices arrived from the Atlantic and were then transported overland to France, Germany, and over the Alps as far as Italy. Merchants from many parts of Europe gathered at the Antwerp market to buy and sell. One industry led to another. For example, sugar refining also called for the production of blue sugar paper to wrap the conical sugar loaves.

The Portuguese and Spanish grew sugarcane on their Atlantic islands and made use of enslaved labor on the plantations. In the 16th century, many African people were transported to European colonies in South and Central America.

Sugar arrived in Antwerp to be refined and traded, a trade from which Antwerp benefited greatly. It cannot be said, though, that Antwerp was built on the sugar trade, as sugar refining was just one of a myriad other crafts and trades. The combination of these trades, manufacturing, and crafts indeed made Antwerp attractive.

The golden years of Antwerp also came with massive urban expansion and development, partly thanks to land developer Gilbert Van Schoonbeke (1519–1556), who was responsible for one-third of the streets developed in Antwerp in the mid-16th century.

The English writer John Evelyn was lyrical about Antwerp in 1641:

Returning hence by the Shop of Plantine, I bought some bookes for the namesake only of that famous printer. But there was nothing about this city, which

SEBASTIAEN VRANCX (1573–1647): *Crane on the Antwerp Quay by the Frozen Schelde*, Rijksmuseum Amsterdam. Two children have vollaard loaves under their arms.

more ravishes me then those delicious shades and walkes of stately Trees, which renders the incomparably fortified Workes of the Towne one of the Sweetest places in Europe. Nor did I ever observe a more quiet, cleane, elegantly built, and civil place than this magnificent and famous City of Antwerp, which caused me to spent the next day in farther contemplation of it…

Van Schoonbeke is also paramount in the history of beer in Belgium and Antwerp, as he created a system to get clean water to the breweries he built in his Nieuwstad (New City). Thanks to the development of the brewery district, Antwerp evolved from a city that had to import beer to an export city. Around 1600, duties on beer accounted for more than 65 percent of the city's total income.[6] Beer, not sugar.

Because of the prosperity in Antwerp, there was so much work it created a whole new class system, unique at that point when everyone in Europe was either rich or destitute: a wealthy middle class. A reference from the period shows that even masons, carpenters, and other craftsmen could afford high rents and that there was a demand for luxurious clothing to mimic the nobles.[5]

This rich middle class had no titles or noble pedigrees, so the way in which they displayed their status was by the houses they owned, the clothes they wore, the art on their walls, and the finery and food on their table.

Antwerp was one of the largest markets for luxury household objects, especially those designed for the table, such as spoons, salt cellars, table bells, drinking jugs, and *roemer* (rummer) glasses. All of which we see appear in the work of Antwerpian still-life painters such as Clara Peeters (see page 195).

These fine tableware items reflected the owner's social status, as only the wealthiest could afford such frivolity. Gifting a couple of solid silver knives and spoons and then, later, cutlery sets, was, for years, a way of helping build the social status of a couple. If they had it to use, they could flaunt it; if they needed money, they could pawn it.

As with the art and frescoes on the dining-room walls of prominent figures in society, these decorated table items all helped with the orchestration of a dinner experience, where topics connected to the visuals could be discussed.[7]

This is also the age when people displayed costly tableware and pottery items, often delftware, without actually using them daily. They were there for validation of wealth only. Delftware tiles surrounded the hearth by the 17th century, because the fireplace gave much-sought-after warmth. The pieces placed on display on the mantelpiece were of great importance as people gathered around it. Today, we still place trophies on the mantelpiece for exactly that reason. The mantelpiece feels like an important location in the house: a place where we gather and where we display our most cherished works of art or a handmade gift from the kids in school, even if the fire is long gone.

By the 1570s, Antwerp was losing its monopoly on sugar refining, as many foreigners and locals who worked in the sugar refineries went abroad to start or help start refineries there, creating competition. The Antwerpian Konrad Rot founded the first sugar refinery in Augsburg, Germany, in 1573. In 1585, the sugar industry emerged in Hamburg, while Dresden followed in 1587.[8] Before this, everyone had imported their refined sugar from Antwerp, which is what kept Antwerp strong in the sugar trade.

The fall of Antwerp and the rise of Amsterdam
In 1576 disaster struck, and the city of Antwerp was looted by mutinous Spanish mercenaries, who murdered close to ten thousand (the actual number is a debated subject) men, women, and children, which at that time was almost 10 percent of the population. This horrendous massacre became known as the "Spanish Fury." In his 1977 book *The Dutch Revolt*, Geoffrey Parker called it "the holocaust of Antwerp."

Antwerp joined the alliance of the Pacification of Ghent, which united north and Southern Netherlands (current Belgium), both Catholics and Protestants, in the fight against the Spanish oppressor. In 1585, however, Antwerp was defeated by the Spanish steward Alexander Farnese after a yearlong siege. After the fall of Antwerp, about half of the population, especially the Protestants, fled the city and migrated to northern Netherlands towns like Middelburg, Haarlem, Leiden, Dordrecht, and, most importantly, Amsterdam. Smaller numbers fled to France, England, and German cities such as Hamburg, Aachen, and Cologne. English merchants, too, left Antwerp and moved to Middelburg.[9] The great

printmaker Christoffel Plantijn also fled from Antwerp, taking up a position at the University of Leiden, although he eventually returned to Antwerp, like many others, when things became less heated.

Antwerp's glory years in trade, arts, and sciences were over and focus shifted to the northern Netherlandish provinces. The Spanish soldiers also burnt the city records, which makes it impossible to grasp the full greatness of Antwerp's Golden Age today.

Cookbook and manuscript authors mentioned in this book, along with artists, merchants, and intellectuals, left Antwerp behind and contributed significantly to the start of the Dutch Golden Age. From then on, all important cookbooks were published in the Netherlands and especially Amsterdam, where previously cookbooks had come from the area of current Belgium.

More than the sugar trade spread with Southern Netherlandish emigration; other industries connected to the colonies also developed in the places where these Antwerpian refugees made their new homes. The influence of the city and port of Antwerp in the Low Countries might have declined when so many merchants and companies left. Still, Antwerp gained trade partners as its refugees set up their connections and businesses all over the Low Countries, France, and England and developed trade there. Many cities' economies flourished thanks to the Antwerp entrepreneurship, most impressively Amsterdam, which took over the crown as the center of Northern European trade and the capital of sugar.

Amsterdam
The Republic of the Seven United Netherlands was founded in 1588 during the Dutch revolt against Spanish rule. The Republic was a confederation of provinces, each with a governing official known as the *stadhouder* (stadtholder or steward), who was usually chosen from the royal House of Orange. Essential to our baking story is that honey cake (gingerbread) molds were often carved into stadhouder figures (see page 239).

The Dutch colonial empire was established when the Netherlands took control of several Spanish and Portuguese colonies. The Republic controlled a network of trade routes through its trading companies, the Dutch East India Company (Vereenigde Oost

Indische Compagnie; VOC) and the Dutch West India Company (Geoctrooieerde Westindische Compagnie; GWC). The income generated from this trade allowed the Republic to finance wars against France, England, Spain, and Portugal.

In 1684, 50 plantations were in Dutch, German, Portuguese, and French hands; by 1778, the number had risen to 450, enslaving around forty-five thousand people into hard labor or as house slaves. By the 18th century, coffee and cacao plantations had joined sugar plantations, feeding the taste for these commodities in Europe.

Joan Jacob Mauricius, who was the governor of Suriname from 1742 to 1751, condemned the misconduct of plantation owners in his poems. An anonymous play from 1771 entitled *The Surinam Life* also told a shocking tale of happenings on plantations. The poet Hendrik Schouten, married to an African woman, protested against racial inequalities in his poems. Paula Keijser wrote in 1985, in her book *Sugar Cane, Sugar Grief*, that although there was opposition to the conduct of plantation owners who lived like kings, actual slavery wasn't openly condemned until the end of the 18th or the start of the 19th century, when a movement was founded to end slavery in the Dutch West Indies. Yet, as Keijser writes, the Dutch publication *De Denker*, in 1764, includes a translation of a letter from an enslaved man to his brother outlining horrific actions by slave drivers, but then notes as justification that sugar would be too expensive if plantations didn't make use of enslaved labor.

The initiative for abolition in the European colonies came from Great Britain. In 1814, the Netherlands signed an international treaty to end the trade in enslaved people. In 1863, slavery was officially abolished in the main Dutch slave colony of Suriname, but it didn't have a large impact, as formerly enslaved people were bound by contract to continue to work on the plantations for at least ten years after the abolition. Meanwhile, teacups, plates, and sugar pots were printed with confronting images of slaves on plantations; sugar pots were branded with a "slave-free" label.

The Netherlands now has the Keti Koti (breaking the chains) festival, which commemorates the date when slavery was abolished in Suriname and the Dutch Antilles in 1863.

Treaty of Münster

The date of 15 May 1648 marks the final blow to Antwerp, when the Treaty of Münster ended the eighty-year war between Spain and the Republic of the Seven United Netherlands or the northern provinces. Antwerp, being in Brabant in Southern Netherlands, lost sovereignty over the river Scheldt to the Republic after a state border was established on the river. Ships could no longer get through and reach Antwerp.

In 1715 there were eighteen to twenty sugar refineries; by 1740 only four to five remained.[4] The difficulty was that raw sugar was no longer brought to Antwerp's shores from its country of origin; it had to come from Amsterdam, which meant Antwerp lost the best position, as there was a large tax to be paid on export to the Southern Netherlands. Antwerp tried to bypass the taxes by buying sugar via Ostend, but the transport through waterways would prove too inefficient and too expensive, as duties had to be paid to Bruges and Ghent. The refineries in Liège also had to import raw sugar from Holland or Zeeland, but they had the advantage of having coals for fuel produced locally, while Antwerp also had to import fuel.

In the following years, there were many mergers between family-owned sugar refineries, creating large sugar companies that made the stand-alone sugar refineries go out of business, as they could no longer compete. By the second half of the 18th century, the whole sugar business was in the hands of just a few companies. The landscape of sugar refining, which used to be mainly family-owned businesses, became monopolized. Because the quality of the end product declined, so did the demand for Antwerp refined sugar. Sugar refineries opened in Ghent and Brussels. By the last quarter of the 18th century, however, more sugar refineries opened all over current Belgium, led by a rise in sugar consumption.[4] The sugar trade, once focused on import and export, now became a domestic industry.

The noble family of Le Grelle founded the sugar refineries Huysmans & Cie in 1756. The family imported textiles, cacao, tea, porcelain, and sugar from England, China, and Portugal in collaboration with the Swedish East India Company. The first reference to the family can be found in 1670 when a Guillaume Le Grelle established himself as a *pasteibakker* (pastry chef) in Antwerp. Members of the family, especially Gérard

Etchings from *De suikerraffinadeur; of Volledige beschrijving van het suiker [The Sugar Refiner]*, by J.H. Reisig (Dordrecht, 1793).

Le Grelle, are responsible for a great part of Antwerp patrimony, several houses on the Meir, the Bourla Theatre, the riverside quay, castles all around Antwerp, and the Antwerp newspaper. Internationally, Gérard was also the architect of the "Iron Rhine" railway connection between Antwerp and Cologne.

From sugarcane to sugar beets
In 1806 Napoleon Bonaparte blocked all imports from England to the Continent with the continental blockade, which meant sugarcane could no longer get through. Napoleon forced French and Belgian farmers to grow sugar beets to become self-sufficient in sugar.

By 1812, conversion to sugar beets had reached fifteen sugar refineries in Antwerp.[4] However, after the blockade was lifted, most refineries turned back to sugarcane, which I find hard to grasp as beet sugar can be derived from a homegrown product, thereby avoiding import duties. But those import duties were lowered in the years after the blockade, and the number of sugar refineries grew again to at least fifty in 1833, only to fall

back to thirty-six one year later.[4] Germany had closed its borders for sugar and was producing its own sugar from sugar beets (see Lebkuchen on page 246).

The Belgian government saw that the sugar beet industry was good for the future, as it supported home agriculture. Protectionist politics grew all over Europe, and Belgian farmers were motivated to grow sugar beets. In 1843 came the *suikerwet*, a sugar law that taxed cane sugar much higher than beet sugar. The centuries-old sugarcane industry collapsed and gave way to the age of the sugar beet and cheap sugar. Recipes in cookbooks became sweeter and sweeter and new recipes were born as a direct result of the new brown beet sugar.

Brown sugar
Candico, one of Belgium's foremost sugar refineries today, was founded in 1832 in Antwerp as a sugar beet refinery. The refinery was a common sight when we drove to that part of town, and thanks to this book, I finally got to go in and see the process. They make *kandij* (brown sugar) by slowly heating white beet sugar

several times and resting it until it creates caramel-colored crystals that form around metal frames, which used to be threads woven through copper sugar-boiling kettles. The slower the sugar is heated, the bigger the sugar crystals.

What is left, after heating the sugar several times until the crystals are the required color – light or dark brown – is the *stroop* (syrup), black as coffee, intensely and uniquely flavored, and the iconic topping of our pancakes and filling of our waffles. It is as dark as molasses but with a gentle flavor more akin to British golden syrup.

A portion of the crystals is kept whole for some uses and the rest is ground into light or dark brown kandij sugar, also known as *cassonade* sugar. This lengthy process allows the sugar refinery to be self-sufficient and use up all of their product, as their only leftovers are the stroop, while other brown-sugar makers need to buy stroop or molasses to color their sugar brown instead of caramelizing it.

Cassonade or kandij sugar (the English term is candy sugar, which I find confusing) is not to be confused with brown *basterdsuiker,* which is popular in the Netherlands and other parts of the world. This is white sugar to which invert sugar is added to prevent hardening, colored with caramel to obtain brown sugar. This is a different product as the process is much less complicated and quicker than cassonade or kandij sugar, but it can also be used for the recipes that require brown sugar in this book. The invert sugar in the sugar will keep bakes moist for longer.

Another type of brown sugar is made by adding sugarcane molasses to refined white sugar – washing this type of sugar will reveal underlying white crystals. This is a process that is common in the United States.

People from Belgium have a taste for beet molasses, while other nations prefer the flavor of molasses that is derived from sugarcane. We have another type of sugar that is never used for baking but only for pancakes. *Cassonade Graeffe* brown sugar, invented by the Belgian Karl Graeffe, who founded a sugar factory in Brussels in 1859, is light brown sugar with a distinctive flavor and scent because it is not made according to the

Candico method used for kandij sugar but instead adds beet molasses to plain white sugar. Its unusual flavor and scent make it an acquired taste, though it is much adored in Belgium. As is the child on the packaging that baptized the sugar *kinnekessuiker* (children's sugar) in the vernacular.

In 1953, the company was bought by Raffinerie Tirlemontoise, which also owns Candico. Conscious of the sentimental value of the name cassonade Graeffe to Belgian consumers, Tirlemontoise decided not to change the name, just as they did not change Candico's name. And, hand on my heart, I would start a revolt if they changed the name of Candico. It seems we Belgians have a thing with brown kandij sugar that no other nation has: brown sugar is the main ingredient in many of our bakes. Whether you prefer kandij sugar or stroop (or both for me) or cassonade Graeffe on your pancake, it is deeply rooted in nostalgic memories of pancake baking at home. Both brands have not changed their packaging since before I was born, and all Belgians are emotionally attached to them. Maybe this attachment to sugar is something that is born out of our past, when sugar was so important.

Recipes & Essays

BRUNO VERGAUWEN *Carnival* (2022)

THE BELGIAN WAFFLE

In this book I am giving an overview of the landscape of waffles of the Low Countries. Winter is waffle time, as stated in *Huishoudelyk woordboek* (1743), and, indeed, waffles appear at all feasts from Saint Martin to Easter. The waffle is spotted in paintings depicting winter festivities as a clear symbol for revelry. Even for the generation of my dad, born in the 1950s, waffles still meant good cheer.

There is no such thing as "The Belgian Waffle," even though in America Belgian waffles are incredibly popular. There is a lot of confusion around which waffle is the true Belgian.

The US concept was born in New York in 1964 when the Belgian Vermersch family opened up their waffle palace on the grounds of the New York World's Fair in Queens. Although their sign said "Bel-Gem Brussels Waffles," people read it as "Belgian waffle." It was reported in magazines such as *National Geographic*, which showed a picture of a woman taking a bite from a thick Brussels waffle covered in cream and strawberries, stating "the Belgian waffle proves a gastronomical sensation."[10]

There are two things very wrong with this picture: the waffle served at the New York World's Fair was indeed from Belgium, but not from Brussels. It was a Flemish waffle (see page 40 for the recipe). Secondly, the World's Fair waffles were eaten as a street food, which is unacceptable behavior in Belgium, as this type of waffle is consumed either sitting down in a waffle house or tearoom or purchased at a *kermis* (fair), wrapped and taken home to be eaten there on a plate while properly seated. The Brussels or Flemish waffle is always covered with a dusting of confectioners' sugar, which explains why it is not a street food.

Before the Belgian waffle took America by storm, it was unthinkable in Belgium to sell the Brussels waffle as a street food, but with American tourists came a demand for Brussels waffles in the streets. It was a phenomenon in the 1990s that has fortunately dwindled today. There are still places offering waffles to go, but people will only get one once and then realize they look like they were in an explosion of confectioners' sugar and end up with a sticky face and hands from all the sweet toppings.

The Brussels waffle was born in 1874 with a recipe in a book by the revered chef Philippe Cauderlier, who wrote the first cookbook that featured a number of recipes with regional Belgian names, such as the Brussels waffle. This doesn't say the waffle was invented by him, because his friend, the Swiss pâtissier Florian Dasher, had already featured *"Grosse gaufre de Bruxelles"* on his business card from his bakery in Ghent.

Cauderlier, as well as Dasher, trained and lived in Brussels before moving to Ghent, where they both set up businesses. Cauderlier had a full and flourishing career behind him by the time he published his first book at the age of forty-nine. He was eighteen when Belgium became a country, which means he grew up in a time when a Belgian identity was being forged. Any gastronome would understand that local specialities are a big seller for any business or region, which would have impacted his choice to include recipes thought of as local in his books.

The original *Brusselse wafel* (Brussels waffle: see page 42), as explained by Cauderlier, is made by whipping up egg whites until stiff, which is what gives this waffle its volume and crisp exterior. Using whipped egg whites in this context was fairly new, as waffles up until then were made using beer, ale barm (a yeasty froth that is scooped off during beer making), or yeast as a leavening agent, or no leaven at all.

Original Brussels waffles were unsuitable for making at a fair, hospitality environment, or a bakery because the batter had to be freshly whipped up or the egg whites would collapse and the batter would be flat. The batter for the *Vlaamse wafel* (Flemish waffle), which contained yeast and whipped egg whites, could be made in advance and was less fickle. Kept in a fridge, it could be used throughout the day. As the Flemish and the Brussels waffle merged into one, few people still remember the name Flemish waffle. For the sake of history I have given the right recipe with the correct name for it on page 40. The Flemish waffle will thus contain yeast and the Brussels waffle will not.

Waffles from Liège
Another waffle that is often depicted when speaking of "The Belgian Waffle" is the *Luikse wafel* (Liège waffle: see page 44). While the Brussels and Flemish waffles are perfectly rectangular and golden, the Liège waffle is oval and golden brown, characterized by speckles of sugar nibs and generous thickness. The thickness is generally the same for the three waffles, though old waffle irons were less deep. The Liège waffle is the only waffle made to be eaten as a street food (not counting the *lacquemant*, page 54, which is fairground food). It is currently marketed in Belgian tourist areas as... The Belgian Waffle.

31

FROM A HOT IRON

In Belgium we have a dedicated glass for every type of beer, so it is not deemed extravagant to have a waffle iron with several interchangeable waffle plates, or several waffle irons so each waffle can be made in its traditional shape. I myself own four electric irons and several antique waffle irons too.

The material culture of waffles

The Gruuthusemuseum in Bruges holds two early 15th-century waffle irons in the collection: they are the oldest known waffle irons in the Low Countries and most likely even the world. One iron, dated by the museum between 1430 and 1450, is intricately carved with the coat of arms of the Burgundian duke John the Fearless on one side and the Star of David on the other side. The second iron has the coat of arms of Burgundian duke Philip the Good on one side and the Lamb of God on the other. These two irons are rectangular, and they do not show the grid pattern we associate with waffles today. In Germany I found a number of similar 15th-century irons,[11] and not just rectangular ones. A round iron is dated 1473 and has the coat of arms of the Archbishop of Salzburg; also in Salzburg is a rectangular iron with a crane, dated 1497. The most spectacularly carved one is a rectangular iron in Nuremberg showing a pelican and her young and a *Reichsadler* (imperial eagle) on one side and a Brunswick lion and entailed fish on the other, with a handy date – 1531 – carved in the middle. In the 16th and 17th centuries we find many more irons, and it is at this time when they are most intricately carved, showing the craftsmanship of the blacksmith who forged them.

In a manuscript from Antwerp dated to around 1580, a recipe for almond waffles calls for a *Ghentsch Yser*[12] "if you have one." It is the only mention of this type of iron so we have no idea how it looked and what kind of waffles it produced.

From the 18th century onward, the carvings become less expert and more naïve. My most prized and possibly oldest iron is naïvely carved, conveniently dated 1886 with the name Anna and a surname that has aged too much to make out (see the photograph on page 34). There is also a very simple tree and geographical shapes and knots. My round flat irons are all carved with simple flower-like illustrations.

It is very possible that there were just a small number of expert waffle-iron forgers who created the still surviving intricate irons from the earlier period and that people commissioned these folk artists especially. It is also very likely, given the subject of the carvings, that these stunning irons were owned by the elite and that they therefore wanted the best waffle-iron maker, just as they would have sought out the most skilled blacksmith for their swords.

As these carved irons became more common, more blacksmiths would have made them, not all of them as skilled as those who were commissioned by the elite. In paintings of the 16th century, by Bruegel for example, they show a different type of iron with the grid pattern we associate with waffles today. This doesn't say, however, that the elite didn't eat grid-patterned waffles, because cookery books of the time confirm that they did.

The design

The earliest waffle irons had long, elegant handles and are tong-shaped, the two iron plates connected by a hinge from the long side. From the 20th century, most irons changed: their handles became shorter, as they were no longer used on an open fire, but on a stove or a burner. The way the waffle iron opens also changed: the hinge that connected the two iron plates now opened from the short side instead. The advantage of earlier waffle irons was that you could place one end of a handle on the floor, while keeping the iron open to be filled with waffle batter, as can be seen in Joachim Beuckelaer's *A Dutch Kitchen Scene* (c. 1561–1570), a painting held by the National Trust in the Treasurer's House, York, UK – and also in the photograph opposite. You cannot do this with the more recent ones, which were clearly made with a kitchen and a burner in mind, rather than for use on an open fireplace or a fire outside. The earliest waffle iron kept the baking iron from touching the floor thanks to the way it opened; if you're using a recent version you'd need to put it on a stool or table.

Grid or decorative

There are two kinds of waffle irons: rectangular grid waffle irons and rectangular or round rimless flat irons that make paper-thin wafers, often engraved with a coat of arms, family and heraldic crests, city crests, mottos, wishes, and biblical scenes, but also the names of a

couple often in combination with a date and hearts, flowers, the tree of life,[11] and even windmills (on a Low Countries iron from the 18th century).

Another remarkable engraving in the irons is the house mark, or house logo, made from rune-like letters. The Gruuthuse also has an 18th-century flat iron with a "Happy New Year" motto engraved into it, and similar examples can be found in Germany too. Flat irons like these can also be found in Belgium, the Netherlands, Germany, France, and Scandinavia.

These rimless flat irons also exist with a very simple grid pattern, where the grid is more an engraving than indentations. The latter have become the most common in the last century, apart from in Scandinavia and Italy where electric waffle irons still depict a simplified version of old-style engravings.

The waffles baked in these flat irons are thin crisp wafers, which usually go by the name *nuwelen* (thin waffles) or *oblyen* in cookery texts up until the 17th century, after which *oublie* becomes the term used in French cookbooks and also in Dutch texts in the Low Countries. *Kniepertjes* or *knijpertjes*, which translates to "squeezies," also appear in Dutch cookery, referring to the action of squeezing the waffle iron to close it in order for the dough to bake, and bake thinly.

The wafers are called *Oblaten* in Germany, coming from the Latin word *oblata* for offerings, as thin wafers were used as communion Hosts. *Krumkake* is their name in Scandinavia and *pizzelle* in Italy. Usually these thin waffles or wafers are rolled up, as we can see in many Dutch Golden Age and Spanish and Italian paintings depicting sweets.

The second kind of waffle iron is the one we most associate with waffles today, with the grid pattern. There were different waffle grids, one deeper than the other, to make either thick waffles or thin waffles.

The different shapes for different waffles, such as the Liège, Brussels, and Flemish, only came to be in the 20th century when, like every Belgian beer needing its own glass, every Belgian waffle needed its own waffle iron. This created a further development of the material culture of waffle irons. The first electric waffle iron was sold in 1911 and was an instant hit because it meant no

more faffing around with the iron on the hob; however, it would take a couple of decades before electric waffle irons became affordable for every family.

My dad remembers when the electric waffle iron came into his life when he was a child. He laments that from then on baking waffles was less of an occasion. With an iron that needed to be held over an open fire or in a stove, the time-consuming process provided not only coveted waffles, but also something to do together as a family. With an electric waffle iron, no one had to tend the fire, keep an eye on the iron, cut away the excess batter from the sides or hold a plate in readiness to catch the baked waffle. From then on, mother made the waffles and no one watched until a stack of waffles appeared.

Waffles for New Year's, Easter, and weddings

Waffle irons were often forged and given as wedding presents (like the one pictured opposite, where the name Anna can be made out in the carving), but they also could have been gifts from one noble person to another. It is possible that the irons of the Burgundian dukes weren't owned by them, but were made as a gift to allies or in honor of the dukes for a certain celebration. One of them depicted the Lamb of God, which is an Easter theme. During the Middle Ages, the new year started at Easter in many parts of Western Europe. With the introduction of the Gregorian calendar, New Year's shifted to the first of January and the custom of baking waffles shifted with it. When genre and still-life paintings show wintertide, waffles always appear on the canvas. In many rural areas, the connection between Easter and the start of the year continued for centuries.

Waffles are eaten throughout winter but especially during the Twelve Days of Christmas, including at Epiphany on 6 January. In recent years Belgium has started to adopt the custom from France of eating *galette des rois* for Epiphany, commemorating the arrival of the Magi.

Because waffles were connected to feasting, they started being sold at Carnival and *kermis* (fairs) too. From the 19th century, opulent waffle palaces moved from town to town with the fair. You could have a waffle there, sitting down, not as a street food. Waffle houses (tearooms) were present in every town, and it became a custom around Christmastime to go out for a waffle with the family.

Waffles with beer 16th century

This recipe for thick beer waffles is one of three thick waffle recipes that I found in a 16th-century handwritten cookery manuscript from Ghent. Its title says "To make thick waffles you do not split," showing that some waffles were split and doused in butter, while these were left whole, though often also doused in butter. All three recipes are made with beer, which gives an interesting flavor note to the waffle. We cannot say exactly what 16th-century beer tasted like; as with many things, flavors, products, and manufacturing have changed over time. But in that period there were two kinds of beer in the region of Ghent: small beer and double beer with names like Crabbelaer and Clauwaert, the latter containing more alcohol. They were flavored with Gruit, a mixture of herbs that varied. Common herbs include sweet gale, yarrow, mugwort, horehound, ground ivy, and common heather, but spices were also added if they could be obtained. A beer with spice notes, or a low-alcohol table beer, would be perfect.

What is different from the 17th-century recipe (on the following page) is that this recipe doesn't create a batter, but makes a firmer dough and also calls for *veel suijckers alsoe dattet welsoet is* (lots of sugar). The author could either mean pounded loaf sugar, which is what we would recognize as confectioners' sugar, or pearl sugar (nib sugar). The latter makes the waffle more related to the thick waffle of Liège (see page 31); in fact, it could be its ancestor if pearl sugar is what the author meant. In any case, after testing the recipe I found that a combination of the two creates the best result.

Historical recipes, especially from this period, can be incredibly vague when it comes to quantities and instructions, and often omit essential ingredients like flour. This recipe was remarkably detailed, for its time. It gives a cue about the consistency of the dough – so that a spoon remains upright in it – and says that you should start half a day before you plan to bake. It even says to make a coal fire to heat your iron. Below is my modern translation, though as always I try to stay as close to the original as I can. The historical recipe makes about forty-two large waffles, but as they are best eaten fresh, I have given quantities for a sixth of the recipe. Feel free to double or multiply by six if you need to.

Makes about 7 large waffles (depending on your waffle iron)

¾ cup (175 g) unsalted butter

½ cup table beer (low-alcohol beer) or beer with spice notes

2 cups (250 g) all-purpose flour

2 Tbsp (25 g) confectioners' sugar

2 ¼ tsp (7 g) instant dry yeast

1 medium egg yolk

¾ cup (150 g) pearl sugar (nib sugar), lightly coated with vegetable oil to prevent the sugar from taking moisture from the batter

oil or lard, for greasing (if you don't have a nonstick waffle iron)

butter and sugar, for serving

Use a plain waffle iron plate (see page 260 for more information).

Melt the butter in a small saucepan over low heat, add the beer, then remove from the heat and set aside to cool until tepid.

Combine the flour, confectioners' sugar, and yeast in a large bowl or the bowl of an electric mixer fitted with the dough hook. Make a well in the center and add the egg yolk, followed by half the butter mixture. Mix until completely incorporated, then pour in the remaining butter mixture and mix well. Cover the bowl and set aside to rest for half a day.

Fold in the pearl sugar and divide the batter into 7 portions. The mixture will have the consistency of thick cake batter.

Preheat the waffle iron. Use a brush to grease the heated iron with oil or lard, if using. Spoon batter onto the waffle plate and close. Bake until golden brown (how long this takes depends on your iron, so check from time to time).

Serve warm with sweet butter if you like (but I find the waffles sweet enough without it). To make sweet butter, simply melt equal quantities of butter and sugar in a small saucepan over medium heat until the sugar has dissolved.

Keep leftover waffles in an airtight container. Waffles may be reheated in a hot waffle iron or simply in a toaster.

Waffles 17th century

Nothing sounds better than a recipe saying, "Hey, this is a recipe from the 17th century; make this to experience something that no longer exists today." In reality, we held on tightly to our historical waffle recipes, we treasured them and took them into the modern age where they are still relevant. If you really want to experience what a 17th century waffle tasted like, you need to bake it using a waffle iron held over an open fire. It takes elbow grease, smoke in your eyes, and sore hands, which is why men eventually took over the job of baking them.

My mum and dad just caught the end of the times when waffles were still baked with handheld waffle irons. My dad explains how his grandfather would bake them and the children would watch. There was no TV in the early sixties, so my dad and his siblings watched the waffle batter being made on the kitchen table, anticipating the rising of the mixture; then excitement came when the batter was poured from a ladle onto the hot iron. The iron was greased between bakes using a piece of wood with a cloth wrapped around the end to distribute lard. The grand finale came in the shape of a stack of waffles and the memory-invoking scent that filled the house. "Those were cozy evenings," my dad says, smiling. But the evenings of watching the waffles being baked ended when my grandmother had finally saved up enough money to buy her first electric waffle iron. Progress is not always positive, though I am grateful for electric waffle irons, and there isn't a family in Belgium that doesn't own one.

The recipe below is indeed a 17th-century recipe, taken and translated from the *Brabants kookboek*, the manuscript mentioned on page 10.

Makes about 20 waffles (depending on your waffle iron)

1 lb (500 g) salted butter

3 cups (700 ml) whole milk

5 ¾ cups (700 g) all-purpose flour

3 ¼ tsp (10 g) instant dry yeast or ale barm (see page 31)

1 Tbsp canola oil

6 medium egg yolks

oil or lard, for greasing (if you don't have a nonstick waffle iron)

Serving suggestions

unsalted butter

confectioners' sugar

whipped cream

fromage blanc (quark)

Use a plain waffle iron plate (see page 260 for more information).

Melt the butter into the milk in a small saucepan over low heat and let cool.

Combine the flour and yeast in a large bowl or the bowl of an electric mixer, make a well in the center, and pour in the oil and the egg yolks followed by half the butter and milk mixture. Mix until completely incorporated, then pour in the remaining butter and milk mixture and mix well.

Preheat a waffle iron and have your batter and a ladle ready, plus a brush to apply the oil or lard.

Grease the waffle iron if it is not nonstick. Ladle batter onto the waffle plate; you will figure out the amount of batter once you get to know your iron. Close and immediately turn the waffle iron 2–3 times (Belgian waffle irons rotate) so that the batter spreads evenly and all around.

Bake to a golden color (how long this takes depends on your iron, so check from time to time) and serve warm. Keep leftover waffles in an airtight container. Waffles may be reheated in a hot waffle iron or simply in a toaster.

The manuscript doesn't mention any serving suggestions, but in the 17th century waffles were usually served doused in melted butter. This is still a practice today, although in tearooms you usually get small packets of butter to spread onto your waffle. If you're lucky, the butter isn't stone cold and melts beautifully onto the crisp, hot waffle. You are more than welcome to serve these waffles dusted with confectioners' sugar and served with whipped cream or, my personal favorite topping, fromage blanc, which makes these waffles great for breakfast.

Vlaamse wafel now also known as Brussels waffles

The *Vlaamse wafel*, or Flemish waffle, is the largest waffle of the bunch: with its sharp corners and thickness, it almost looks like a caricature of itself. The waffle is made from a light yeast batter, made even lighter thanks to whipped egg whites and a dash of baking powder. When baked properly the exterior should be crisp and the interior soft.

This is my adaptation of the recipe for Flemish waffles by the father of Belgian cuisine, Philippe Cauderlier, who was the first chef after the creation of Belgium in 1830 to publish cookbooks containing recipes with Belgian regional names. With his books he helped build a Belgian culinary identity.

However, if you looked for this waffle today, you would not find it because somewhere in the early 20th century it was renamed "Brussels waffle," and the term "Flemish waffle" wholly disappeared. In cookery books from the last century, this waffle is usually named "batter waffle"; however, Vlaamse wafel is the most frequent dish with a Flemish heritage to appear in cookery books from before 1851. This was discovered by the Academie voor de Streekgebonden Gastronomie (ASG) in 2006. The reason we lost the name "Flemish waffle" is unknown, but I tend to blame our language divide in Belgium. This waffle is, after all, being marketed as "the Belgian waffle" abroad, and Brussels is our capital city, the city that is supposed to unify this country (see pages 30–31).

The proper way to eat the Flemish/Brussels waffle is sitting down in a tearoom for a special occasion: with the waffle on a plate, cutting off row by row and square by square of the waffle. My husband and I had waffles at our favorite waffle house after our civil wedding; that is how special it is!

Makes about 12 waffles in a deep iron and about 22 in a plain one

14 Tbsp (200 g) unsalted butter

3 ⅓ cups whole milk

4 medium eggs

4 cups (500 g) all-purpose flour

4 ¾ tsp (15 g) instant dry yeast

pinch of ground cinnamon

½ tsp salt

oil or lard, for greasing (if you don't have a nonstick waffle iron)

confectioners' sugar, for dusting

Serving suggestions

unsalted butter

whipped cream

fresh strawberries

Use a deep or plain waffle iron plate (see page 260 for more information).

Melt the butter into the milk in a small saucepan over low heat, then set aside to cool. Meanwhile, separate the eggs.

Combine the flour, yeast, and cinnamon in a large bowl or the bowl of an electric mixer, make a well in the center, and pour in the egg yolks followed by half the butter and milk mixture. Stir until completely incorporated, then add the salt and pour in the rest of the butter and milk mixture and mix well.

Whisk the egg whites to stiff peaks and fold them into the batter with large, gentle movements in order to keep in as much air as possible. Set the batter aside to rest for 1 hour at room temperature, or in the fridge until you need it.

Preheat your waffle iron to the hottest setting and have your batter and a cup measuring tool (which works perfectly for my iron size) ready.

Grease the waffle iron if it is not nonstick. Ladle batter onto the waffle plate swiftly, spreading it into all the holes. The deep iron will need 2 cups of batter, the plain one needs 1 cup. Close and immediately turn the waffle iron 2–3 times (Belgian waffle irons rotate) so that the batter spreads evenly and all around. Bake to a pale golden brown color, which will take just under 2 minutes.

Dust generously with confectioners' sugar before serving: this is a must because the waffle itself isn't sweet. Then offer toppings of butter to spread on top or whipped cream to pipe into the holes. I find fresh strawberries are too extravagant, but that is how the waffle was served at the New York World's Fair in 1964 (see page 30).

My husband and many other people like this waffle served in an old-fashioned, even historical, manner, topped with cold butter so it melts into the holes.

Brusselse wafel 19th century

This recipe is adapted from the first recipe for Brussels waffles published by Philippe Cauderlier in 1874. If you want the thick yeast-leavened Brussels waffle you remember from a trip to Belgium, you need to follow the recipe for Flemish waffles on the previous pages. Read about their history and the mix-up of their names on pages 30–31.

Brussels waffles are a treat saved for the first days of the new year. Traditionally my mum and dad and I, like so many Flemish families, would head to a famous tearoom in our town of Antwerp, situated at the corner of the high street and the Grand Place. We would have to queue for a table, and my dad would get nervous. As I remember it was always raining, and the tearoom was always too hot, too loud, too full, and smelling like wet carpet. But the thought of the waffle made me endure my father's nerves and the hurdle to get to that table. The waffle, baked to a golden color, arrived crisp on the outside and, if done right, still doughy on the inside, dusted generously with confectioners' sugar and finished with a dot of cold freshly whipped cream in each hole. As there is no sugar in the batter, the waffle benefits from the toppings; it is rather dull without them.

Makes about 10 waffles (depending on your waffle iron)

1 cup (250 g) unsalted butter

1 cup whole milk

1 cup cold water

3 ⅓ cups (400 g) all-purpose flour

⅔ cup (100 g) rice flour or ¾ cup (100 g) cornstarch

1 tsp salt

2 tsp ground cinnamon

4 medium eggs, separated

butter or lard, for greasing (if you don't have a nonstick waffle iron)

confectioners' sugar, for dusting

Serving suggestions

whipped cream

unsalted butter

fresh strawberries

platte kaas (thick quark)

Use a plain waffle iron plate (see page 260 for more information).

Melt the butter into the milk over low heat, then pour in the cold water to cool it down.

Combine both flours, salt, and cinnamon in a large bowl or the bowl of an electric mixer, make a well in the center, and pour in the egg yolks followed by half the milk and butter mixture. Mix until completely incorporated, then pour in the rest of the milk and butter mixture and mix well.

Let the batter rest while you get your waffle iron ready.

Whisk the egg whites to stiff peaks, then fold them into the batter with large, gentle movements in order to keep in as much air as possible.

Grease the waffle iron with butter or lard if it is not nonstick and ladle in the batter; you will figure out the amount of batter once you get to know your iron. Bake the waffles until golden (how long this takes depends on your iron, so check from time to time).

The best way to keep these waffles is to bake them and freeze them, then thaw for about 30 minutes and heat them up in a hot waffle iron. When kept in an airtight container they will still be good the next day when reheated.

Dust with a generous layer of confectioners' sugar.

Classic serving style
Pipe whipped cream into each hole and serve.

Another way
Many people prefer this waffle with butter instead of cream. Just spread soft butter all over the hot waffle so it melts. Scatter with strawberries if you like.

My way
For breakfast I prefer filling the holes with platte kaas (thick quark).

Luikse wafel

The *Luikse wafel* (Liège waffle) is the traditional street food waffle from Liège in Wallonia, where they call it *wafe* in Walloon, etymologically related to the Frankish *wafla* – as opposed to *gaufre* in modern French.

It wouldn't be an iconic bake without a good story: for the Liège waffle, the legend goes that its origin dates back to the 18th century when the Prince–Bishop of Liège asked his cook to create something sweet for him.

These waffles and their scent were a big part of my childhood in Antwerp, where they were sold from small waffle stands that were squeezed into buildings. While I associate the scent and experience of eating this waffle in the street with my home city, it was a phenomenon of the 1990s, and it's just my generation that has the scent imprinted on our memories. Today the scent has gone; even though a few waffle stalls remain, they aren't plentiful enough for the scent around town to be so significant. Today you will find the Liège waffle more represented in Ghent and Bruges, and less so in Liège.

When made well and baked twice – because baking it twice, as is done in street stands, caramelizes the sugar better – these waffles are an absolute delight. To experience a Liège waffle to the fullest, bake it and take it for a walk on a crisp winter day, holding it with a piece of paper as it warms your hands.

Makes 8 waffles

4 cups (500 g) bread flour

2 Tbsp (25 g) demerara (coarse raw) or superfine sugar

4 ¾ tsp (15 g) instant dry yeast

½ tsp ground cinnamon

½ cup water

3 ½ Tbsp whole milk

1 Tbsp runny honey

1 medium egg

½ tsp sea salt

⅛ tsp baking soda

1 cup (250 g) unsalted butter, softened

1 cup (200 g) pearl sugar (nib sugar), lightly coated with vegetable oil to prevent the sugar from taking moisture from the batter

butter or lard, for greasing (if you don't have a nonstick waffle iron)

Use a deep or plain waffle iron plate (see page 260 for more information).

Combine the flour, sugar, yeast, and cinnamon in a large bowl or the bowl of an electric mixer fitted with a dough hook. Pour in the water, milk, honey, and the egg and knead for 5 minutes. Let the dough rest for 5 minutes.

Add the salt and baking soda on one side and the softened butter in chunks on the other side and knead for 10 minutes. After 10 minutes gently knead in the pearl sugar so that it is well distributed throughout the dough, then let rest for 5 minutes. After resting, the dough will no longer appear wet and will have started to embrace the pearl sugar so the nibs no longer drop out.

Line a tray or large airtight container with parchment paper. Divide the dough into 8 pieces (about 5 ½ oz/150 g each) and place on the tray or in the container. Transfer to the fridge to proof slowly – overnight for the best flavor.

Take the dough out of the fridge 30 minutes before baking. Heat the waffle iron. Grease the waffle iron with butter or lard if it is not nonstick and bake the waffles until they are golden brown (how long that takes depends on your iron – mine take 5 minutes).

The first waffle will come out fairly clean, but the second will have some caramelization from the melting pearl sugar nibs, which is what you want. Greasing with butter or lard for every bake will create a nice layer of caramel on the outside of the waffle. There is nothing more disappointing than a Liège waffle without any caramel because the waffle baker is trying to keep the iron from getting sticky.

Transfer the baked waffles to a wire rack to cool. When ready to serve, reheat waffles as needed: this second time in the waffle iron will add some more caramel to the waffle. When cold, these waffles seem dense as bricks! Baked waffles that you don't eat straight away can be frozen, thawed overnight in the fridge, and heated up in a hot iron for that perfect fresh-baked experience.

Oublie

Oublies are paper-thin waffles, or wafers, that were popular at the banqueting table throughout the Middle Ages and up to the 19th century. "Oublie" (*"Oblaten"* in German) comes from the Latin *oblatus*, or "offering." Oblaten are hosts for communion, also used as a base for marchpane (marzipan) in the Middle Ages and Lebkuchen in Nuremberg.

These waffles don't just appear in cookery texts: they are plentiful not only in Flemish and Dutch 17th-century paintings, but also in Spanish and Italian still-life artworks. They were originally made in elaborately carved waffle irons, which could be rectangular or round. They were the privilege of the rich, forged for state banquets and weddings, with city crests, heraldic emblems, flowers, names, and biblical and folkloric scenes. Apart from round irons with flower carvings, I own a rare rectangular one from the 1800s that was forged for a wedding, with names and a date carved into it. The result is almost like a baked wedding card, using dough and a carved iron instead of ink, paper, and a printing press (see page 34).

Recipes vary in that either water or wine, or a mixture of the two, is used in early recipes, though later this becomes Cognac. Some recipes call for spices and rosewater. Eggs are also not always used. *Eenen Nyeuwen Coock Boeck*, printed in Antwerp in 1560, calls the waffles *Nuelen*, as in New Year's. These waffles were indeed connected to New Year's celebrations as *lukken* (see page 51), and the rolled *Nieuwjaarsrolletjes* (see page 48) still are. This recipe is adapted from a manuscript that is written into the blank pages of a 19th-century cookbook I own. The author calls them "Prauweltjes." These waffles are also called *kniepertjes* (squeezies) because they are made by squeezing the iron closed to get a perfect imprint from the carving.

**Makes 30 oublies,
5 inches in diameter**

½ cup (125 g) unsalted butter, plus extra for greasing

1 ¼ cups (250 g) light brown sugar

1 medium egg

¼ tsp ground cinnamon

¼ tsp ground aniseed

pinch of ground ginger

pinch of salt

2 cups (250 g) all-purpose flour

1 cup water

Variation: Replace half the water with white wine, or replace 1 Tbsp of the water with 1 Tbsp of Cognac.

Use a shallow waffle iron (see page 260 for more information).

Melt the butter in a saucepan over low heat, remove from the stove, and add the sugar. Set aside to cool. Whisk the egg, cinnamon, aniseed, ginger, and salt and stir in the butter and sugar mixture. Fold in the flour, then add the water in small batches until the batter has the consistency of yogurt.

You can use the batter immediately, but it's better to leave it to rest, covered, in a cool place for at least 24 hours. The flavor and texture of the waffles improve after resting. I have left the batter for up to a week at times.

Heat the waffle iron. Grease the iron with butter and scoop 1 teaspoon of batter onto one side of the iron. You might need to adjust the quantity of batter depending on the iron, so start by testing how much batter you need for one waffle. Squeeze closed and bake for 3 minutes on each side, though this timing does depend on how hot you can get your iron, so please test.

Use a wooden spatula to remove the waffle from the iron, and have a wooden spoon or pie dolly ready and a folded piece of paper towel. Transfer the waffle onto the folded paper towel, holding it in the palm of your hand (be aware, it can be hot) and mold the oublie around the spoon handle or dolly with the help of the paper towel. Let it rest for a minute or two until the waffle has set, then you can remove the dolly to use again for the next waffle. If you feel confident, you can also roll straight off of the iron.

Arrange the rolled oublies high on a plate to serve after dinner with sweet or spiced wine, and other stiff drinks.

Nieuwjaarsrolletjes

In Flanders, these rolled *Nieuwjaarswafels* (New Year's waffles) or *ijzerkoeken* (iron-cakes, as they are baked in an iron) aren't very common, but they are a tradition in Wallonia and in the Netherlands. In the Netherlands the waffles are made flat on the days leading up to 1 January because the year has been rolled out, and on New Year's Day the waffles are rolled up because the year has yet to unroll itself.

These sweet treats are descendants of the delicate rolled *oublie* waffles (see page 46) that we see in 16th- and 17th-century paintings. As waffle irons evolved, they became less intricately carved and produced less delicately thin waffles, so the oublie waffles transformed into these New Year's waffles.

These waffles are made from a wetter dough than the *lukken* waffles (see page 51) from West Flanders. When baked, they are rolled up as soon as they come out of the iron and filled with whipped cream if you are Dutch, and vanilla or coffee buttercream if you are Walloon. Or you can leave them as they are, which is just as nice.

Makes around 16 (depending on your waffle iron)

½ cup (125 g) unsalted butter, plus extra for greasing

1 ¼ cups (250 g) light brown sugar

1 medium egg

¼ tsp ground cinnamon

¼ tsp ground aniseed

pinch of ground ginger

pinch of salt

2 cups (250 g) all-purpose flour

⅔ cup water

whipped cream or flavored buttercream, for serving

Use a shallow waffle iron (see page 260 for more information).

Melt the butter in a large saucepan over low heat, then remove from the heat and stir in the sugar. Set aside to cool before you whisk in the egg, cinnamon, aniseed, ginger, and salt. Fold in half of the flour and all of the water; when fully incorporated, add the rest of the flour.

You can use the batter immediately, but it's better to leave it to rest, covered, in a cool place for 24 hours. The flavor and texture of the waffles improve after resting. I have left the dough for up to a week at times.

Heat the waffle iron. Grease the iron with butter and scoop 1 tablespoon of batter onto one side of the iron. You might need to adjust the quantity of batter depending on the iron, so start by testing how much batter you need for one waffle. Squeeze closed and bake for 3 minutes on each side, though this timing does depend on how hot you can get your iron, so please test.

Use a wooden spatula to remove the waffle from the iron and have a wooden spoon or pie dolly ready and a folded piece of paper towel. Transfer the waffle onto the folded paper towel, holding it in the palm of your hand (be aware, it can be hot) and mold the waffle around the spoon handle or dolly with the help of the paper towel. Let it rest for a minute or two until the waffle has set, then you can remove the dolly to use again for the next waffle.

Pipe in the filling of your choice. Stack the filled waffles high in a pyramid on a board or plate to serve.

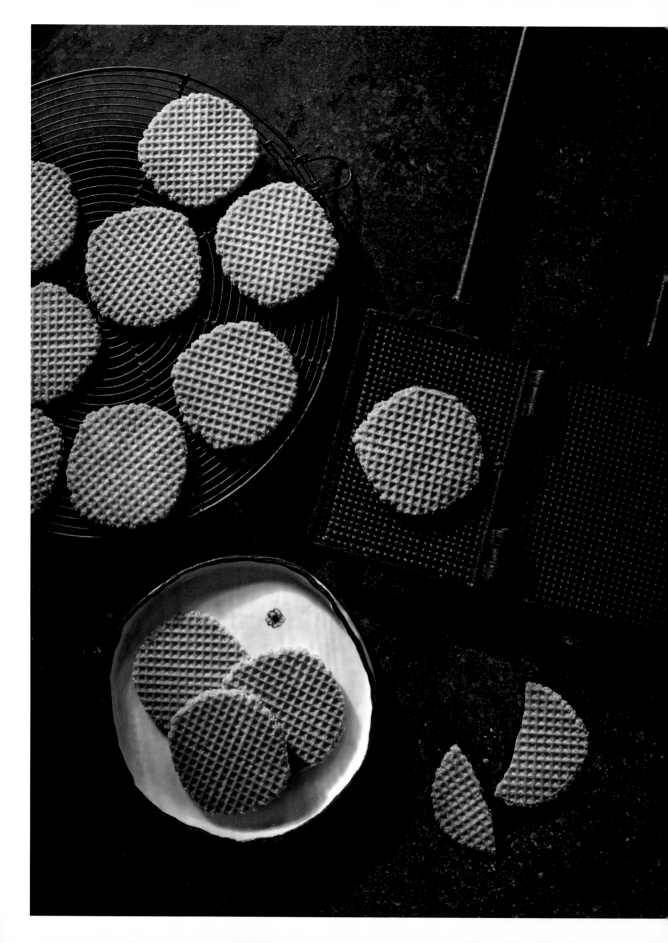

Lukken

These brittle, buttery waffles are traditionally made for New Year's in West Flanders in Belgium. They are a descendant of the *oublie* (see page 46), but they are slightly thicker and are not rolled. The name, *luk*, comes from the Dutch *geluk* (luck) as a wish for luck in the new year.

In the 16th and 17th centuries these waffles were eaten after a festive meal and served with sweet or spiced wine.

In 1890, local baker Jules Destrooper started producing these waffles using his secret recipe and making them available all year round as *galettes au beurre* (galettes with butter). They became such a favorite cookie all over the country that people from outside of the region no longer associated the buttery cookie with the lukken waffles or New Year's.

Since 1904 a biscuiterie in Dunkirk, French Flanders, has also baked these lukken waffles all year round as the *gaufre Dunkerquoise*. They do note, however, that this is a Flemish waffle. Some areas of French Flanders still have a lot of affinity with Flanders, and they even have a Flemish dialect, though sadly the latter is disappearing.

After the war, in 1949, Jules Destrooper's son started exporting his waffles to New York, where they were equally well received. Every year in the weeks leading up to New Year's, the *Gazette van Detroit*, founded in 1914 and published for more than a hundred years in both English and Dutch, ran advertisements for lukken waffle irons. This shows not only that Destrooper's waffles took off, but that people were baking them at home too.

The recipe below is one that was given to me ten years ago; it has been a favorite in our house ever since. The waffles can be made in a shallow electric waffle iron, an ice-cream cone iron, or a stovetop iron. There is a lot of weighing and rolling of dough involved, hence baking these waffles used to be a family activity – in many families in West Flanders, it still is to this day.

Makes 63 small waffles

1 cup (250 g) unsalted butter

2 medium eggs

2 ½ cups (475 g) superfine sugar

pinch of salt

2 Tbsp Cognac or rum
(or water if you don't want
to use alcohol)

4 cups (500 g) all-purpose flour

Use a shallow waffle iron (see page 260 for more information).

Melt the butter in a small saucepan over low heat and let cool. In a large bowl, whisk the eggs with the sugar, salt, and Cognac, then add the melted butter and combine well. Sift in the flour and knead to a smooth dough. Transfer the dough to an airtight container and leave to rest overnight in a cool place (not in the fridge).

The next day, measure ¾-oz (20-g) nuggets of dough and shape them into balls or fat cigars, depending on the shape you want to achieve.

Let your electric or stovetop waffle iron get very hot and bake each waffle for 2–3 minutes until they are a deep golden color. Seconds mean the difference between golden and dark brown. There is no need to grease the irons as the dough doesn't stick if the iron is hot enough.

Keep the waffles in an airtight container for up to 3 weeks.

Cinnamon waffles

These *Zimtwaffeln* appear in centuries-old Dutch language and German cookery books, but a culture of cinnamon waffles further developed in German Saarland, where they have specialized decorative waffle irons for the purpose. In Belgium and Holland we favored other waffles, so we lost our taste for strongly flavored cinnamon waffles at some point in the early 19th century.

Cinnamon waffles are baked throughout Advent. The man from whom I bought the antique heirloom *Zimtwaffeleisen* pictured opposite also gave me two of his family recipes. One was from his wife's grandmother and dates to the 1920s, the other is from around the 1960s.

I wondered why he was selling his precious waffle iron, but he explained that he didn't use it anymore, since the same intricate carvings are now available as an electric iron. He assured me that during the Advent season his house is still filled with the fresh scent of butter and cinnamon from cinnamon waffles. So I got myself the electric version too as, being a waffle-iron collector, I like to have the correct waffle iron for every waffle and I also like to make it easy by going electric. When it comes to stovetop irons, heat is key: if the iron is not hot enough, the dough will stick.

The *Frankfurter Kochbuch* from 1789 has a recipe for these Zimtwaffeln: you'll find it below. The modern recipe is still exactly the same as this one, although the family recipe given to me by the seller of the waffle iron also includes almond meal and chocolate, which appears to have been a trend in the 1920s. Luckily it didn't stick around, as these waffles are perfect the way they are.

Makes 60 thin waffles

½ cup (110 g) superfine sugar

1 cup (225 g) unsalted butter, melted and cooled

1 medium egg

2 Tbsp ground cinnamon

1 ¾ cups (225 g) all-purpose flour

Use a German *Zimtwaffeleisen,* a shallow or decorative waffle iron, or *Krumkaka* iron (or see page 260 for more information).

Combine the sugar, butter, egg, and cinnamon in a bowl and whisk until creamy, then add the flour gradually until well combined.

Leave the dough to rest overnight, covered, in a cool place (preferably the fridge) so that the flavor can develop.

Shape the dough into balls about the size of walnuts.

Let your electric or stovetop waffle iron get very hot, then place the balls of dough into the iron and bake for 1–2 minutes until golden brown. There is no need to grease the iron, as the dough doesn't stick if the iron is hot enough.

Keep the waffles in an airtight container for up to 3 weeks.

Lacquemant

A *lacquemant* (also spelled *lacment, lacquement,* or *lackman* and also often called *galette*) is a crisp, thin yeast waffle that is split when still steaming hot from the waffle iron and smeared with a runny syrup made with honey, *kandij* syrup (see page 27), or brown sugar and flavored with a hint of orange flower water.

Served in a pointy paper bag like *frites* (fries), the warm syrup seeps out of the waffle and into the tip of the bag, and the last piece of the waffle is used to dip into the syrup. When buying several in one bag (they are traditionally sold as six to share), it was always a fight as to who was going to be the one dipping their waffle into the syrup.

Waffles that are split after baking and then covered with a simple filling of melted butter, or butter and sugar, appear in the early Dutch-language cookbooks of the 16th century. This waffle is a logical evolution of those early split waffles.

The lacquemant waffle was invented in 1903 by a man called Désiré Smidts. He named the waffle after his employer, a pâtissier in Lille (French Flanders) called Berthe Lacquemant who toured with waffle palaces on *kermis* (fairgrounds). The inspiration behind this waffle is the *gaufre fourrée* or the Flemish waffle, which is popular in Lille and a descendant of those early split waffles. The *Bredasche Courant* of 28 September 1917 gives an account from someone remembering the fair in Rotterdam in Holland, where he ate beignets from "the famous Max" (Consael), the profiteroles with ice cream from Lacquemant de Lille, the *poffertjes* from Consael, and the waffles from Vulsma. Désiré Smidts had his own kermis waffle palace selling his lacquemants from at least 1912 when he was seen at the Liège fair.

Marc Stoffels, the grandson of Désiré Smidts, continued his grandfather's work, first at fairs and then, from the early 1980s, in his tearoom Désiré de Lille in Antwerp. In 2016 he sold his business and it is now beyond recognition, waiting for much needed renovations. Luckily another descendant of the family, Anne-Marie Stoffels, still travels around with the actual Désiré de Lille waffle palace, keeping the family business and history alive.

This is *gastronomie foraine*, or kermis gastronomy: foods exclusively available at *grandes foires*, or great fairs. My father remembers lacquemants at the fair vividly and took me to get a lacquemant when I was a little girl. He'd say to me, *"Moete ne lekman hebbe?"* ("Do you want a lackman?" in Antwerp dialect), and for years I thought the waffle's name was "lick-man" because you had to lick the syrup. My dad says that, like the Brussels waffles, these waffles were hardly ever consumed at the fair; the custom was to buy them and take them home to enjoy with the family. Today they are a street food, but they are becoming increasingly rare.

When it comes to gastronomic treats that are traditionally eaten on the street (in my generation anyway – my dad would disagree), the manner in which they are eaten contributes to the experience and therefore flavor. The paper cone is essential, as it allows you to dip your lacquemant into the tip where the syrup has gathered. It also prevents your shoes from getting dripped all over with syrup. I've given instructions to make your own paper cone because I do think it is essential. Another thing is the waffle imprint, which is rather wide on these waffles. It is possible to bake them in the same irons as the *lukken* (see page 51) or *stroopwafel* (see page 59), but I've found that the larger imprint, which is traditional to this waffle, keeps hold of the syrup better on the outside, therefore contributing to the flavor. I managed to get a great result using an inexpensive ice-cream cone iron. You can decide for yourself if you want to add another waffle iron to your collection: the *lukken* and *stroopwafels* can also be made in the cone iron. In Belgium it is completely normal to own several irons, but that's because waffle baking is in our blood.

Makes 30 lacquemant

7 Tbsp (100 g) unsalted butter

2 ½ Tbsp whole milk

4 cups (500 g) bread flour

¼ cup (50 g) brown or white superfine sugar

½ tsp instant dry yeast

½ tsp ground cinnamon

1 medium egg

½ cup water

1 tsp salt

For the syrup filling

scant 1 cup (200 g) brown sugar

4 Tbsp (50 g) unsalted butter

1 Tbsp honey

1 Tbsp water

1 Tbsp orange blossom water

1 tsp ground cinnamon

Use a shallow waffle iron (see page 260 for more information).

In a small saucepan over low heat, melt the butter into the milk and set it aside to cool.

In a large bowl or the bowl of an electric mixer fitted with the dough hook, add the flour, sugar, yeast, cinnamon, and the egg. Pour in the butter and milk mixture along with half the water and knead together until fully incorporated, then add the rest of the water and knead for 2 minutes. Leave to stand for 5 minutes, then add the salt and knead for 10 minutes. Cover and set aside to rest for 1 hour until doubled in size.

Meanwhile, for the syrup filling, combine all of the ingredients in a saucepan, bring to a boil over low heat, stirring constantly, then set aside to cool.

Prepare the waffle iron with the galette, ice-cream cone, or thin waffle attachment.

Weigh out 1-oz (30-g) pieces of dough and shape into balls. Heat the waffle iron, roll out the dough balls to oblong shapes roughly 5 x 3 inches, and bake in the iron for 2 minutes until pale golden brown. How long that takes depends on your iron, so please test the cooking time with the first waffle.

While still warm, split the waffle horizontally with a sharp knife and spoon in the syrup filling. Serve warm in a paper cone, turning it around in the syrup accumulating in the tip.

You can keep the uncooked dough balls covered in the fridge for 2 days. These waffles are best eaten immediately after baking them.

For the paper cone
Make paper cones by taking a sheet of paper and folding the bottom right corner up toward the left side of the sheet. You now have about 3 inches left over at the top, so fold that down and fold the corner around the cone to the back. (It is a good idea to secure the base tip with some adhesive tape so the syrup doesn't seep out all over: it is a sticky mess!)

Gaufre de Tournai

Also called *gaufres fourrées*, split waffles, or *Poperingse spletters* (Poperinge splitters), these are very thin, soft waffles, split and filled with a mixture of butter and light brown sugar. Traditionally, these waffles were baked around New Year's by the grandmothers of West Flanders and French Flanders, particularly in Tournai, which used to be part of the Duchy of Flanders but is now in Wallonia. Although bakers in Tournai still freshly bake these waffles to their own recipe, the ones made by Gaufrerie Marquette & Fils for four generations are the ones that are most widespread in Belgium. I often bought these waffles, among others, from a vending machine at my school.

Just around 15 miles away, we find these waffles in Lille, a town that was part of Flanders until 1713. In 1849 the Flemish Michael Paulus Gislinus Méert took over ownership of an iconic pâtisserie in Lille. He brought the tradition of this waffle with him, and for the past 170 years, it has been its most famous article.

A bakery in Antwerp, just around the corner from our house, sold these waffles filled with vanilla buttercream and dusted with confectioners' sugar. It had divine status at my primary school. Children who were allowed to go home for lunch would often come back flaunting their waffles in the playground. I hated those kids! We kids who had eaten lunch at school would look at the waffles with big longing eyes, knowing that by the time school ended, they were always sold out. While buttercream is, of course, lush, this is the recipe for the traditional filling made with *cassonade*, a light brown beet sugar. In West Flanders, the sugar mixture is called *stierenboter*.

Makes 30 waffles

4 cups (500 g) all-purpose flour

¼ cup (50 g) white or light brown superfine sugar

½ cup (125 g) unsalted butter, softened

2 ¼ tsp (7 g) instant dry yeast

6 Tbsp whole milk

3 medium eggs

pinch of salt

For the filling

1 cup (250 g) unsalted butter, softened

2 cups (250 g) confectioners' sugar

1 ¼ cups (250 g) soft light brown sugar

Note: 1–2 Tbsp of rum is often added to the filling, which can be fun, but is not really to everyone's taste. Feel free to add it if you want a boozy waffle.

Use a shallow waffle iron (see page 260 for more information).

Combine the flour, sugar, butter, and yeast in a large bowl or the bowl of an electric mixer fitted with a dough hook. Pour in half of the milk and the eggs and start kneading. When the liquid is completely absorbed, pour in the rest of the milk and knead for 5 minutes. Set aside to rest for 5 minutes.

Add the salt and knead for 10 minutes, scraping the dough off the dough hook and sides of the bowl if needed, until it has come together in a smooth and elastic dough that is neither too dry nor terribly wet. Cover the dough and set aside for 1 hour until it has doubled in size.

Meanwhile, make the filling by whisking the butter and confectioners' sugar together until soft and creamy, then fold in the light brown sugar with a spatula. Set aside until needed.

Briefly knead the dough, then divide it into 30 equal pieces, rolled into smooth balls.

Heat the waffle iron, then flatten and stretch each dough ball into an oval shape, place it in the iron, and press to close. Bake to a golden color: how long that takes depends on your iron, so please test the cooking time with the first waffle.

Remove each waffle from the iron and immediately split it using a sharp knife. While there is still some warmth left in the waffles, finish them with the filling.

Serve immediately, or keep the filled waffles in an airtight container for up to 3 days.

Stroopwafel

This thin waffle filled with honey or a sugar syrup mixture is popular in Flanders and the Netherlands, which is the place most people associate them with. It was in the Dutch town of Gouda in the 19th century that the first bakers started to produce these waffles as *Goudse stroopwafels*, but the exact history is impossible to trace. Like the *lacquemant* (see page 54) and other filled waffles, this too is a descendant of the historical split waffles.

When I was a child it was one of the treats my mother often bought, filled with honey, although usually sugar syrup is used. The beauty of this waffle happens when you put it on top of a mug of coffee or hot chocolate, and the syrup or honey inside becomes runny and peeps out around the edge. In the Netherlands, there is also a version of this waffle made with thin cookies instead of waffles, called *stroopkoek*.

These waffles are cut out into a neat round after baking and then split, thus yielding a lot of offcuts, which, in the Netherlands, are sold in bags as a real treat for snacking. You may skip cutting the waffles, or develop a fondness for snacking on offcuts as the Dutch do.

Makes about 34 large ones (3½-inch diameter) or 39 small ones (2½-inch diameter)

4 cups (500 g) bread flour

1 cup (250 g) unsalted butter, softened, plus extra for greasing

½ cup (100 g) demerara (coarse raw) or superfine sugar

4 ¾ tsp (15 g) instant dry yeast

½ tsp ground cinnamon

½ tsp sea salt

¼ tsp baking powder

3½ Tbsp whole milk

1 Tbsp runny honey

1 medium egg

For the filling

1 ½ cups (300 g) white or light brown superfine sugar

2 Tbsp runny honey

2 Tbsp glucose syrup

6 Tbsp water

7 Tbsp (100 g) unsalted butter

pinch of ground cinnamon

Use a shallow waffle iron (see page 260 for more information) and a 3½-inch or 2½-inch round cutter. If you have a waffle iron with two shallow waffle imprints, you will need to use the smaller size; if you have a round waffle iron, you can make the large ones.

Combine the flour, butter, sugar, yeast, cinnamon, salt, and baking powder in a large bowl or the bowl of an electric mixer fitted with the dough hook attachment. Pour in the milk, honey, and the egg and knead for 5 minutes. Let the dough rest for 5 minutes. Knead for a further 10 minutes, then cover the bowl and set aside to rest for 1 hour.

Meanwhile, make the filling by combining the sugar, honey, glucose, and water in a medium-sized saucepan, stir over low heat until the sugar dissolves, then add the butter. Bring to a boil and then simmer until the mixture reaches 210°F on a sugar thermometer. Add the cinnamon and continue to boil until the syrup reaches 234–240°F: this is called soft ball stage. It will foam up in large bubbles at first, appearing creamy, then the bubbles will get smaller. I am not giving timings as I want you to focus on your thermometer and your caramel and not a timer. Remove the saucepan from the heat and set it aside: you can warm it again when you need to fill your waffles.

After the dough has risen, weigh 1- to 1½-oz (30- to 40-g) pieces and place them on a tray lined with parchment paper or in an airtight container. You can allow them to slow-rise in the fridge overnight, or bake them immediately.

Heat the waffle iron. Grease with a small amount of butter, press one of the dough balls flat, and bake until golden brown, which takes about 2 minutes in my iron.

While the waffles are still warm, use a round cutter to cut out perfect rounds (you may omit this if you don't mind them rustic). Split each waffle horizontally with a sharp knife and smear on the filling. Gently press the waffle halves together: the bits of filling that peep out around the edge are the best bits!

Savory sweet potato waffles

These waffles are the best savory waffles you will ever make – in my humble opinion, anyway. The spices provide a subtle flavor in the background: they aren't meant to be pronounced, just to support.

I serve them with our traditional *platte kaas* (quark or fromage blanc), which is also used in the cheesecakes of Wallonia or smeared onto bread, topped with radishes, and served with Gueuze beer.

Makes 10 medium waffles (2 per person, for lunch or breakfast)

14 oz (400 g) sweet potato

3½ Tbsp (50 g) unsalted butter

4 oz (100 g) semifirm cheese, such as semi-mature Gouda, Cheddar, or red Leicester

¾ cup (100 g) bread flour

¾ cup (100 g) all-purpose flour

¼ tsp baking powder

¼ tsp sea salt

¼ tsp smoked paprika

¼ tsp ground cumin

1 Tbsp dried bruschetta herbs or oregano

2 medium eggs, separated

3½ Tbsp whole milk

To serve

flat-leaf parsley

platte kaas (fromage blanc, quark) or sour cream or skyr (Icelandic-style yogurt)

cracked black pepper

chervil sprigs

Use a plain waffle iron (see page 260 for more information).

There are two ways to go about cooking the sweet potato: if you are feeling organized, you can put the whole unpeeled potatoes into the oven along with your evening meal and bake them until soft (this is the way that will yield the most flavorsome result, and it's so easy you will definitely remember to pop in a sweet potato or two next time). The oven temperature isn't important as long as you don't go over 400°F – just squeeze the potato after 30 minutes to see if it is soft; the skin will be wrinkly if it's ready. You can keep the cooked potato in the fridge for up to 3 days after cooking.

The second way is to cook the sweet potato on the day you're making the waffles. If you can find small ones, cook them whole as it will improve the flavor, but if they're large, peel them, cut them into cubes, and keep an eye on them so they don't fall apart. Depending on the size of the potatoes, cooking them will take about 20 minutes.

Scoop the flesh out of the potato peel or toss the cubes into a food processor and blend to a purée, then let it cool.

Meanwhile, melt the butter in a small saucepan over low heat so it doesn't bubble, then let it cool. Grate the cheese.

Put both the flours, baking powder, salt, spices, and herbs into a large bowl and mix well.

In a separate bowl, whisk the sweet potato purée and the melted butter together until well incorporated. Add the egg yolks and milk, then, add this mixture to the flour mixture. Stir until combined, then whisk the egg whites to stiff peaks and fold them into the batter with the grated cheese.

Heat a plain waffle iron. Place a dollop of batter on the iron and bake each waffle for 3 minutes until golden.

For serving, chop some parsley and add it to the cheese or sour cream. Add the pepper, as much as you like, and stir to combine.

Serve the waffles with the cheese mixture, scattered with the dainty leaves of chervil, which will give a delicate flavor. Other delicate salad leaves will work too.

Freeze leftovers or keep in an airtight container. The next day, or after thawing, simply heat up in a hot waffle iron or a toaster.

Regula's waffles

This recipe started with one I found in the single tattered cookbook we had at home when I was growing up. Having just a handful of recipes at my disposal meant that I always felt the recipes were there as a guide only, and I could experiment to create my own result. My mother helped me make the first batch according to the recipe, which was just a few lines, and I went on from there, experimenting. The result was these soft waffles. They are often known as household waffles in Belgium because they keep for over a week when properly stored. This means they are perfect for *wafelenbak*, a festivity where waffles are baked and sold. They are also often baked at children's parties and small fairs, where local women are doing the baking on domestic irons. Waffle trucks baking this kind of waffle have popped up in recent years at antique and garden fairs: they are a different breed from the waffle palaces of the *kermis* (fair), in that they are usually not passed on through generations of the same family. A bakery stall at the weekly market in the Flemish town of Mechelen is revered for its waffles, which are just like these, baked on the spot on several irons and sold by weight.

I've halved the recipe here. As a child I always forgot to halve the recipe, and the whole of our tiny flat would be full of trays of cooling waffles. I'd then make my own wrapping and boxes and give the waffles to elderly family members as "Regula's waffles" with handpainted labels.

I always made the waffles quite small to bake four in one go and eat two rather than one large one, but recently I've started making them larger. This is the recipe that has evolved the most throughout my life, and it had its final tweak while I was writing this book.

Makes about 14 large waffles

½ cup (125 g) unsalted butter

1 cup whole milk

5 medium eggs, separated

1 ½ cups (280 g) superfine sugar

2 tsp natural vanilla extract, or
   seeds of 1 vanilla pod

4 cups (490 g) all-purpose flour or
   white spelt flour

1 Tbsp baking powder

pinch of salt

oil, for greasing

Use a plain waffle iron (see page 260 for more information).

In a small saucepan, melt the butter in the milk and let the mixture cool. Meanwhile, whisk the egg yolks with the sugar and vanilla until the mixture is light and creamy.

In a large bowl, combine the flour, baking powder, and salt, pour in the milk mixture, and stir with a wooden spoon until the batter is smooth and no flour pockets remain. Now work in the egg yolk mixture, stirring until well combined.

Whisk the egg whites to stiff peaks and fold into the batter in large slow movements, because you want to keep the air bubbles in.

Heat a waffle iron with the plain waffle attachment. Have a bowl of oil and a brush ready to grease the iron between bakes. Use 1 or 2 tablespoons of batter and see if you like the size. Bake the waffles to a pale golden brown color and transfer to a wire rack. How long this takes depends on your iron, so please test the cooking time with the first waffle.

Eat them warm, preferably, but they are also very good cold, though they will be less fluffy. Reheating cold waffles in a hot waffle iron revives them beautifully and gives them a little crisp exterior.

Keep leftover waffles in an airtight container for up to 1 week; they also freeze very well.

HANS FRANCKEN (1581–1624): *Winter still life with pancakes, waffles and duivekater*, KMSK Brussels. You can see (clockwise from top left) a decorated vollaard, peperkoek, waffles, pancakes, fritters, lemon (which is often squeezed over pancakes and fritters), a letter cookie, syrup, white bread rolls, nuts, apples, and medlars.

A MIDWINTER FEAST

Bread is life. It's therefore no wonder that bread plays an important role in festival events and seasons. This isn't exclusive to the Low Countries. Celebratory decorative loaves are a part of the culture of feasting in many countries; their shapes often associated with religious, symbolic, or superstitious beliefs. Bread can be shaped like bundled babies, animals, saints, and eternity symbols, or peculiar shapes where the meaning is lost to time. Festive breads most often appear around New Year's and Easter, but also at the feasts of certain saints and heroes.

When the Gregorian calendar replaced the Julian, it moved the start of the new year from March to January. This is why many cultures have the custom of giving a large rich festive loaf around Christmas and New Year's and at Easter.

Easter bread was baked to celebrate the return of butter and eggs after winter and Lent, something that made baking rich breads possible again. The egg symbolizes the rebirth of spring. This is why the loaves we now consider to be Christmas or New Year's loaves often contain eggs and butter.

The *vollaard* in Belgium or *duivekater* in the Netherlands are the main historical festive winter loaves of the Low Countries. They are made out of sweet yeast dough, and the decoration varies from region to region and even from town to town.

In the Netherlands, the duivekater – in some regions called *scheenbeenbrood* or *krulkoek* ("shinbone bread" or "curl cake") – is oval or rectangular and usually decorated by carving the egg-washed dough to reveal the pale interior. The top and bottom are often cut into and the tips curled outward like a moustache (hence "curl cake").

Although widely available in the Renaissance, the loaf now solely remains in the Zaan district and northern Amsterdam. Today the most famous duivekater comes from an eponymous bakery "De Duivekater": they purchased the recipe from the legendary baker Kroes, who was known for his excellent duivekater loaves. The family bakery proudly keeps this tradition alive, and people travel from afar to buy their festive loaf each winter, as I've done since discovering it.

Written sources can be found from the 17th century, but none explain the curious name, which has been wildly speculated about. From references to the devil to poor French pronunciation, the explanation might be as simple as it being the surname of the first baker who made it. We will probably never know unless a new historical source is discovered. An early mention of the word appears in Cornelis Kiliaan's *Etymologicum* (1599). He gives the Latin translation for "duyven-kater" as *"Libi genus, quod strenae loco datur"* (a type of cake that is given as a New Year's gift). Another significant mention appears in *Moortje*, a comedy play from 1617 written by Gerbrand Bredero. There the winter customs connected to Saint Nicholas, Christmas, and Three Kings day are explained, mentioning that, at Epiphany, a *"moye Duevekater"* was received as a gift.

From folk custom to art, the patacon

Unlike the duivekater, the vollaard is decorated with shields and swaddled babies made out of fine white pipe clay. The shields are called "*patacons*," after the Spanish–Dutch coin, the patagon. They are a form of folk art that is very rare today. I have met one of the only two people still known to create this form of art, and she is the only one who still makes them to be baked into vollaards for a Christmas craft market in Bruges, once a year. She has taught me the process, and my husband and I have started making our own patacons, as this custom and form of folk art are too precious to lose.

The delicate clay discs for patacons are usually imprinted with a bas relief and painted in bright colors. The subjects can range from biblical to legendary. The top patacon as seen on Hans Francken's painting (opposite) is a common one depicting the Lamb of God. This links the loaf to Easter, which was, before the calendar changed, the start of the year.

These small works of art baked into loaves were once produced all over the region of current Belgium. The patacon artist I visited told me that people had to go to the baker before Christmas to order and pay for their patacon, as it was costly to make. It really was a treat for children, who would collect the patacons each year.

The festive loaf of the Netherlands, the duivekater, has managed to survive in one region; however, while the imposing vollaard in Belgium is now almost lost, it can be traced in other breads, such as the *cougnou, mantepeirden,* and *klaaskoeken.*

Shaping the bread
In the Netherlands, the duivekater appears for Christmas, New Year's, Pentecost, and Easter; in Belgium, the loaves of bread morphed into different forms spreading across regions. If not called vollaard, the loaf is called *engelenkoek* or *engeltje Gabriel* (angels' cake or angel Gabriel) in Bruges, and *toteman* in Tienen.

Cougnou (see page 74) became the end of the year, winter, and New Year's bread of Wallonia and around the language border between Flanders and French Flanders. It is roughly shaped like a swaddled baby with one small ball for the head, a larger oval shape for the body, and another small ball for the feet. We still see the afterimage of patacons in the chalk buttons and sugar baby Jesus baked into festive cougnou loaves. It is sold from October to January. In France, the festive loaf is called *mannele* and shaped like a little man.

Klaaskoeken (Saint Nicholas cakes) and mantepeirden (man on a horse) were linked to the feasts of Saint Nicholas and Saint Martin (see page 216). They were shaped into a naïve figure with a mitre, a man on a horse, or a horse alone, and at times were impaled on a stick to parade around and referred to as "Saint Martin on a stick." They are sold from September until Christmas, and in some localities only in December. In Horst in Dutch Limburg, there was a Christmas tradition of a large loaf shaped like a horse, although the tradition disappeared around the time of the Second World War.

Loaves made in the image of a horse were linked to the Scandinavian yule horses and going back even further to the horse Sleipnir, the eight-legged horse ridden by Odin. Interestingly, Odin is also mentioned as one of the origin stories of our custom of Saint Nicholas.

Greefkoeken are made in the image of the *Graaf van Halfvasten* (the Earl of Midfast or Laetare Sunday: see page 127) in northern France, Brabant, Antwerp, and more recently Halle. The greefkoek wasn't impaled on a stick, but a little rooster-shaped bread was. We see an example of this "rooster on a stick" peeping out of the child's basket in Jan Steen's painting of *The Feast of Saint Nicholas* (see page 207).

A man-shaped figure called Pichou is baked in Tournai for their Carnival between March and April. In Germany a *Wekkeman* is still baked: a little man with a white clay pipe patacon. In Dutch Limburg, it is called *buikman* (bellyman).

Festive loaves in art
Art also gives us insight into the culture of these loaves. For example, a large decorated festive loaf is shown being carried under the arm of a man in one of the miniatures in the Dutch illuminated manuscript the *Hours of Catherine of Cleves* from around 1440. One with a familiar shape is seen in Bruegel's *The Battle between Carnival and Lent* (see page 12), where one is held under a child's arm, and also in Bruegel the Elder's *Children's games* (1560, held in the Kunsthistorisches Museum, Vienna).

In the 17th century, depictions of festive loaves in art become more frequent. A painting celebrating midwinter bakes by the Flemish Hans Francken (see page 66) displays a large vollaard decorated with several patacons, peperkoek, waffles, pancakes, fritters, a letter cookie, syrup or honey, and fine white bread buns. The story is in the detail often missed: the two red flowers shown are hellebores, an evergreen flowering plant also known by the name winter rose and Christmas rose. Next to the flowers appears a dainty little tree made out of wire with golden pendants and red and green tassels. Could this be an early Christmas decoration, perhaps even a Christmas tree? Though at this time people didn't have a Christmas tree as we know it today.

I've found a similar decorative little tree with pendants planted into the middle of a large tart in one of Clara Peeters's still-life paintings (*Still life with vlaai,* c. 1615, held in a private collection); in the center of the painting, under the tart, lies a red hellebore flower, which can be easily missed. Are these two paintings depicting the same festivities? Would the combination of the small decorated trees with the hellebore be an obvious sign of Christmas or New Year's festivities to the 17th-century viewer?

The little tree and the smaller ones seen in Clara Peeters's work do not look like they are made from wire as the one in Hans Francken's work is. It appears they are decorated rosemary sprigs. Rosemary symbolizes remembrance, as mentioned by Ophelia in *Hamlet,*

ER SNIJERS (1681–1752): *Aquarius (The month of January)*, KMSK Antwerp. This painting shows a large and small vollaard, each with figures and patacons. In the background you can see "three kings" singers for Epiphany.

Act IV, Scene V: *"There's rosemary, that's for remembrance; pray, love, remember."* The 17th-century poet Robert Herrick writes in his couplet "The Rosemary Branch":

Grow for two ends, it matters not at all,
Be't for my bridal, or my buriall.

There is a duality in rosemary that could represent the old year and the new, as the Christmas tree and Christmas greenery represents life and death, past and present.

On page 23 of this book you can see a painting by Antwerpian Sebastiaen Vrancx. A keen eye will spot two children with vollaards under their arms on the quay of Antwerp. Another Antwerp artist, Peter Snijers, painted a winter allegory (see previous page) entitled *Aquarius*, which shows, in the background, children holding a big star, singing for Three Kings: a custom still alive today where children go from door to door on Epiphany to sing and receive sweet treats. In the foreground there is an impressive vollaard held by a wealthy lady, decorated with a great number of white patacons and other clay or sugar figures. The bread appears excessive, showing off its owner's wealth. Right next to her a woman, perhaps a servant, has a large *peperkoek* under her arm decorated with cloves. It was the custom to give employees a peperkoek around New Year's, a practice that has only started to wane as recently as the 1990s. On the right-hand side of the painting, a child and mother of modest appearance are holding a smaller vollaard with a couple of painted patacons. While the wealthy woman smiles smugly, the poor woman and her child simply appear grateful for the treat, and behind them a little girl is holding out her hand in the hope of receiving charity. This work is remarkable as it clearly places the vollaard at the center of attention, meaning it had to be important to people of all social classes and emblematic of the period of the year.

For a northern Dutch example of a duivekater, see Jan Steen's *The Feast of Saint Nicholas* on page 204, which shows a duivekater leaning against a table in the bottom right corner. In his painting of *Baker Arent Oostwaard and his Wife Catharina Keizerswaard* (see page 112), Steen depicts a different style of duivekater and an array of bakes, such as pretzels and fine white bread buns. Duivekaters are never decorated with the pipe clay decorations we see on the vollaard of the Southern Netherlands (current Belgium). Their decoration is solely in the carving and adding decorations in dough.

Complimentary bread
For many village bakeries, a complimentary end-of-the-year loaf was a way to thank villagers for their custom. In the 17th century, this was often seen as a breach of the bread-price law. So deeply rooted were the customs of giving bread or *koek* for Saint Nicholas or New Year's, it was hard to eradicate, so it was condoned.

The size of the gifted bread depended on how much the customer had spent at the bakery that year, which led to jealousy between neighbors if one family's complimentary loaf was larger than another's. Even in the early 20th century, the tradition was still alive; it was not the bread law or ordinances, but an eye on profits that motivated the end of free festive bread.

Banning the bread
Many historical sources concerning the luxurious festive loaves deal with banning or regulating the baking of these large fine wheat loaves. The people of Amsterdam went outside the city walls to avoid the regulations concerning the duivekater, a practice that was also banned in an ordinance, kept in Stadsarchief Amsterdam,[13] from 13 December 1542. In 1649 bakers were banned from gifting duivekaters to their customers. And an ordinance in Amsterdam from 26 November 1698 bans the baking and selling of duivekater loaves because they were made of white flour, but bran was being added to loaves for less affluent customers, thereby lowering the quality of their loaves.

In Namur in current Belgium, an ordinance from 22 December 1698[14] forbade the baking of cougnous because grain was scarce and could not be wasted on white loaves for children.

Baking was banned during the night in closely built villages and towns for fear of fire. This is because houses were made of wood and fire could spread quickly, as happened with the Great Fire of London in 1666.

The baker blew his horn in the morning to alert the villagers that the bread was ready. This phenomenon is depicted in several 17th-century Dutch genre paintings. On page 112 you can see an example of the bakery horn in the background of the Jan Steen painting.

FROM WHITE WHEAT TO DARK RYE

Ever since the Middle Ages, everyone in every layer of society has had bread on their table. The class difference didn't show in whether or not you could afford bread, but what type of bread you could afford. Dark rye bread was the bread of the poor when they were lucky. In dire times, poor people would have to eat bread that was baked for animals, often consisting of legumes and sand.

In many of the Golden Age paintings, you will spot small white bread buns. These were a sign of wealth and considered celebratory, as witnessed in the painting on page 66 by Hans Francken depicting celebratory bakes. That bread bun is today's *pistolet* (see page 76).

Herenbrood, or gentleman's bread, was the whitest and finest bread, made from sifted wheat flour. But it is a misconception that the well-to-do ate only white bread. The Flemish Rembert Dodoens wrote in his *Cruydeboeck* in 1554 that the gentleman's bread is the healthiest, while the second healthiest is the bread where the coarsest bran has been sifted out. The worst bread consists almost only of bran, and he claimed rye bread to be healthy but hard to digest. A bread made with rye and wheat was called *masteluinbrood* (strangely, this became the name of a fine white bun at some point. In Wallonia, the fine white sugar tart on page 176 is called *mastelles*, but elsewhere a white bun flavored with cinnamon – see page 80 – is known as a *mastel*). The two grains were also often grown together on one patch of land. Masteluinbrood was still eaten by people who were well off and by working-class people on feast days, if they could afford it. Just over a century later, Stephanus Blankaart in his *De Borgerlyke Tafel* chooses bread still containing some bran over the white wheat bread, for good health.

Dark rye bread had a fixed weight, but the price varied; for white wheat bread, the price was fixed and the weight of the bread varied. Prices could fluctuate greatly, and notices detailing the price of bread were displayed on the walls of churches and other important buildings. The price and weight of bread for the week was often announced in churches on Sundays. Bread was the staff of life: its price meant the difference between a full belly and famine.

Next to festive loaves, *peperkoek*, rusks and daily bread, small white buns, pistolets, *kadetjes*, or *stoetjes* (rolls) were also baked for special occasions and became customary for Sundays. *Schootjes* – eight little buns stuck together – and also *Leidse hoogjes* (high-top bread made in a tin by stuffing buns in together) are both seen in some Golden Age paintings.

Bakers used to buy grain and store it in the attic. Some customers, often farmers who grew their own grain, brought in their grain for the baker to use for their bread. In a little book of interviews with bakers who operated in the early 20th century, I read that bakers loathed the custom, as it meant having to separate one bag of grain from another from a different family. Baking bread from each family's grain was too fiddly, so many bakers stopped allowing customers to bring their own grain. Many customers did, however, continue to bring in their own bread dough to be baked. Early 20th-century bakers started buying from traveling grain merchants instead of farmers and, with that, the link between farm and baker was forever broken.

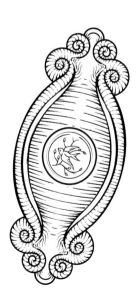

Vollaard

As described in the previous pages, *vollaard* is the primary festive loaf of the Southern Netherlands, which is current Belgium. Its earliest mention in print is as an ingredient for waffles in a cookery book printed in Antwerp in 1560. Recipes are rare because this loaf was always made by the bakery and never at home. Therefore it appears only once as a recipe in its own right, in a practical bakery guide from 1898. This book is held in the museum of folklore in Bruges, and tells us that there are two kinds of this festive loaf, the common vollaard and the large vollaard.

The common vollaard contains butter, eggs, and sugar or honey but no milk; the large vollaard requires more sugar, milk, and a little cinnamon. It needs to be baked at a hotter temperature than the common vollaard. One curious thing is that the book also tells the reader to let the vollaard rest overnight before eating it, because it would otherwise be too heavy on the stomach.

In the photo opposite, inspired by the painting by Hans Francken (see page 66), you can see on the left the vollaard of Wallonia (the French region of Belgium and French Flanders), called *cougnou* (recipe on page 74), with a *patacon* (decorative clay buttons); in the center is a Flemish vollaard with three patacons; and to the right is a *duivekater* (recipe on page 75) from the Netherlands.

A vollaard using the traditional recipe with 2 kg (4 ½ lb) of flour doesn't fit into any domestic oven, so I have halved the recipe here.

Makes 1 medium vollaard

8 ⅓ cups (1 kg) bread flour, plus extra for dusting

6 Tbsp (50 g) confectioners' sugar

3½ Tbsp (50 g) unsalted butter, softened

4 ¾ tsp (15 g) instant dry yeast

2 cups whole milk

2 medium eggs

½ tsp ground cinnamon

1 beaten egg + 1 Tbsp milk, for egg wash

clay buttons, for decorating (optional)

If you have a ridiculously large oven, perhaps a wood-fired one, you can double the recipe and increase the cooking time to 1 hour to make a large vollaard. You can also halve the recipe for a smaller loaf, which will need 30–35 minutes cooking time.

Combine the flour, sugar, butter, and yeast in a large bowl or the bowl of an electric mixer fitted with the dough hook. Pour in half of the milk and the eggs and start kneading. When completely absorbed, pour in the remaining milk and knead for 10 minutes. Let the dough rest, covered, for 30 minutes and then knead briefly.

Cover the dough and set aside for 1 hour until it has doubled in size.

On a floured work surface, briefly knead the dough, folding it inward and shaping it into a large sausage. Pat it out until it is about 24 inches long and 6 inches wide, then make two 6-inch cuts at each end and flatten the center part so that it looks like a wrapped sweet. Stretch out the 3 strands at each end to make them longer and leave to rest for 2 minutes. Roll the middle strand at each end to form a curl. Now roll the outer strands away from the center curl, as shown in the photograph.

Cover the sheet with a light kitchen towel or piece of cheesecloth and wrap it in a large plastic bag (I keep one especially for this purpose). Rest the loaf for 1 hour.

Toward the end of the resting time, preheat the oven to 400°F. Do not use the fan setting. Brush the loaf all over with the egg wash and place clay buttons in the center of the loaf, if you have them. Alternatively, you can cut patterns into the egg-washed dough using a sharp knife. Bake for 35–40 minutes until the bread is brown and sounds hollow when you tap on the bottom. Transfer to a wire rack to cool.

Cougnou

The region of Wallonia and French Flanders has managed to keep a *vollaard*-like loaf (see page 72) alive with the *cougnou* (or *cougnolle*, depending on the region). The shape can be interpreted as a swaddled child, a baby Jesus with a clay button as his belly button. But often the loaf is left plain or a sugar Jesus figure is baked into the dough. These simple buttons are what we have left of the entire art form of *patacons*, or clay buttons, which are connected to the decorative *Oblaten* that were stuck to Lebkuchen in Germany (you can see examples of Oblaten on page 246). My mother-in-law remembers sugar figurines that were stuck to her Christmas *peperkoek*. All these decorative items that were attached to loaves come from the older custom of gifting a loaf with a coin.

Makes 1 cougnou (see photograph on page 73)

4 cups (500 g) bread flour, plus extra for dusting

2 Tbsp superfine sugar

2 Tbsp (30 g) unsalted butter, softened

4 ¾ tsp (15 g) instant dry yeast

1 ¼ cups whole milk

1 medium egg

1 tsp sea salt

1 beaten egg + 1 Tbsp milk, for egg wash

clay button or sugar figurine, for decorating (optional)

Combine the flour, sugar, butter, and yeast in a large bowl or the bowl of an electric mixer fitted with the dough hook. Pour in half of the milk and the egg and start kneading. When completely absorbed, pour in the remaining milk and knead for 5 minutes. Let the dough rest for 5 minutes.

Add the salt and knead for 10 minutes. Let the dough rest, covered, for 30 minutes and then knead briefly.

Cover the dough and set aside for 1 hour until it has doubled in size.

On a floured work surface, briefly knead the dough, folding it in on itself, then divide it in half. Take one half and divide it in half again, so you have 1 large and 2 smaller parts.

Take one piece of the dough and lightly flatten it on your work surface, then pull the outer parts in like a purse and gently squeeze together like a dumpling. Turn the dough over so the squeezed ends are on the bottom. It should be nice and smooth on top. Do the same for all the pieces; this ensures that the dough will not split open while rising.

Assemble the cougnou by placing the largest piece of dough in the middle of a large baking sheet lined with parchment paper. Push it into a slightly oval shape, then place the smaller balls of dough at the top and bottom. Cover the sheet with a light kitchen towel or piece of cheesecloth and wrap it in a large plastic bag (I keep one especially for this purpose). Set aside to rest for 1 hour.

Toward the end of the resting time, preheat the oven to 350°F. Do not use the fan setting. Brush the cougnou all over with the egg wash. Place a clay button or sugar figurine, if you have one, on the middle of the loaf, and bake for 30–35 minutes until the cougnou is browned and sounds hollow when you tap on the bottom.

Transfer to a wire rack to cool.

Duivekater

Cornelis Kiliaan (c. 1530–1607) described in his *Etymologicum* the word *"duyvenkater"* as a kind of cake that is given as a New Year's gift. This festive loaf of the Netherlands has managed to survive while the *vollaard* in Belgium has been almost completely lost, though living on in the *cougnou*, *mantepeirden*, and *klaaskoeken*.

When you ask elderly people from the Netherlands about duivekater, they will tell you that the main flavor was lemon. This makes me believe that the recipe contained candied lemon peel at some point. Recipes for duivekater in historical cookbooks are nonexistent because the loaves were baked at the bakery, not at home. The same goes for *vollaard* (see page 72). For clues about these two loaves it is 17th-century art that enlightens us. You'll see them in many of the paintings reproduced in this book.

We cannot know if duivekater and vollaard were made to the same recipe, but in the paintings it sure looks like they are the same type of dough. Small variations from baker to baker and region to region are normal. This is my recipe, which unfortunately couldn't be based on a historical source, but makes a loaf that I judge as similar to the artworks and to the Kroes duivekater I buy in a small town north of Amsterdam.

Makes 1 loaf (see photograph on page 73)

4 cups (500 g) bread flour, plus extra for dusting

¼ cup (50 g) superfine sugar

7 Tbsp (100 g) unsalted butter, softened

4 ¾ tsp (15 g) instant dry yeast

¾ cup whole milk, at room temperature

2 medium eggs

grated zest of 1 lemon

1 tsp natural lemon extract

1 tsp sea salt

1 beaten egg + 1 Tbsp milk, for egg wash

Tip: This loaf makes excellent French toast (*pain perdu*), the lemon making it extra flavorsome. I coat the baked slices in cinnamon sugar and serve it with a dollop of fromage blanc or *platte kaas* (thick quark).

Combine the flour, sugar, butter, and yeast in a large bowl or the bowl of an electric mixer fitted with the dough hook. Pour in half of the milk and the eggs and start kneading. When completely absorbed, pour in the remaining milk and knead for 5 minutes. Let the dough rest for 5 minutes.

Add the lemon zest, lemon extract, and salt and knead for 10 minutes. Let the dough rest, covered, for 30 minutes and then knead briefly.

Cover the dough and set aside for 1 hour until it has doubled in size.

On a lightly floured work surface, knead the dough, rolling it and folding it inward, then flattening and repeating the rolling, folding, and flattening. Shape into a large rectangle of about 4 x 16 inches.

Transfer the loaf to a baking sheet lined with parchment paper. Make a 2-inch cut into either side at the top and bottom and curl the ends outward (see photo on page 73). Cover the bread with a light kitchen towel or piece of cheesecloth and wrap it in a large plastic bag (I keep one especially for this purpose). Set aside to rest for 1 hour.

Toward the end of the resting time, preheat the oven to 350°F. Do not use the fan setting. Brush the loaf all over with the egg wash and use a sharp knife to score in decorations.

Bake for 30–35 minutes until the bread is browned all over and sounds hollow when tapped on the bottom.

Transfer to a wire rack to cool.

Pistolets

The *pistolet* is the typical bread bun of Belgium. The bun is made of the whitest flour, baked at a high temperature so that the result is pale golden, with the texture outside very crisp and the inside soft. A good pistolet should have a pocket of soft dough in the middle, which could be taken out and kneaded, then eaten or, as we did in school, used as an eraser in charcoal drawings. The hole left in the pistolet could then be used to hold your filling if it's a salad, but the traditional pistolet is eaten with a slice of ham or Gouda cheese on top of a generous layer of butter. The pistolet is then squeezed, pushing the bottom up into the top so you end up with almost a bowl-shaped bun. This makes the otherwise tall pistolet fit into your mouth more easily. A pistolet that doesn't have the pocket of dough you can remove, and doesn't allow you to push the bottom up into the top half, is not the right bun and is probably too dry.

You can find pistolets in the Flemish, French, and German parts of Belgium. You could say that this bread unites the whole of the country, which is no mean feat in a country with so many differences brought on by language barriers. The language of the pistolet is the same: its size might vary according to the generosity of the baker, but the recipe does not change much from baker to baker and region to region.

Other names are *kadetje* or *mikje*. "Pistolet" was also the word for a coin, the coin that could buy you one of these buns. Sometimes the origins of a name can be as simple as that.

The long version of this bun, with a deep cut in the middle, is these days only carved in Ostbelgien. In other regions, long pistolets are no longer carved. The carved pistolets, called *Lange Brötchen* in German, can be seen in still-life paintings of the 17th century.

Until twenty-five years ago, these buns were exclusively for Sundays, feast days, and for funeral or mourning meals. Today most bakeries have given into the demand for pistolets on regular days and will bake them every day. I absolutely adore that first whiff of their freshly baked scent when I open the paper bag they came in from the bakery. If you're an early bird you could be in luck and they might still have some heat of the oven in them.

Makes 10 pistolets

4 cups (500 g) bread flour

1 ½ Tbsp (20 g) unsalted butter,
 softened

4 ¾ tsp (15 g) instant dry yeast

1 ¼ cups water

2 tsp sea salt

Combine the flour, butter, and yeast in a large bowl or the bowl of an electric mixer fitted with the dough hook. Pour in half of the water and start kneading. When completely absorbed, pour in the rest of the water and knead for 5 minutes. Set aside to rest for 5 minutes.

Add the salt and knead for 10 minutes until the dough has come together in a smooth and elastic dough that is neither too dry nor terribly wet. Cover the dough and set aside for 1 hour until it has doubled in size.

Knock out the air from the dough and knead by making folding movements pulling the dough inward. Divide it into 10 equal pieces. Take one piece of dough and lightly flatten it on your work surface, then pull the outer parts in like a purse and gently squeeze them together like a dumpling. Turn the dough over so the squeezed ends are on the bottom, so the dough will not split open while rising. It should be nice and smooth on top: if not, flatten it and start again. Shape into a round ball or a long bun, roll in flour so it is completely coated, then place each pistolet on a tray or board and cover with a light kitchen towel or piece of cheesecloth and wrap it in a large plastic bag (I keep one especially for this purpose). Rest the buns for 10 minutes.

After 10 minutes use a pastry scraper to make an indent in the middle of each bun, then cover the tray again and rest the buns for 1 hour.

Toward the end of the resting time, put an empty baking sheet in the oven and preheat the oven to 450°F. Do not use the fan setting.

When you are ready to bake, take the hot baking sheet out of the oven and transfer the buns to the sheet.

You need steam to obtain the crisp crust of these pistolets (no steam means soft buns). Lightly spray the shaped pistolets with water and place them in the middle of the oven. Then spray the inside of your oven all around. Bake for 15–20 minutes until golden.

Eat on the same day and freeze leftover buns. Thaw at room temperature an hour before you want to eat them: no need to heat them again.

Kramiek and craquelin

Kramiek or *krentenbrood* is a rich loaf studded with raisins or currants. *Craquelin* or *suikerbrood* (sugar loaf) uses the same dough, but is made with pearl sugar instead.

The raisin loaf is the older of the two recipes, and was traditionally baked and gifted for New Year's or Easter because of the rich nature of the dough, which contains eggs, butter, sugar, and currants or raisins. The sugar loaf became more popular when sugar beets took over from sugarcane in sugar production.

Makes 1 loaf

For the kramiek

8 oz (235 g) currants or raisins

2 Tbsp rum

For the craquelin

1 cup (200 g) pearl sugar
   (nib sugar), plus extra
   for decorating

2 Tbsp melted butter, cooled

4 cups (500 g) bread flour, plus
   extra for dusting

¼ cup (50 g) superfine sugar

7 Tbsp (100 g) unsalted butter,
   softened, plus extra for greasing

4 ¾ tsp (15 g) instant dry yeast

¾ cup whole milk,
   at room temperature

2 medium eggs

1 tsp sea salt

1 beaten egg yolk + 1 Tbsp milk,
   for egg wash

Use a loaf tin or bake it free-form.

For the kramiek, soak the currants or raisins in the rum for 1 hour, then drain.

For the craquelin, put the pearl sugar in a bowl and add the cooled butter, stirring so that all the nibs have a coating of butter: this will prevent the sugar from taking moisture from the dough, resulting in a dry loaf.

Combine the flour, sugar, butter, and yeast in a large bowl or the bowl of an electric mixer fitted with the dough hook. Pour in half of the milk and add the eggs and start kneading. When completely absorbed, pour in the remaining milk and knead for 5 minutes. Let the dough rest for 5 minutes.

Add the salt and knead for 10 minutes. Let the dough rest, covered, for 30 minutes and then knead briefly.

Incorporate the kramiek: Add the soaked currants or raisins to the dough and knead carefully, or on slow speed, to mix in the fruit without crushing it. Cover the dough and set aside for 1 hour until it has doubled in size. Meanwhile, butter the loaf tin. Shape the dough into a square brick, then roll it up and place it in the loaf tin, seam down. Cover and set aside to rise again for 1 hour.

Incorporate the craquelin: Take a quarter of the dough and roll it out to a 6 x 16–inch rectangle. Scatter the buttered pearl sugar over the top, then roll it up into a sausage shape. Fold up the sausage and shape it into a ball. Now roll out the remaining dough (that doesn't contain sugar) and wrap it around the dough with sugar. Cover and set aside to rise again for 1 hour. Brush the top of the loaf with the egg wash and use a small, sharp knife to carve a circle into the top of the loaf. Sprinkle on a handful of pearl sugar. Place the loaf on a baking sheet lined with parchment paper.

Meanwhile, preheat the oven to 400°F. Do not use the fan setting.

Bake on the second rack from the bottom of the oven for 35–40 minutes until it is cooked and sounds hollow when you tap on the bottom.

Gentse mastel

Mastellen, *huubkes*, or *hupkes* are round dimpled or crossed cinnamon buns. Since medieval times the bun was consecrated by a priest and eaten as a preventative against hydrophobia (rabies) on the feast of Saint Hubert on 3 November. In a magazine from 1879,[15] it was claimed that blessed bread would never rot. If no bread was blessed there would be a lot of rabid dogs that year. The correct way to eat the blessed bread was to ensure that it was the first food eaten that day; one had to make the sign of the cross and take the first bite of the bun plain, with no butter or any other topping.

The custom of eating consecrated bread on Saint Hubert's day comes from the story that the saint cured a man of rabies by giving him bread to eat. Saint Hubert was the bishop of Liège and the patron saint of hunters. On 3 November an event takes place in Liège where the hunting hounds, masters, and staff are blessed by a priest. This date also marks the start of the hunting season. The saint is also known for evangelizing pagans in the Ardennes forest in Wallonia.

In the villages around Essen in Belgium the buns are called huubkes after Saint Hubert, and they do not have a dimple, but have an indentation of a cross. In areas of East Flanders, of which Ghent is the capital, the dimpled mastel is available all year round, and many bakeries omit the cinnamon these days. In the Dutch town of Breda in Brabant, the buns are called hupkes. God-fearing farmers ordered the consecrated buns to feed to their livestock to protect them from disease. Some bakers have to go to church with their baskets of mastellen, huubkes, or hupkes, while some priests come to the bakery to give their blessing there.

Mastellen are also used for making *Oost Vlaamse vlaai* (see page 158) and the dried-out bun was also often soaked in buttermilk to eat as a gruel. In Ath in Wallonia they are also used for making *tarte à Mastelles* (also called *tarte Gouyasse*) along with macaroons for almond flavor. Mastel buns are also sold for the Ducasse d'Ath festivities, at the end of August.

In Geraardsbergen, where we find the *mattentaart* (see page 162) and the *Geraardsbergse krakelingen* (page 116), mastellen are also sold in bakeries.

A baker there told me that many people believe that mastellen are in fact the Geraardsbergse krakelingen, because the krakelingen are only seen in the town around the krakelingen festival.

Ironed mastellen

It is in the beautiful town of Ghent that these mastel buns are mostly found today.

They have a custom of the "ironed mastel," in which a mastel bun is sliced in two and spread with butter and a generous topping of brown sugar. The bun is then crushed under the weight and heat of an old-fashioned heavy cast-iron clothes-pressing iron: the kind that was kept on the stove and filled with coals. The result is a crisp cookie that resembles a *lacquemant* waffle (see page 54): truly delicious.

This ironing of the mastel is popular on the first weekend of August during the Patershol Festival, a jolly folk festival in the Ghent neighborhood of Patershol, one of Ghent's most culturally diverse areas. If you don't have a heavy iron like that, you can use a heated cast-iron pan to do the trick, as I do.

To make your own, halve a mastel bun and spread the cut sides generously with butter. Add a layer of brown sugar on one half, replace the top, and place the mastel between two layers of parchment paper on a wooden board. Place an old-fashioned iron or a heavy cast-iron pan on the stove and allow it to get really hot, slowly. Place the hot iron or pan on the mastel, cover it with a kitchen towel, and press down using your weight. The mastel should be as flat as a cookie and lovely and crisp with caramelized sugar around the edges. If you own a sandwich press, you could use that, but an old-fashioned iron is definitely the most romantic option.

Makes 12 buns
(see photograph on page 82)

4 cups (500 g) bread flour

⅓ cup (60 g) superfine sugar

5 Tbsp (70 g) unsalted butter, softened

1 tsp ground cinnamon

4 ¾ tsp (15 g) instant dry yeast

1 medium egg

1 cup whole milk, at room temperature

1 tsp fine sea salt

1 beaten egg + 1 Tbsp milk, for egg wash

Combine the flour, sugar, butter, cinnamon, and yeast in a large bowl or the bowl of an electric mixer fitted with a dough hook. Pour in the egg and half of the milk and start kneading. When completely absorbed, pour in the remaining milk and knead for 5 minutes. Let the dough rest for 5 minutes.

Add the salt and knead for 10 minutes. Let the dough rest, covered, for 30 minutes and then knead briefly.

Cover the dough and set aside for 1 hour until it has doubled in size.

Knock out the air, knead the dough briefly, and divide it into 12 equal pieces. Take a piece of dough and lightly flatten it on your work surface, then pull the outer parts in like a purse and gently squeeze together like a dumpling so that the dough will not split open while rising. Turn the dough over so the squeezed ends are on the bottom. It should be nice and smooth on top: if not, flatten it and start again. Place each bun on a baking sheet and cover the sheet with a light kitchen towel or a piece of cheesecloth and wrap it in a large plastic bag (I keep one especially for this purpose). Let rest for 1 hour.

Press your thumb into the smooth bun, then take the bun in one hand, place both thumbs in the middle, and squeeze while turning the bun so you end up with something that looks like a doughnut, making sure you do not pierce right through the thin layer of dough that remains in the middle.

Cover again and let the buns rest for 30 minutes. Toward the end of the resting time, preheat the oven to 400°F. Don't use the fan setting.

Uncover the buns and brush them all over with the egg wash, not missing the hole. Bake in the middle of the oven for about 15 minutes until they are golden brown.

Eat them plain, though some people are partial to having them with a slice of Gouda, but I like just butter on them. You can also make "ironed mastellen," using the method described opposite.

The next day, the buns can be revived in a hot oven for a few minutes. You can also freeze them, thaw, and then pop them in a hot oven for a few minutes so your mastellen are just as they were when they were first baked.

Gentse mastellen and ironed mastellen

Piot

Piot means a small person, but can also mean a soldier. Whichever you prefer, it is also a small long bun packed with raisins, sold in the market in Antwerp, and it is one of the treats I longed for each Friday when it was market day. These piot buns are placed close together on the baking sheet, to cozy up against the other buns so they can be torn apart. They look a bit like soldiers in a regiment, so maybe that is why they are called piotten. This is a type of special-occasion bun that was also baked with enriched dough, much like the *kramiek, craquelin,* and other celebratory loaves. In the Netherlands these buns are called *schootjes.*

Makes 16 buns

7 oz (200 g) raisins or currants

9 Tbsp water

4 cups (500 g) bread flour, plus extra for dusting

2 Tbsp (25 g) superfine sugar

5 Tbsp (75 g) unsalted butter or lard, softened, plus extra for greasing

2 ¼ tsp (7 g) instant dry yeast

1 medium egg

⅔ cup whole milk

1 tsp sea salt

1 beaten egg yolk + 1 Tbsp milk, for egg wash

Soak the raisins or currants in 2 tablespoons of the water for 1 hour, then drain.

Meanwhile, combine the flour, sugar, butter, and yeast in a large bowl or the bowl of an electric mixer fitted with the dough hook. Add the egg and pour in the milk and start kneading. When completely absorbed, pour in the remaining water and knead for 5 minutes. Let the dough rest for 5 minutes.

Add the salt and knead for 10 minutes. Let the dough rest, covered, for 30 minutes and then knead briefly.

Finally add the soaked currants and raisins and knead carefully, or on slow speed, to mix in the fruit without crushing it. Cover the dough and set aside for 1 hour until it has doubled in size.

Divide the dough into 16 portions and shape into long narrow finger buns of 6 x ¾ inches. Place the buns close together on a baking sheet lined with parchment paper, with not too much space in between as they are supposed to stick together. Cover and set aside to rise again for 1 hour.

Preheat the oven to 400°F. Do not use the fan setting. Brush the top of the piot buns with the egg wash and bake for 15 minutes until golden brown.

Cool on a wire rack.

The best way to eat these piot buns is from a paper bag in the street.

Rogge verdommeke

Rogge verdommeke translates freely to "damned rye," but the actual meaning of this bread is "bread of the damned." In the early 16th century there was a businessman in Antwerp with the name Pieter Pot. He built a chapel and an abbey, and he also had a large personal grain store full of precious rye. Because he was so charitable, he had bread made for the poor as alms. Legend goes that during festivities he would order the plain rye bread to be enriched with raisins for the prisoners – otherwise known as the damned – in the Steen (the fortress in the city center of Antwerp). So goes the legend of the name rogge verdommeke.

Pieter Pot did indeed do great works for the poor and the damned of Antwerp, but whether the rogge verdommeke loaf received its name at that time is difficult to determine, since most of the city's archives were burnt in 1576 during the sack of Antwerp, when mutinous Spanish soldiers burnt down the city hall. What is a fact is that this loaf is still a much-loved bread in Antwerp, especially from the oldest bakery in the city, Bakkerij Goossens, which has been keeping the rogge verdommeke tradition alive for generations.

Makes 1 loaf

6 oz (150 g) raisins or currants

2 ½ cups (300 g) whole-grain rye flour, plus extra for dusting

1 ⅔ cups (200 g) bread flour

1 ½ Tbsp (20 g) unsalted butter or lard, softened

3 ¼ tsp (10 g) instant dry yeast

1 ¼ cups water

1 tsp sea salt

butter, for serving

In a small bowl, cover the raisins or currants with water and soak them for 1 hour, then drain.

Meanwhile, combine the flours, butter, and yeast in a large bowl or the bowl of an electric mixer fitted with a dough hook. Pour in half of the water and start kneading. When completely absorbed, pour in the remaining water and knead for 5 minutes. Let the dough rest for 5 minutes.

Add the salt and knead for 10 minutes more, scraping the dough off the dough hook and side of the bowl if needed, until the dough has come together in a smooth and elastic dough that is neither too dry nor terribly wet.

Cover the dough and set aside for 1 hour until it has doubled in size.

On a floured work surface, knead the bread for 5 minutes by stretching parts of it inward as if you were trying to stuff a winter coat into your backpack. Finally, add the soaked currants or raisins and knead carefully to mix in the fruit without crushing it. Shape into a round loaf and place on a baking sheet. Cover with a kitchen towel and set aside to rise for 1 hour.

Preheat the oven to 425°F and place a baking sheet, bread cloche, or enamel cast-iron pot inside to get hot. Do not use the fan setting. When you are ready to bake, lower the temperature to 400°F. Score the top of the bread to control how it will crack. Place the loaf on the hot sheet or inside the cloche or cast-iron pot and bake for 40 minutes until the loaf sounds hollow when tapped on the bottom.

Cool on a wire rack and serve spread with butter.

Donker rogge

This is the dark rye bread I grew up with in Flanders, though it isn't traditionally associated with the region today. Both of my great-grandmothers and my great-aunt ate it with stinky Brussels cheese. My grandmother and my mother and I loved eating it as open tartines, spread with *platte kaas* (fromage blanc or thick quark) or cream cheese and topped with thinly sliced white-fleshed radishes with brightly colored red skins. This combination is one of my strongest childhood flavor memories. I was probably the only child who cried when given a choc-hazelnut spread sandwich instead. Although it's an everyday bread, dark rye with platte kaas and radishes was a feast to me, and a cunning way for my mother to get me to eat fiber, protein, and one of my "five a day."

Rye bread in general used to be the principal food of the Low Countries before the potato arrived and, even after the potato arrived, the regional rye breads survived. Bakers made use of the falling heat of the oven for baking dark rye bread. But as wood-fired ovens were replaced by modern ones in the 1950s, the process moved from the village baker to the large factory bakery. This didn't impact quality, even though there is something to be said about regionality.

The Low Countries have many regional variations on rye bread, ranging from a dark and sticky type of bread in the north to a lighter bread with a finer structure in the south. The rye bread of the northern Low Countries and Germany – where it is called pumpernickel – is usually made with broken rye groats rather than rye flour. The groats are combined with a small quantity of rye flour, scalded with boiling water, and left overnight, during which time the saccharification of starch happens. Often the bread was made by using a portion of crumbs from previous loaves, creating the sweetness from the long and low baking process rather than letting the fresh dough sweeten before baking. The baking process also varies from four hours for a lighter bread to twenty-four hours for a very dark rye.

Dark rye bread today comes ready-sliced super thin, and wrapped in plastic. You can no longer buy it from small bakeries as ovens are no longer designed for making this type of slow-baked bread. The slow baking caramelizes and coagulates the grain to form the structure of the

bread, which makes it very sticky and impossible to slice neatly at home. In fact, when I make it at home, my knife is usually taken hostage by the dark sticky loaf.

I've developed a recipe for you so that you can bake this bread at home. It requires patience and some energy, which is dear today, but the low temperature will make a difference for sure. It will also help those who have an old-fashioned stove with a warmer compartment or a range cooker such as an AGA or Esse, who want to make use of the ovens while they heat the house or cook something else. Of course, if you happen to be one of those lucky bakers who have a wood-fired oven, you can make the most of your wood with this recipe, which will need some trying out, as all wood-fired ovens have their own temperaments.

Makes 1 loaf

2 cups water

4 cups (500 g) broken rye groats

1 Tbsp appelstroop or blackstrap molasses

1 ½ tsp salt

¾ cup (100 g) whole-grain rye flour

½ cup (50 g) fine rye bran

quark or cream cheese and sliced radishes, for serving

Use a large 9 x 5 x 3-inch loaf tin.

Pour the water into a large saucepan and bring to a boil, then add the rye groats, syrup, and salt and stir well. Remove from the heat, cover with the lid, and let it stand overnight or for at least 6 hours.

The next day the groats will have swelled and all you need to do is add the rye flour to create more binding in the structure of the bread. Knead in the rye flour for as long as it takes for the flour to be completely taken up by the dough and there are no dry patches left. Shape the bread roughly a little smaller than the size of your tin.

Preheat the oven to 140°F.

Scatter the rye bran onto a large baking sheet or board, place the dough on top, and turn it over until it is completely covered in bran. You can omit this step for a smooth finish, but I prefer the look of the bran on the finished loaf.

Wrap the loaf in a layer of parchment paper, then in two layers of foil. Place the loaf in the tin: if it doesn't fit, that's okay; you can bake it on a baking sheet as the bread won't expand.

Place the bread in the middle of the oven and let it "sweeten" for at least 6 hours or overnight. The next morning, raise the oven temperature to 225°F and bake for 8 hours.

The bread is ready if it springs back when you push in your thumb; if your thumb leaves an imprint it needs longer in the oven. If you push in your thumb and the mixture still acts like dough, you're hours away from a finished loaf.

Unwrap and let cool on a wire rack. Keep in an airtight container for up to a week, or freeze in slices.

Serve spread with quark or cream cheese, topped with slices of radish.

A note on *platte kaas* and radish tartines
In the Pajottenland, the region around Brussels also famous for its remarkable Lambic and Gueuze beers, it is tradition to combine one of these beers with a large slice of light rye bread (use the recipe for Rogge Verdommeke on page 87, omitting the raisins) spread with *platte kaas* (fromage blanc or thick quark) topped with slices of radish. This can be found in nearly all traditional Belgian beer cafés in Brussels. The flavor of the beer with the simple bread, cheese, and radish is a marriage of simple beauty with extraordinary heritage.

Worstenbrood

It is tradition in Antwerp to eat *worstenbrood* (sausage bread) on the first Monday after Epiphany, a day known as Lost Monday. In 1879 a journalist[15] writes under the heading *"Verloren Maandag"* (Lost Monday) that the day is also called *poefdag* (credit day). On that Monday, the workers went to their masters' clients wishing them a happy New Year and gathering tips that were noted down on a credit list with the donator's name. They then went to the bar to drink as many tips as they had gathered on their list. It was also customary for the landlords of the bars and inns to pay the brewery on that day, and in return the innkeeper would be given a free cask of beer that he could then use to sell pints for half price to his customers. Meaning the customers had more beer they could afford.

The journalist wrote that the custom was dwindling by 1879 and almost forgotten, and that the traditional worstenbrood was now only eaten in the home, apart from in Antwerp, where he thought they were delicious. Interestingly, today Antwerp is the only city in Belgium that still has the tradition of eating sausage bread on Lost Monday. The custom is generally believed to be connected to the workers who had their day of drinking and needed a snack in the bar or café to line their stomachs. For at least the past fifty years, traditional Antwerp cafés serve sausage bread to their loyal customers; especially in the harbor of Antwerp, where the custom has been kept alive. Families now eat sausage bread and apples baked in a pastry jacket, the latter being a custom that came from Wallonia, where the *rombosse de Mariembourg* (apples baked in pastry) is popular.

In an article in a newspaper comparing the bakeries of 1925 and 1965, a baker says that in 1925 worstenbrood was a Christmas bake, and that his bakery would be full of them. And indeed in the Netherlands, in Brabant, it's the custom to eat worstenbrood during Advent, throughout the pre-Lent Carnival period, and after evening mass at Christmas.

While today the worstenbrood of Antwerp uses puff pastry, this wasn't the case in old recipes. In *Nieuwe Vaderlandsche Kookkunst*, published in 1797, I found a recipe for *saucijzenbroodje* (sausage bread) that asks for fine dough, which I interpret as an enriched bread

dough like that used today for *Brabants worstenbrood* in the Netherlands (Antwerp is, after all, originally county Brabant). It is a great sausage bread to make at home. In March 2016, the Brabant sausage bread was included in the List of Intangible Cultural Heritage by UNESCO.

A necessary word on meat

I adore worstenbrood though I didn't eat any when I was growing up, because I didn't want to eat meat. The first time I found a producer who made worstenbrood using organic higher-welfare meat was a happy day. I think I was twenty-four years old, so I waited a long time for it. So please, if you eat meat, that's totally fine, but consider where you get it. I've purchased my meat from certain farms for sixteen years now. It takes some planning, but I always have a stocked freezer and don't need to go grocery shopping every week. It allows me to support a farm directly rather than filling the pockets of supermarket chains.

The difference in flavor when animals have not been stuck in barns or feedlots all their lives is enormous. Treat an animal with respect and it will reward you with tasty meat. And looking at it from a holistic viewpoint, I wouldn't want to put meat from a stressed and miserable animal into my system. You are what you eat, after all...

Makes 12 sausage rolls

For the pastry

4 cups (500 g) bread flour, plus extra for dusting

14 Tbsp (200 g) unsalted butter, softened

¼ cup (50 g) superfine sugar

3 ¼ tsp (10 g) instant dry yeast

¾ cup water

2 tsp salt

1 beaten egg, for egg wash

For the filling

1 ¾ lb (770 g) organic/humane ground pork or a mixture of pork and beef or veal, with not too much fat or the meat will shrink in the pastry; ask your butcher to grind you some lean meat for sausages, or buy unseasoned sausage meat

2 medium eggs

1 ½ cups (75 g) panko or homemade breadcrumbs from Pistolets (see page 76) or Beschuit (page 94)

1 tsp salt

2 Tbsp finely chopped fresh flat-leaf parsley

1 tsp freshly ground black pepper

¼ tsp ground mace or nutmeg

For the pastry, combine the flour, butter, sugar, and yeast in a large bowl or the bowl of an electric mixer fitted with the dough hook. Pour in half of the water and start kneading. When completely absorbed, pour in the rest of the water and knead for 5 minutes. Let the dough rest for 5 minutes.

Add the salt and knead for 10 minutes until it has come together in a smooth and elastic dough that is neither too dry nor terribly wet. Cover the dough and set aside for 1 hour until it has doubled in size.

Meanwhile, prepare the filling by combining all the ingredients and kneading until all the flavorings and breadcrumbs are well distributed.

Divide the meat filling into 12 portions of about 2 ½ oz (75 g) each and shape each piece into a sausage about 6 inches long. If you start the filling early you can put it in the fridge until needed.

Preheat the oven to 325°F. Do not use the fan setting. Line a baking sheet with parchment paper.

Divide the dough into 12 equal pieces and roll out on a floured work surface into ovals about 8 inches long and about 4 inches wide. Place a sausage in the middle of each oval and fold the top and bottom inward, followed by the left and right sides. Crimp the edges tightly and place on the baking sheet with the crimped side down.

Brush the tops of the rolls with the egg wash and bake for 50 minutes until golden brown.

Cool on a wire rack.

These worstenbrood freeze perfectly: just thaw overnight in the fridge, then bake for 15 minutes at 400°F.

Beschuit

Often called *tweebak*, meaning twice baked, these are not to be confused with the spongy cake the French and indeed Dutch-speaking people call "biscuit," or biscuits in the English sense of the word. *Beschuiten* are twice-baked bread buns of the rusk family. The name comes from the Latin *bis* (twice) and *coctus* (cook), which gave the Italians the word *biscotto* and us the word biscuit. They are first baked as buns, then halved and baked until crisp. Some recipes use a loaf that is sliced and, often, coated in sugar before being baked again (as seen in Osias Beert's painting on page 197). This type of beschuit still exists in Bruges today as *Brugse beschuiten*, although the modern eye would categorize them as toast.

Beschuit was around in medieval times, but it was in the 17th century that it began to be produced in large bakeries. One town in the Netherlands, Wormer, had over 150 beschuit bakeries in the 17th century. Baking during the night wasn't allowed for fear of fires – most of the buildings were made of wood – so every morning, the baker's tower clock rang the bell to announce the start of the day and at night the clock rang to turn off the ovens.

Because beschuit had a long shelf life it was also taken on board ships, along with ship's biscuits or hardtack. Ship's biscuits were for every day, while beschuit was a treat, as it was made from a richer dough. Beschuit was versatile, eaten plain, but also frequently crumbled to thicken sauces and to replace flour in part or altogether.

In the 20th century, the baking of beschuit moved to the local bakery, partly motivated by the two world wars when bakeries were forced by the authorities to switch from, for example, *peperkoek* to beschuit as the need for the latter was much greater.

Unlike the much flatter beschuit of the past, today's beschuiten have a raised disc shape. This shape is obtained by letting the dough balls rise, then baking them stuffed underneath *beschuitdoppen* (small round cake tins with holes to let the air out; see the photograph on the previous pages). The tin forces the dough to rise into shape. After baking, the doppen are removed and the beschuit buns are halved and then baked again to dry them out.

In the past, beschuiten were sold from large tins in the bakery, but for the past hundred or so years they have been sold in rolls or tins of thirteen: a baker's dozen.

Beschuit to celebrate the birth of a child

Beschuit is often seen in art of the 17th century, mostly in breakfast still-life paintings. At times when bakers were not allowed to bake during the night, there was no bread for breakfast, so beschuit, thanks to its long shelf life, stepped in to save the first meal of the day. At that time, fine beschuit was food for the rich and that is why, in the Netherlands, the custom remains to serve beschuit sprinkled with anise sugar comfits (*muisjes* or *mice*) to celebrate the birth of a child, blue for a boy and pink for a girl (or was it the other way round?). History continues to surprise me, and a "Eureka!" moment came when I found a recipe for *muysjes* – aniseed in a sugar coating – in the confectionery chapter of an 18th-century Dutch cookbook. I have several recipes for comfits (seeds in a sugar coating), but that they called it muisjes, the name we still use for this particular comfit, was a great surprise.

Spreading beschuit with butter and topping it with sprinkles is a very satisfying way to eat them and felt like a feast to me as a child. At children's parties we were often given beschuit to decorate with sprinkles and candy. In fact the first-ever "cake" I made was smearing beschuit with a mixture of margarine and sugar, stacking a couple, then covering them in chocolate sprinkles. I served it with pride to my parents in bed. It was seven o'clock in the morning and I was about six years old. To my disappointment, they didn't eat it.

Beschuit as an ingredient

In historical cookery books of the Low Countries, beschuit crumbs are often called for as an ingredient for waffles or for thickening sauces. And while we no longer use it for waffle batter, every clever cook keeps a roll or two in the cupboard for using as breadcrumbs to thicken sauces. When stored well, they keep for ages. Beschuit crumbs can be used in the following recipes in this book: Spice Cookies (page 200), Oost Vlaamse Vlaai (page 158), and Lierse Vlaaike (page 160).

Modern beschuit is a featherlight cake, made possible by a cocktail of additives called *beschuitgelei*. My recipe yields a more firm rusk, which is also more natural and more akin to its ancestor.

Makes 10 beschuiten (see photograph on pages 92–93)

4 cups (500 g) bread flour

2 Tbsp (45 g) glucose, corn syrup, or honey

1 ½ Tbsp (20 g) butter, softened

4 ¾ tsp (15 g) instant dry yeast

1 ¼ cups water

1 medium egg yolk

2 tsp sea salt

vegetable oil, for greasing

A word on beschuitdoppen

I understand not every baker is keen enough to buy new kit for every bake they want to try, so if you want to make these you can either bake them without tins or you can search out tins that are about the same size and adjust your ball of dough. People often use the tops of metal tins. You can get creative, or you can splurge on beschuit tins, which are inexpensive enough to make up for the shipping cost. I can testify that using the tins is very satisfying.

Use 5–10 beschuitdoppen or small round baking tins 4 inches in diameter and 1¼ inches deep, greased.

Combine the flour, glucose, butter, and yeast in a large bowl or the bowl of an electric mixer fitted with the dough hook. Pour in half of the water and the egg yolk and start kneading. When the liquid is completely absorbed, pour in the remaining water and knead for 5 minutes. Let the dough rest for 5 minutes.

Add the salt and knead for 10 minutes until the dough has come together in a smooth and elastic dough that is neither too dry nor terribly wet.

Cover the dough and set aside for 1 hour until it has doubled in size. Line 2 baking sheets with parchment paper and lightly grease the beschuitdoppen, if using.

Briefly knead the dough and divide it into 10 equal pieces. Take a piece of dough and lightly flatten it on your work surface, then pull the outer parts in like a purse and gently squeeze together like a dumpling so that the dough will not split open while rising. Turn the dough over so the squeezed ends are on the bottom. It should be nice and smooth on top – if not, flatten it and start again. Shape into a round bun and place the buns on the sheets. Cover with a large plastic bag (I keep one especially for this purpose) and rest the buns for 1 hour.

Flatten the risen buns with the palm of your hand and place the beschuitdoppen or tins over the buns. Cover and rest the buns again for 1 hour.

Toward the end of the resting time, preheat the oven to 450°F. Do not use the fan setting.

Transfer the sheets of buns covered with the tins to the middle of the oven and bake for 20 minutes until golden – it is difficult to check with the tins but try, carefully, lifting up a tin wearing an oven glove.

After baking, remove the tins, and transfer the buns to a wire rack to cool. You can eat them as buns, but if you want to go ahead and make the rusks, leave the buns overnight.

The next day, preheat the oven to 400°F. Do not use the fan setting. Halve the buns and lay them cut-side up on the baking sheets. Bake for 12 minutes, then turn off the oven and leave the door slightly ajar to let out any steam (a wooden spoon placed between the door and the side of the oven will make just the right-sized gap). Let the beschuiten dry in the oven for 15 minutes. Put your ear close to the oven...the cooling rusks make a soothing sound that I can only describe as rain gently hitting a window. The beschuiten will keep for several weeks stored in an airtight container.

Pain à la grecque

Pain à la grecque is linked to the founding of the Augustijnenklooster (Augustinian monastery) in Brussels in 1589. It was a significant moment, as the Netherlands had gone through the Reformation, and the founding of this cloister was part of the revival of Catholicism in the region. The monks taught lessons in their cloister, acted as firefighters to the community, and, according to legend, on feast days they also baked cookies with leftover bread dough and sugar and handed them out to the poor.

The name pain à la grecque is deceptive: it was originally bread *(pain)* from the *grecht* – the city canal or waterway that surrounded the cloister where the cookies were distributed. (It was also nicknamed *wolvengracht brood* or wolf canal bread, as the canal was called the Wolvengracht or Wolf Canal.) Frenchification of the name made it *"pain à la grecque,"* which is often misunderstood as "Greek bread," although it has nothing to do with Greece. A book from 1829[16] mentions pain à la grecque as the speciality of Brussels together with *pistolets* (see page 76); however, several bakeries in Antwerp used to sell the cookie by weight. My mum grew up with it and so did I.

A recent addition is pearl sugar (nib sugar), but traditionally it is made with rough sugar crystals that do not melt during baking. These are harder to obtain, so feel free to use small pearl sugar instead.

Makes 18 large pieces

4 cups (500 g) bread flour

10 Tbsp (150 g) unsalted butter, softened

1 tsp ground cinnamon

3 ¼ tsp (10 g) instant dry yeast

1 medium egg

1 ¼ cups whole milk

pinch of salt

1 ½ cups (320 g) large nonmelting sugar crystals or tiny pearl sugar (nib sugar)

3 Tbsp superfine sugar + 3 Tbsp water, for glazing

Tip: You can use leftover Vlaai dough (page 148), which is very similar.

Combine the flour, butter, cinnamon, and yeast in a large bowl or the bowl of an electric mixer fitted with the dough hook. Pour in the egg and half of the milk and start kneading. When completely absorbed, pour in the remaining milk and knead for 5 minutes. Set aside to rest for 5 minutes.

Add the salt and knead for 10 minutes, scraping the dough off the dough hook and side of the bowl if needed, until it has come together in a smooth and elastic dough that is neither too dry nor terribly wet. Cover the dough and set aside for 1 hour until it has doubled in size.

Weigh 7-oz (200-g) chunks of dough and set aside to rest while you prepare your baking sheets. You need four sheets lined with parchment paper, depending on how large your oven is: you might need more, or you could adjust the strips of dough to fit your sheets. On another sheet or your work surface, scatter the sugar.

Roll each chunk of dough in the sugar and shape into a thin sausage, transfer to the baking sheets, and flatten until they are half as high. Let the dough rest, covered with a kitchen towel, for 15 minutes.

Meanwhile, preheat the oven to 400°F. Don't use the fan setting.

Flatten the rolls of dough further until they are 3 inches wide, and sprinkle the leftover sugar over them. Place the sheets in the middle of the oven, one at a time, and bake for 25–30 minutes until golden brown. They should not be pale, but if some bits of sugar are black, it has gone too far.

While baking, make a glaze by melting the superfine sugar into the water over low heat. Brush the pains à la grecque with the sugar syrup as soon as they come out of the oven, using a pastry brush, then turn over on the sheet. While they are still warm, cut them into 4-inch-long cookies, then transfer them to a wire rack to cool.

Keep in an airtight container.

CANDLEMAS AND PANCAKES

"On Candlemas, no woman is too poor to heat her pancake pan."
Flemish saying

In our house, making pancakes for Candlemas was a sacred thing. Not for religious reasons, but because it was tradition. Even though my mother's sister and aunt are nuns, we never went to church and, outside of school, I never had to read the Bible or pray. Religion was used to teach me lessons of morality, though: my mother taught me when I was little that I couldn't lie because it would make baby Jesus cry. We were, however, very religious when it came to heating our pan at Candlemas for pancakes.

Candlemas is celebrated on the fortieth day after Christmas – on 2 February – and in Europe it signals the end of the winter season. In honor of Mary, a candle procession is held, and candles are blessed. Hence the name "Candle mass."

Many theories exist as to why, in Belgium, France, and Switzerland, we eat pancakes on this day. One is that the pancake is a descendant of sacrificial bread, symbolizing the sun and the return of spring after the dark and cold of winter.

In the Netherlands, and in the past in current Belgium, pancakes were also eaten on Shrove Tuesday, but we called it Vastenavond (Fast Night), the evening before Ash Wednesday and the end of the Carnival season.

Anglo-Christians eat pancakes for Shrove Tuesday or Fat Tuesday (Mardi Gras), the day before Ash Wednesday. They call it Pancake Day, these days, to give it a more secular appeal. While Candlemas is always on 2 February, Shrove Tuesday is a moveable feast that occurs forty-seven days before Easter Sunday.

Making pancakes for Shrove Tuesday or Vastenavond gave people the opportunity to use up eggs, milk, and butter before embarking on the Lenten fast. That is, if you were wealthy enough to have them spare and in need of "using up." For common people, the pancakes, fritters, and other rich foods eaten on the days leading up to Lent were a treat.

Wheat pancakes were not the only kind of pancakes made for Candlemas or Vastenavond: buckwheat pancakes, savory and sweet too, were also made – depending on your social status in the past and taste for buckwheat today. Seventeenth-century paintings depicting poor people's meals show thick buckwheat pancakes, while the rich collection of winter bakes in the painting by Hans Francken (see page 66) clearly shows fine wheat pancakes.

Old recipes for pancakes call for triple the amount of eggs compared with modern recipes; they also include spices such as nutmeg, mace, and sugar. Today, recipes usually contain milk, flour, eggs, melted butter, and a pinch of salt, with the odd recipe calling for cinnamon or vanilla, the latter not being traditional at all.

It feels a little odd to give a recipe for simple pancakes, which are the easiest thing to make, and I've never used a recipe for them. Instead, I find it liberating to take a bowl, scoop flour from a jar using a teacup, add an egg or two, and then whisk in milk until the consistency seems right. If the first pancake fails, it is not the end of the world. With pancakes, as in life, you can always pivot to obtain a better result.

If you haven't yet mastered the art of "winging it" when making pancakes, then here are the quantities for a stack of 12–14 paper-thin pancakes: 7 oz (200 g) plain flour, 17 fl oz (500 ml) whole milk, 3 eggs, 20 ¾ oz (20 g) butter (melted), ¼ teaspoon salt, and 1 teaspoon sugar. Follow the method on page 109, adding the whole eggs to the flour and half the milk in step 1, then add the remaining milk with the sugar, salt, and melted butter.

I hope that after trying a few of the recipes in this book you will gain confidence, and experience the exhilarating feeling of not having to stick to measurements when making these pancakes. Baking doesn't always have to be an exact science.

MARDI GRAS AND BINCHE CARNIVAL

Mardi Gras also means pancakes, especially in the carnival town of Binche where they maintain the iconic Gilles parade.

On Mardi Gras, hours before dawn, everywhere in the Belgian town of Binche in Wallonia the Gilles are waking up. Dressing up as these Carnival creatures is the privilege of male citizens of Binche from as soon as a boy can walk. It is a four-hundred-year-old tradition deemed so important that it was granted UNESCO cultural heritage status in 2004.

The whole day is dictated by rituals. First the Gilles are ceremonially dressed by their family in their precious traditional red costume patched with crowns, lions, stars, and frills in the colors of the Belgian flag. The jacket is stuffed with barley straw to create the unique hunchback silhouette.

All dressed, they then go door to door to gather fellow Gilles, accompanied by tambourines and the clanking sound of their wooden clogs on the pavement. As the parade grows it also becomes louder, an age-old tradition to chase away the darkness of winter from the streets.

Armed with their *ramon*, a bunch of willow branches that is also traditionally seen in the hand of other winter figures, and each with the same eerie wax mask in the shape of a pink face with red hair and green glasses, they look like an army of light marching in tiny steps on their wooden clogs to the beat of the drums. Off they all go to City Hall, where the mayor of Binche will honor the Gilles who have fifty years of service under their belt of bells. After a celebratory meal of oysters and Champagne, the Gilles part ways to go home and swap their wax masks for enormously tall ostrich-feather hats and wicker baskets of oranges. Hungry Gilles will enjoy a plate of *doubles de Binche*, buckwheat pancakes filled with a typical local strong cheese (see page 105 for the recipe): a perfect meal to keep Gilles, young and old, going on their wooden clogs.

The merry men then regroup and head for a large square from which they will hold the big cortège, accompanied by other traditional figures, such as harlequins, peasants, and pierrots. The Gilles are stamping the ground with their clogs as they walk to the mesmerizing tune of the tambourine. With each thump of a clog they wake up the Earth from its deep winter sleep, while the oranges are thrown into the crowd as a sign of fertility and prosperity. The parade of the Gilles marks the last day of the three-day Binche Carnival.

Doubles de Binche

The batter for these thin buckwheat pancakes should be made with half buckwheat and half all-purpose flour, which is a common ratio in most recipes for buckwheat pancakes. The pancakes are then filled with a very strong local Walloon cheese called *boulette* (a rind-washed aged soft cheese).

Locals these days also add blond Binchoise beer to the batter, a top-fermented, unfiltered beer with a gentle bitterness and aromatic notes of coriander and citrus. You can find a beer with these flavor notes to use if you are opting to make the modern version. While modern recipes do not use any eggs, I am adding an egg, as I am recreating Catherine Bernard's *doubles* (see page 106) in her honor.

The doubles are also a very popular dish in Nivelles, a town south of Brussels.

Variation: All over Belgium and the Netherlands these crêpes are eaten with a sweet topping, such as *stroop* (syrup) or sugar, or with strips of bacon baked into the batter. In Liège, raisins are added for *boûkète* (see page 106).

**Makes 30 pancakes,
6 inches in diameter**

4 ¾ tsp (15 g) instant dry yeast

1 qt milk or water or half milk and
    half water, lukewarm

2 cups (250 g) buckwheat flour

2 cups (250 g) all-purpose flour

1 medium egg

1 ½ Tbsp (20 g) unsalted butter,
    melted and cooled

2 tsp sea salt

butter or lard, for frying

8 oz (225 g) cheese (see note)

Add the yeast to half of the milk or water. In a large bowl, combine both flours and blend well. Make a well in the center and add the egg, followed by the yeast mixture and the butter. Now gradually add the rest of the milk or water until well incorporated and smooth. Stir in the salt. Cover the bowl with a kitchen towel and set aside to rest for 1 hour, or refrigerate overnight.

Cook the crêpes in a generous amount of butter or lard in a 8-inch frying pan, or use whatever pan you have. I use about 1½ scoops of a 2-tablespoon ladle to get the right amount of batter for each pancake. The batter should be pourable, as for crêpes. As you add the batter, tilt and rotate the pan to coat the bottom with a thin layer.

When 2 crêpes are cooked, add dots of cheese on one, leaving ½ inch around the edge of the crêpe, and place the second crêpe on top. Set aside to be refried later, and continue making crêpes. Keep any crêpes you don't use immediately in an airtight container in the fridge for up to 3 days, or freeze and simply thaw them an hour before you need them, refrying them in butter or lard.

Refrying is essential to obtain the crisp exterior of the crêpe: we don't want soggy pancakes, we want crispy crêpes! To refry, add some more butter or lard to the pan, then place a filled pair of crêpes in the pan and cook for 2 minutes until crisp, turning once.

On cheese
After talking to cheese experts, I have to conclude that the Walloon cheese used in the original recipe is unique and doesn't really have a counterpart anywhere else in the world. For the sake of completeness I'm listing the traditional cheeses, but as an alternative shredded mature Gouda or Cheddar is a very good choice.

The traditional cheeses include: bètchéye, boulette, boulette de Falaën, boulette de Namur, boulette de Nivelles, boulette de Romedenne, boulette de Surice, and cassette de Beaumont.

CATHERINE À DOUBLES

Frédéric Ansion, the president of the oldest Gilles society in Binche and author of several books on the town's history, told me a story about *doubles de Binche* (see recipe on page 105). In a small house behind the town hall of Binche, Catherine Bernard was born on 29 November 1828. She was known locally as "Catherine à Doubles" because she baked the famous buckwheat crêpes (pancakes) outside her house. Women baking pancakes on open fires in makeshift stalls by the road is seen in several Dutch genre paintings of the 17th century. Catherine might have been one of the last pancake ladies that we have on record.

In his book, Ansion has the lyrics to a song about Catherine and her "Double Binchoises." The song tells us the ingredients of the pancake and a little something about Catherine's character:

To make it we use flour, buckwheat, butter, eggs and cheese. From September to Maundy Thursday. It can be eaten hot, no one is complaining. The brave woman who cooks them is called "Catherine à Doubles." She asks everyone, "What news! Do you want double?" It's cheap – yes really! Fifteen cents, nothing more. And for a little extra, you get more butter and cheese.

It's generally accepted that the name "doubles" comes from eating the pancakes in pairs, but the song leads me to believe the name came from the dear lady Catherine's nickname, because the song highlighted that she always tried to upsell her pancakes. Ansion kindly gave me a photograph of Catherine sitting in front of her house. She is of a mature age, flowers in her hair, dressed in a white blouse and stiff white apron, her legs straight and her ankles probably crossed, waiting patiently by the flat table-like coal-fired griddle with the wooden bucket of batter and ladle by her feet.

The doubles de Binche are eaten between Candlemas and Mardi Gras today, although the song tells us that it used to be from September until the Thursday before Easter. Many Gilles will eat them for lunch during Carnival when they go home to change into their afternoon costume with feathers. Mind you, after a breakfast of oysters, doubles for lunch are ideal for a busy day dancing the winter away in the streets of Binche.

Boûkète

In Liège a similar buckwheat pancake is baked, with raisins added to the batter, around Christmastime and for the town's festival on 15 August. It is not served with cheese, but with sweet toppings, such as *stroop* (syrup).

Boûkète is Walloon for the Dutch word *boekweit* (buckwheat). The Walloon language has Celtic, Romance, and Germanic influences. The language has become very rare, as most Walloons speak French now.

CRÊPES IN THE MANNER OF TOURNAI

Pancakes (*pannekoeken* in Dutch and *crêpes* in French) first appear with a Belgian connection in the 14th century in *Le Ménagier de Paris* (The Parisian Household Book), which was written as a treatise on morality and domestic economy by a wealthy man for his young bride.

A recipe titled "Crêpes à la guise de Tournay" (crêpes in the manner of Tournai) is not the only recipe connected to the town of Tournai, or Doornik, included in this book (see pages 57 and 166). The town was at that time in the possession of the dukes of Burgundy. The city was thrown around like a ball throughout history; in 862 CE Charles the Bald made Tournai the capital city of the County of Flanders. After the partition of the Frankish empire it became part of France. In 1513 it was captured by Henry VIII of England, which made it part of England. In 1668, the city returned to France for a short while, and in the 18th century it formed part of the Austrian Netherlands. Following the Napoleonic Wars, Tournai, then part of France, became part of the United Netherlands and, after 1830, of the newly independent country, Belgium.

While the city of Tournai was once one of the greatest cultural and economic centers of Flanders because the river Schelde connects it to Antwerp, today it is not situated in Flanders but in Wallonia, the French-speaking region of Belgium.

The recipe
This recipe as it appears in *Le Ménagier* is an incredibly detailed recipe for thin pancakes made using white wine and butter, which the reader is told to "unsalt" before use. This was at a time when recipes were merely *aides-memoire* rather than step-by-step instructions. The recipe is not just important in the history of recipe writing, but also as part of the history of the formation of the Low Countries and Belgium.

Crêpes in the manner of Tournai
Translation by Dr Annie Gray.

First, you should provide yourself with a copper or brass pan holding a quart, the mouth of which should be no wider than the bottom, or only very little, and the sides of which should be four or three and a half fingers high. Item: put in salted butter, melt it, skim it and clean it and then pour into another pan, and leave all the salt behind. Add to it fresh fat as clean as can be. Then take eggs and fry them, and take the whites away from half of them and beat the remaining whites and all of the yolks, and then take a third or a quart of lukewarm white wine, and mix all of this together: then take the finest white wheaten flour that you can have, and beat everything together bit by bit, enough to tire out one or two people, and your paste should be neither thin nor thick, but such that it can gently run through a hole as big as a small finger; then put your butter and your fat on the fire together, as much of one as the other, until it boils, then take your paste and fill a bowl or big spoon of pierced wood and pour this into your fat, first in the middle of your pan, then turning it until the sides are filled; and keep beating your paste without ceasing so that you can make more crêpes. And for each crêpe that is in the pan you should lift it with a stick or skewer and turn it over to cook, then remove it, put on a plate, and start another; and remember to always be moving and beating the remaining paste without stopping.

Paulette's Diestse kruidkoek

Also known as *Diestse cruydtcoeck*, this is a thin pancake that is known in historical English cookbooks as a "tansy." This is because it uses the herb *Tanacetum vulgare*, or tansy. In Dutch the herb is called *boerenwormkruid* or *reynvaert*, as it was called when the great father of botany Rembert Dodoens wrote poetically about the *cruydt* and the custom of making egg cakes with it in his *Cruydeboeck* published in 1554.

Another recipe appeared as "Engelschen Cruytcoeck" in the *Cocboeck* by Carolus Battus, published in 1593. It uses tansy and spinach, eggs, sugar, and mace or nutmeg but no flour. Dodoens doesn't call for flour either. Historical recipes for English tansies are usually without flour or use just a small amount, creating something that is more like an omelette.

While these green-speckled pancakes were eaten widely, it is in the town of Diest in Flanders where they remain a much-loved treat to celebrate the start of spring. In many modern recipes the tansy is partly swapped out for dandelion leaf, so if you cannot find tansy, dandelion leaf is a good alternative for flavor; for color you could also use young spinach or chervil.

The Confrerie van den Cruydtcoeck (Association of the Kruidkoek) keeps alive the tradition of picking young shoots of tansy at the start of spring and making them into pancakes. But I am quite certain my dear friend Krikke's mother, Paulette, who is an absolute gem, is the master baker of these *kruidkoeken*. She doesn't stop making them when the plant matures and brings my friends stacks of green pancakes all year round. I've known Paulette for years and she has always been so motherly to me: this is her family recipe.

Serves 4–8 people

3 ⅓ cups (400 g) all-purpose wheat, spelt, or rye flour

1 qt whole milk

2 medium eggs, separated

1 Tbsp vanilla sugar, or 1 Tbsp superfine sugar + 1 tsp natural vanilla extract

3 Tbsp superfine sugar

pinch of salt

2 oz (50 g) young (small) tansy or dandelion sprigs (use as much as you like, but do not overdo it or the kruidkoek will taste bitter)

butter, for frying

Put the flour into a large bowl, pour in half of the milk and 2 egg yolks, and whisk to combine. Beat the egg whites with the vanilla sugar to stiff peaks.

Set aside ⅓–½ cup of milk and add the rest to the batter along with the egg whites, superfine sugar, and salt.

Tear the leaves off the tansy stalks if the stalks are woody and brown. If you have young green shoots, leave them whole.

In a blender, purée the tansy leaves with the reserved milk. Stir this mixture into the batter. The batter should have a runny consistency; if it looks too thick, add a dash of milk to thin it out.

Melt a teaspoon of butter in a 9-inch (23-cm) base crêpe pan over medium–high heat. Pour in a ladleful (1 fl oz/30 ml) of batter and quickly tilt the pan around to distribute the batter evenly.

Fry until the pancake has pulled away from the sides a little and the edge has turned golden, then flip the pancake with the help of a spatula and cook the other side until golden.

Geutelingen

The *geuteling* is a thick pancake from the Flemish Ardennes. The batter is poured with a long ladle straight onto the red-hot tiles of a wood-fired oven. In the past, families brought their own batter to a communal oven, where they baked *geutelingen* together. The demise of the geuteling came with the demise of the wood-fired oven. But one village is keeping this heritage alive by baking large quantities of geutelingen every year. And much of that is thanks to Pieter de Koekelaere, who is a third-generation geuteling baker and owner of a geuteling bakery in the village of Elst.

Geutelingen were traditionally baked on 9 February during Carnival time, for the feast day of Saint Apollonia, who was known as the "toothache saint." People believed that eating geutelingen on that day would shield them from toothache, so many traveled to the village of Elst on a pilgrimage. While the geutelingen appear humble to us today, the amount of wood needed to fire the oven classified these thick pancakes as a feast day treat.

The pancakes used to be transferred onto straw to cool, but today wire racks do the trick just fine. The batter contains just flour, milk, eggs, and yeast. The result is a spongy pancake with a large air bubble. They should be eaten fresh, topped with butter or brown sugar, but I rather like making them savory, topping a cooled geuteling with a mixture of Cheddar and Emmenthaler cheese and popping it back in the searing hot oven to melt. I then add chopped tomatoes, spring onions, and chile and spoon some quark or sour cream over the top. Two per person make a great lunch. This isn't traditional, though it has become tradition in our house.

But there is a catch: you cannot bake geutelingen in a regular oven or pan – I've tried. The heat from a wood-fired oven or electric pizza oven is essential to puff up the batter. Cooked in a pan or poured onto a hot stone at 475°F, it's just a pancake. I have one of those funky electric pizza ovens, so I am able to bake these geutelingen at home. I use a small ladle that will fit under the roof of my oven.

Makes 20 geutelingen, depending on your ladle size

4 cups (500 g) all-purpose flour

3 ¾ tsp (12 g) instant dry yeast

pinch of salt

3 cups whole milk

4 medium eggs

butter and dark brown sugar, for serving

Use an electric pizza oven or a woodfired oven.

Put the flour, yeast, and salt into a large bowl and add the milk. Whisk until smooth, add the eggs, and whisk until well combined. The batter should be pourable, as for crêpes. Cover and set aside to rest in the fridge overnight.

If you have an electric pizza oven, preheat the oven to as high as it goes (mine goes to 750°F). If you have a wood-fired oven, you know how to fire it up. Otherwise, put your oven on maximum heat and bake a little longer.

When ready to bake, give the batter a calm stir. I use a small 2-tablespoon ladle to swiftly spoon two ladles full of the batter for each geuteling on top of the hot stone in the oven. Then leave it alone because the batter starts to make air pockets immediately when it touches the hot surface. Bake for 2 minutes until golden brown and puffy in the middle, then transfer to a wire rack or serve immediately.

The warm geutelingen are traditionally spread with melting butter and topped with dark brown sugar to serve. See above for my savory suggestion. Reheating is possible in a toaster or oven. Leftover geutelingen can be frozen.

JAN HAVICKSZ. STEEN (c. 1626–1679): *Baker Arent Oostwaard and his Wife Catharina Keizerswaard*, 1658, Rijksmuseum Amsterdam. In the painting we see krakelingen (pretzels) hanging from a pretzel stand, as well as duivekater, beschuiten, and several white buns. In the background a little boy is blowing the bakery horn to alert the villagers that the bread is ready.

KRAKELING, BRETZEL, PRETZEL

The shape of the *krakeling* or pretzel, this twisted strand of dough, symbolizes the eternal cycle of life and death. It can also be seen as a symbol of marriage or the crossed arms of someone in prayer. With concepts as old as a pretzel, different meanings could all have been relevant at one point in history or in some locality. The legends surrounding its origins, too, are plentiful.

The earliest surviving depictions of a pretzel can be found in a couple of "Last Supper" illuminations from the 11th and 12th century. The *Hortus deliciarum* (Garden of Delights) is a 12th-century illuminated manuscript created as an educational tool for young novices at the convent of the Hohenburg Abbey in Alsace, and shows a pretzel on the table. Alsace today is still known for its *bretzels*: the name is clearly related to the German word *Brezel*.

A striking image of intertwined pretzels used as a garland held by fools in each corner can be found in a vividly colored illuminated manuscript produced in about 1440 by the anonymous Dutch artist known as the Master of Catherine of Cleves. On the right side of the illustration is a row of flatbreads or crackers, which I believe could be Jewish matzoth, baked for Easter.

The Morgan Library in New York, where this manuscript is held, reports that the link between the saint depicted on the page, Saint Bartholomew, and the pretzels is unknown. Yet, Bartholomew appears to be patron saint to bakers, among many other professions, which could be an explanation. More interestingly, in Belgium he is also the patron saint of Geraardsbergen, where his relics are held. Every year, the pretzel is celebrated here with a procession and the custom of throwing them from the top of a hill.

What's in a name?
The name pretzel, or Brezel in German, comes from the Old High German *brezita*, *brezin*, *brezta*, and *brezitella* and Middle High German *brezel* and *prezel*.

It is possibly connected to the Latin *bracteatus*, meaning gilded or shining like gold, or the medieval Latin *brachitella* and *bracchialis*, meaning folded arms or bracelet. Digging further, there is *pretium*, which translates to price or reward, because these breads were often used as alms or handed out at festivities. As the

pretzel is centuries old, there could be various sources for the name. Yet the Dutch name, krakeling, isn't linguistically related to any of the Latin words, not even to Brezel, unless you count variations on the Middle Dutch *brootjen* or *brotchen* (meaning "little bread").

The Dutch word krakeling, freely translated, means crackling, and tells me that early examples of this bread were very brittle. This makes sense, as pretzels had a Christian religious significance at Lent when eggs and animal fats were not allowed to be used. Pretzels feature in artworks such as *The Battle between Carnival and Lent* (see page 12) by Pieter Bruegel. If you look closely at the gaunt Lady Lent depicted in the work, you can spot pretzels, herring, mussels, and simple bread, the staples of Lenten meals.

The pretzel as symbol
Because of its distinctive shape and symbolic meaning, artists frequently included these twisted breads in their art and, thus, in their story. In art the pretzel can represent eternity, but also the fragility of life, as demonstrated in Jan Van Bijlert's *Pulling of the Pretzel* (c. 1630–1640) and Pieter Bruegel's *Netherlandish Proverbs* (1559), where two people are each holding one end of a pretzel (see page 144). You can spot pretzels hanging from a pretzel stand in the painting by Jan Steen (opposite page), and if you look closely, you'll also spot pretzels decorating the large *duivekater* loaf, as good wishes for the receiver. In Luxembourg and more recently also in Namur in Wallonia, it is a tradition for a man to give a woman a pretzel on mid-Lent (Laetare) Sunday as a confession of love. With great contrast, pretzels were eaten at weddings and, in some areas in Flanders, the Netherlands, and Friesland, also at funerals.

From the Middle Ages, pretzels appeared across the whole of mainland Europe. The pretzel also became the symbol used by bakers as a guild symbol and so you see it in shop signage all over north and western Europe.

Today pretzels are still most frequently found and celebrated in Austria, Switzerland, Alsace, Sweden (where they are called *kringlor*), the Netherlands, and Belgium. There are Swabian, Bavarian, and German stories claiming its invention, and they all make the pretzel differently, with many regional varieties.

In Belgium, pretzels – or more correctly krakelingen – are still found today in Geraardsbergen, where they are made of a basic bread dough in the shape of a ring (see page 116). *Brugse achten* (see page 124) are figure-eight unsweetened cookies that are covered in sugar and then baked. A traditional figure-eight laminated dough pastry found all over Belgium is a pretzel too, but in disguise because custard in the two holes obscures its shape. Namur takes its pretzel from Luxembourg, and in Liège recently a pretzel bakery opened with a whole array of pretzels in different styles and shapes.

In the Netherlands there are puff pastry pretzel cookies and small salty shortcrust pretzels at the iconic bakery Holtkamp in Amsterdam. *Nonnevotten* (see page 140) often share the pretzel shape.

The knot-shaped bread pretzel as seen in 16th- and 17th-century Flemish and Dutch paintings is forgotten, and so are the almond cookie versions found in old cookbooks (see page 120). They appear more frequently in art than they do in cookbooks of the period, in general.

In Germany, savory pretzels are sprayed with a solution of lye before going into the oven. The resulting alkalinity enhances the Maillard reaction, a chemical reaction that causes the protein in the flour to brown. It is what gives pretzels that silky, shiny surface texture. Sweet pretzels too are baked: the *Martinsbrezel* for Saint Martin festivities; the *Weidenberger brezen* or *anisbreze* is made with aniseed.

The simplicity of pretzels also made them ideal for handing out as alms to the poor, something still remembered in the gifting of pretzels to bystanders at the European folkloric festivals where pretzels feature, such as at Geraardsbergen.

Geraardsbergen krakelingen feast and fire

A legend tells us of the siege of Flemish Geraardsbergen in 1381 by a fearless local nobleman, Walter Van Edingen. His strategy was to starve the people of Geraardsbergen, but when the last remnants of bread and herring were thrown over the city wall as a signal of abundance, the besiegers gave up, discouraged and tired of waiting. The people of Geraardsbergen then waited for dusk and created a bonfire on the mount of their town to let the neighboring towns know they got rid of the enemy and needed help. And every year since, a barrel of tar would be taken up to the same mount and a fire would be lit.

Reality, however, was less romantic, as the whole town of Geraardsbergen was actually destroyed that day. But the people of Geraardsbergen refuse to tell that story, although they recognize that it happened. They choose to tell the tale of nonviolent resistance instead.

To commemorate the siege, Geraardsbergen started celebrating the *krakelingenfeest* (pretzel feast) on the first Sunday of Lent, making it the carnival of this quaint town in the Flemish Ardennes. The festivities of the day start with a parade through the streets depicting the history of the town. Wicker baskets filled with pretzels are carried along with the procession and up the cobblestone path of the Oudenberg, the mount from the legend. The mount was adorned with a chapel in 1640 (the current structure is a copy from 1906), but the belief is that the mount was used by druids for rituals on solstices and equinoxes. *De Volksstem* newspaper of 1 September 1900 tells of a belief that the hill used to be where witches gathered for Sabbath.

Whatever the meaning given to the mount through the ages, it was common to build a chapel on a location that had been important to pre-Christian traditions, thereby Christianizing the customs connected to it instead of eradicating it and risking public outcry.

Today the mount and its narrow cobblestone path is mainly known abroad as the finale of one of the most challenging stretches of the Tour of Flanders cycle race.

The fish mentioned in the myth also have a place in the celebrations. After the parade has arrived at the mount, the dean, the mayor, the aldermen, and the municipal councilors each drink a small living fish from a bowl of wine. Some say it is a sign of celebration and fraternity; others say it is a symbol of new life as spring is coming. It can also be seen as sacrificial.

Between 1590 and 1608, Josse Schollaert, a local poet, playwright, and school principal, wrote a poem in Latin about the annual celebration in Geraardsbergen, showing us that in the 16th century, the tradition was already in full swing.[17]

After the fish were ceremonially gobbled up, it was time for the krakelingenworp to throw the pretzels from the top of the mount and into the greedy hands of the public.

A magazine[15] from 1879 describes in great detail and with much spectacle the happenings of the festivities and the joy of the spectators. At this time it wasn't just pretzels, but also wicker baskets filled with dried herrings and oranges that were carried up to the mount. These would all be tossed from the hill into the crowds, the herrings making a clattering sound like hail hitting the cobblestones. I imagine there would have been injuries at this annual event in the past, as the magazine mentions that after the pretzels, herrings, oranges, and figs, whole baskets filled with goodies were chucked down at the people who all desperately tried to catch them. In any case, those who were unlucky not to have caught any prize could buy something from the many stalls that had set up around the hill, for exorbitant prices, the author claims.

A British priest wrote a letter about this custom to the novelist Guido Gezelle in 1858.[18] He had just witnessed what he described as a "strange custom" on the hill in Geraardsbergen, where many people had flocked to witness the mayor drink from an ancient cup that contained a live fish. Afterward, fish and bread were thrown to the crowd.

The pretzel from Geraardsbergen is made as a ring just like the Swedish kringlor pretzel. An article from 1895 in *De Volksstem* reports that the pretzels were baked hard. Crucial to the story of Belgium, the author also mentions that Walloons and Flemings came together to take part in the celebrations and to battle it out for a *koek* (cake). Geraardsbergen is situated just a few kilometers from the language border.

Bonfire
The barrel of tar from the myth lives on in the name of the next and final stage of the pretzel feast, the *tonnekensbrand* (barrel fire). Every year after the wicker baskets of pretzels were emptied and dusk had set around the rolling countryside, a bonfire made of straw was lit, and the fire was answered by counter fires from the surrounding municipalities. In the olden days, torches were lit from the fire and taken down to the town and to the fields and orchards to bring light and to wake up nature for spring. It is a pagan custom akin to Apple Wassailing in Britain.

The Geraardsbergen festival was included on the UNESCO cultural heritage list in 2010. According to the annals of the town, a city account from 1393 mentions the expenses for the tonnekensbrand. Since then, there is evidence of both krakelingen and tonnekensbrand in the city accounts, with the exception of during the religious wars in the 16th century and the First and Second World Wars.

While many centuries-old cookies and baked goods have been lost to time, the pretzel's iconic shape has managed to save it from oblivion.

Geraardsbergse krakelingen

These buns are the pretzels from Geraardsbergen (see page 114). They are shaped into rings and made with a basic bread dough (less yeast, no fat) that creates a denser ring. They are related to other European ring-shaped breads, which are often no longer linked to pretzels, as we have come to associate just one shape with them and that is the figure-eight knot.

I often visit the Broodhuis bakery in Geraardsbergen, where they decorate the shop window with the *krakelingen* hung from the ceiling on strings. The baker told me the krakelingen aren't made to be eaten, but to decorate shops and most importantly to be thrown to the public from a nearby hill for the Krakelingenworp festival. To make them nicer to eat, a very small proportion of butter or fat is added to the dough. The baker from Broodhuis told me that many people confuse *mastellen* (see page 80) sold in his bakery with krakelingen these days, but they are not the same.

Geraardsbergen is also the town known for *mattentaart* cheese pies (see page 162).

Makes 6 krakelingen

4 cups (500 g) bread flour

1 ½ tsp (5 g) instant dry yeast

1 ½ Tbsp (20 g) unsalted butter or lard, softened

1 ¼ cups water

2 tsp sea salt

Combine the flour and yeast in a large bowl or the bowl of an electric mixer fitted with the dough hook. Add the butter or lard and half of the water and start kneading. When the liquid is completely absorbed, pour in the rest of the water and knead for 5 minutes. Leave the dough for 5 minutes to rest.

Add the salt and knead for a further 10 minutes. Let the dough rest, covered, for 30 minutes and then knead briefly.

Cover the dough and set aside for 1 hour until it has doubled in size.

Knock out the air, briefly knead the dough, and divide it into 6 equal pieces. Take a piece of dough and lightly flatten it on your work surface, then pull the outer parts in like a purse and gently squeeze together like a dumpling so that the dough can no longer split open while rising. Turn the dough over so the squeezed ends are on the bottom. It should be nice and smooth on top: if not, flatten it and start again. Cover with a large plastic bag (I keep one especially for this purpose). Rest the buns for 1 hour.

To create the ring shape, press your thumb into the smooth bun. Take the bun in one hand, place both thumbs in the middle, and squeeze through the dough while turning the bun so you end up with something that looks like a doughnut but with a much larger hole. The ring should be 1¼ inches thick and 5½–6 inches in diameter in total.

Place each krakeling on a tray or wooden board lined with parchment paper and dust with flour. Cover and rest the krakelingen for 20 minutes.

Toward the end of the resting time, preheat the oven to 450°F and put an empty baking sheet in the middle of the oven to get hot. Do not use the fan setting.

Transfer the krakelingen with the paper they sit on onto the hot baking sheet and bake for 15–20 minutes until they are golden brown.

If not eaten immediately, the krakelingen can be revived in a hot oven for a few minutes.

Zoute krakelingen

Although *krakelingen* (pretzels) feature prominently in 17th-century Netherlandish art, recipes for them are rare in 16th- and 17th-century Dutch cookbooks. They do appear frequently in cookbooks of the 18th century. In a small book book titled *'t Zaamenspraak tusschen een mevrouw, en een banket-bakker en Confiturier* from 1758, I found this recipe for salty krakelingen, which I have developed for you. They are made of a short pastry but you cannot exactly say they crack. They remind me of the tiny salty krakelingen that Cees Holtkamp has been making at his bakery in Amsterdam. These are delicate krakelingen, and because of the hint of salt, I can never stop myself from eating them. They are an elegant accompaniment to aperitifs at dinner parties.

Makes 16 krakelingen

1 ¾ cups (225 g) all-purpose flour

1 tsp salt

½ cup (115 g) unsalted butter, softened

1 medium egg

1 extra egg yolk, lightly beaten, for egg wash

Preheat the oven to 350°F. Line a large baking sheet with parchment paper.

Put the flour in a bowl, stir in the salt, then rub the butter into the flour until the mixture resembles breadcrumbs. Add the egg and mix to combine. Knead to a supple dough and shape into pretzels by dividing the pastry into 16 chunks and rolling them into 12-inch ropes. Shape into pretzels or figure eights and place on the baking sheet.

Brush all over with the egg wash and bake in the middle of the oven for 20–25 minutes until golden brown.

Transfer to a wire rack to cool. Store in an airtight container.

Serve as they are or as a snack with wine or beer, as they were intended to be served.

Amandel and anijs krakelingen

This recipe for sweet almond and aniseed *krakelingen* comes from *De Volmaakte Hollandse Keuken-Meid* from 1746. It is one of the earliest Dutch pretzel recipes in print, although I have found an earlier recipe for almond pretzels in a 17th-century German book.

According to the author, these pretzels are excellent, and I agree. They are chewy with a hint of marzipan, coriander, and a lot of aniseed flavor (if you hate aniseed, leave it out). The recipe calls for an obscure ingredient called "gum tragacanth," which is frequently used in sugarwork. Although not necessarily familiar to the home baker, it is easy to get online or from specialty cake-making stores. It is used to stabilize the pastry.

These krakelingen were historically served with sweet or spiced wine after a meal; they are a great way to let your guests taste the flavors of the past.

Makes 10 krakelingen

½ tsp aniseeds

¼ tsp coriander seeds

8 oz (225 g) blanched almonds, or use almond meal if you don't want to process it yourself

1 tsp rosewater

1 cup (110 g) confectioners' sugar

⅛ oz (5 g) gum tragacanth (E413)

1 medium egg

1 extra egg white, lightly beaten, for glaze

Preheat the oven to 300°F. Line a large baking sheet with parchment paper.

For the best result, grind the seeds yourself so you still have some larger bits and the spices won't color your pastry. Put them in a mortar and grind with the pestle until none of the seeds are left whole.

Put the blanched almonds and the rosewater into a food processor and process to a fine meal. Add the sugar, spices, and gum tragacanth and combine well.

Add the egg to the almond mixture and knead to a dough. It will appear dry, but kneading will bring the dough together thanks to the warmth of your hands and the emulsifying nature of the egg. Don't add water, or the dough will become too sticky.

Divide the dough into 10 chunks and roll out to 14-inch-long strands. Shape into knots or figure eights and transfer to the baking sheet. Brush all over with the egg white. Bake in the middle of the oven for 10 minutes, then brush again with egg white and bake for 10 minutes more until they are still pale but with a golden blush.

Transfer to a wire rack to cool. Store in an airtight container.

Brood krakelingen

These are the common *krakelingen* seen in the paintings of Bruegel and other Flemish and Dutch masters of the 16th and 17th century, some of which are included in this book. These pretzels are more bread-like, and even though the dough is without embellishment, the krakelingen look incredibly appetizing – especially when you serve these in your bread-and-butter basket at a dinner party. The dough is forgiving, and shaping it is not complicated. These are like Italian grissini breadsticks, but with a far more attractive shape.

As seen in the painting on page 112, in the past these krakelingen were hung on wooden krakelingen stands. Because they are not made from an enriched or luxurious dough, they were considered perfect for Lent. We are reminded of that by Pieter Bruegel's incredible painting *The Battle between Carnival and Lent* (see page 12). If we look closely at the gaunt Lady Lent, we find krakelingen by her feet and attached to the belt of one of the followers in her parade.

Makes a baker's dozen (13)

2 ¼ cups (270 g) bread flour

2 Tbsp canola or olive oil

1 tsp superfine sugar

1 tsp (3 g) instant dry yeast

¾ cup water

½ tsp salt

Combine the flour, oil, sugar, and yeast in a large bowl or the bowl of an electric mixer fitted with a dough hook. Pour in half of the water and start kneading. When completely absorbed, pour in the rest of the water and knead for 5 minutes. Set aside to rest for 5 minutes.

Add the salt and knead for 10 minutes until it has come together in a smooth and elastic dough that is neither too dry nor terribly wet. Cover the dough and set aside for 1 hour until it has doubled in size.

Toward the end of the resting time prepare two or three baking sheets by lining them with parchment paper. Preheat the oven to 450°F.

Knock the air out of the dough and divide it into 13 equal pieces. Have a small bowl of water handy. Take a piece of dough in your hand and stretch, then moisten your hands with a little water and roll the dough into a 24-inch strand that is just under ½ inch wide.

Sprinkle each lined sheet with some flour to prevent the dough from sticking. Shape the strand into a pretzel straight onto the sheet by twisting the ends of the strand together once or twice, depending on your preference. Moisten your index finger and thumb and then stick the twisted ends onto the middle of the loop. You can correct the shape if needed while the krakeling is on the sheet.

Bake the krakelingen for 10–12 minutes until they have a golden blush, then transfer to a wire rack to cool. Keep in an airtight container.

Brugse achten

"Bruges eights" are small, sugary *krakelingen* shaped like the number eight, which is an old pretzel shape and the shape of eternity. A chef at the court of Maria van Bourgondië is said to have invented them when she grew tired of tarts and wanted something different... or so the legend claims.

Amand Deman, a baker, and his wife, Stefanie Vervarcke, set up shop in the Braambergstraat 20 in Bruges in 1880. They baked mostly bread, but also *pain à la grecque* (see page 96), *eierkoeken* (egg cakes: a type of spongy cookie), *Brugse beschuit* rusks, and *Brugse achten*. Today two female bakers from the same family are continuing the family business under the name "Oud Huis Deman." They continue the tradition of baking these pretzels.

This recipe is based on one in the 285th edition of the iconic *Ons Kookboek*, published by the Farmer's Wives' Union; however, the original creates a total mess. As always with historical recipes, it needed the hands and head of an experienced baker to come up with a good result.

Makes 20

⅔ cup (150 g) unsalted butter, softened, plus extra for greasing

2–2 ½ Tbsp water, plus extra for dipping and sprinkling

2 cups (250 g) bread flour

⅓ cup (15 g) crumbled *beschuit* (see page 94), rusks, or panko breadcrumbs

½ cup (100 g) soft light brown sugar

Melt the butter in a small saucepan over low heat. Remove from the heat, pour in the water to cool it down, then add to the flour in a bowl, kneading it into a compact dough. Set aside to rest for 15 minutes.

Prepare a baking sheet by greasing it and creating a base with the crumbled beschuit, rusks, or breadcrumbs for each pretzel. Put the sugar into a bowl and have a spray bottle or small bowl with water ready.

Preheat the oven to 400°F. Do not use the fan setting.

Roll the dough to the thickness of a pencil and cut strands of 8 inches in length. Shape the strands into a figure eight or pretzel shape, dip them into the sugar, then place them on the crumbs on the baking sheet. Toss the remaining sugar over each pretzel and give each pretzel a light spritz of water from the spray bottle or by flicking it over with your fingers.

Bake in the middle of the oven for about 20 minutes until golden.

Cool the Brugse achten on the sheet until the caramelized sugar solidifies. For the picture opposite, I've separated them too wide on the baking sheet: the best result is obtained when they are placed almost touching so the caramel glues them together.

Our six-year-old godson adores them because of the pieces of caramel attached to them.

SINTEGREEF, THE EARL OF LAETARE

In 1508 a ship carrying oranges, figs, and raisins arrived in the port of the city of Antwerp. The townspeople, wary of the exotic sweet treats for fear they would make them sick, were apprehensive about buying the cargo. And this is where the legend starts; the Margrave of Antwerp, eager to boost trade in the city, ordered the cargo to be distributed among the people of Antwerp, knowing that if the goods were free, the people would accept them with eager hands. It would have given many Antwerpians a first taste of the sweet exotic treats that would become an integral part of the Golden Age in Antwerp.

Each year from then on, on the day – which happened to fall on Laetare Sunday – the generosity of the Margrave was remembered and the *Sintegreef, Sanct* or *Graaf van Halfvasten* (Earl of mid-Lent or Laetare) appeared as the personification of the feast.

He can be recognized by his distinctively large nose, a sack of toys, and a rod, in depictions carved in gingerbread molds. He is often accompanied by his wife, Sanctin, on the flipside of the mold, their figures far less elegant than that of the royal Orange couple or the lovers (see page 240) and oddly resembling the English Punch and Judy. Sintegreef is the forerunner of the *Prins Carnaval* figure, similar to the Lord of Misrule around Christmastime in medieval England.

He appears in French Flanders, Halle, Ypres, Brabant, and specifically Antwerp, where a gingerbread mold carver specialized in carving Sintegreef figures.

Poems and songs about Sintegreef refer to figs and raisins and also mention the custom of carrying a tiny loaf on a stick in the shape of a rooster. We see an example of this "rooster on a stick" peeking out of the basket of the child in Jan Steen's painting *The Feast of Saint Nicholas* (see page 207).

There are resemblances to Saint Nicholas and Saint Martin. Sintegreef also rode on a white and gray horse or a donkey in other stories, bringing children not only sweets but also gifts. And in case children had been bad, he also brought the rod, showing the figure to also have a disciplinary function.

It shows that the celebratory customs of the three saint figures overlap and are interchanged, ambivalent. Jan Steen might have included the symbolism of Sintegreef on purpose to include a symbol of the secular Graaf van Halfvasten for people to identify with. At the time he painted the work, Calvinists were trying to outlaw Saint Nicholas. Although referred to as Sintegreef in some regions, he wasn't a saint figure, but usually depicted as an 18th-century nobleman.

Greefkoeken were baked for the occasion, made just like the *mantepeirden* and *klaaskoeken* out of enriched bread dough (see page 216); or honey cake and later *speculaas*. However, greefkoeken seem to have disappeared completely in the past thirty years. Sintegreef, too, will soon be lost to time.

KERMIS GASTRONOMY

As a child I was rarely allowed to go to the *kermis* (fair) because my mother thought it wasn't proper. One of the few times we went, I was allowed to fish for a prize: I chose a goldfish. I remember the scent of the fair vividly, though I can't remember ever eating something bought from the colorful waffle and *oliebol* wagons, to my great disappointment.

"Kermis" comes from the Western European custom of Church (*kerk*) mass (*mis*), the holy mass conducted in honor of the patron saint of the mother church or in commemoration of its consecration. This happened every year on the patron saint's name day, but later when the religious character started to fade, kermis started to move to other important feast days. These could be Carnival on the eve of Lent, the change of the season, or important moments on the agricultural calendar, such as harvest time, reclaiming the pagan nature of the custom.

Another term often used interchangeably with kermis in Belgium is *foor*, or *foire* in French. While they are now considered the same event, *"foor"* comes from the Latin *forum* and refers to the medieval trade fairs where traveling and local tradesmen offered their wares and farm animals were judged and sold.

In medieval times, as witnessed in the paintings of Bruegel, the festivities were centered around food and drink, dancing, and rural games and sports. This is something still seen in today's Vlaamse Kermis (Flemish Fair), an activity in which rural games and sports are played, accompanied by feasting and dancing.

This is the time when the *hylickmaker* makes an appearance (see page 231). This form of *peperkoek* (see page 226) is given by a boy to a girl as a gesture of courtship. Peperkoek and kermis have always gone hand in hand. Later *oliebollen* (doughnuts) and waffles appeared. Oliebollen especially were something a common family wouldn't be able to cook, even though the ingredients are humble, because the amount of oil or lard needed to fry them in was costly. So oliebollen became, and still are, an emblematic food on kermis.

The oldest kermis still occurring in Belgium is in Leuven. It commemorates the defeat of the Vikings by Arnuld, king of East Francia and Lorraine, in 891. The Battle of Leuven has been celebrated ever since with

a trade fair and kermis. The iconic Antwerp Pentecost *Sinksenfoor* has existed in different locations within the city walls since the 13th century. The equally iconic October foor on the other side of the language border in Liège is eight hundred years old. In Ghent, a very important city in the Middle Ages, Philip the Fair, Duke of Burgundy, gave perpetual permission to set up a Laetare Sunday Fair in 1497. It still exists today.

Kermis could be a rowdy affair, often leading to peasant revolts, so much so that at different moments in history the clergy tried to either control or ban it. But in times of poverty and hard labor, working-class people lived for these occasions when the light shone a little bit brighter and spirits were lifted.

While initially a festival of rural games, dancing, and feasting, among the traveling tradesmen were also artists and people with certain talents. Inventors also showed up to demonstrate their latest inventions. Menageries appeared and so did curiosity shows, theaters, puppet shows, phantasmagorias, and circus acts, such as rope walkers, clowns, and acrobats. It was a place of wonder and imagination. Around 1800 the circus started pulling away, prompted by the trend set by the English circus pioneer Philip Astley. In 1787 he set up his circus in the Warandepark in Brussels. After that, kermis and circus were no longer entangled.

Another phenomenon that gave an excuse for kermis was the giants' procession: a parade of huge puppets, usually made of papier mâché, operated by a puppeteer inside their bodies. In Borgerhout, Antwerp, the first giants' procession was held in 1712, but there were older ones that no longer exist in their original form. My godfather was a giant carrier; I remember going to greet him underneath the skirt of the 10½-foot-high giant character while he was marching in the procession.

In the postwar period, the kermis evolved into an amusement park with an emphasis on fun attractions. Luckily for our story, the festive kermis foods remained a paramount part of the experience. Kermis traders lovingly named these treats *foor gastronomie*.

These are peperkoek, oliebollen, waffles thick and thin, potato fries (not considered dinner in the olden days,

but a sort of fritter), and, in Limburg (and for Belgian communities in the United States), *vlaai*.

Waffle palaces

Early 19th-century foor wagons were still rather primitive: Antwerps Gebak began its life in 1835 as just a board on wooden trestles. By 1925, the next generation was traveling around with what is beginning to look like a waffle palace. Waffle palaces were opulent wagons with mirrors, frescoes, and often even seating areas, which made them into traveling tearooms.

I spoke to a fourth-generation waffle palace or *gebakkraam* (pastry stand) owner, Paul-Jan, whose wife descends from the family who owned Antwerps Gebak. Paul-Jan's grandfather started Booms Frituur in 1895, and the two businesses merged when Paul-Jan and his wife took over the reins. Until the mid-1990s this family lived in their wagons, moving from kermis to kermis. Paul-Jan says much has changed since kermis people started living in houses, as the families are no longer living together on the road.

When I asked him whether or not kermis gastronomy has a place in modern times, he told me that he can tell by people's faces that the need for nostalgic treats like oliebollen, waffles, and fries is still very much part of today's world. He has added churros to his offerings because demand is simply too high to refuse it, but he doesn't believe it will replace the traditional kermis food. When I tell him that churros also appear in Dutch 18th- and 19th-century cookbooks, he is pleasantly surprised.

Nostalgia is a powerful seasoning, and Paul-Jan enjoys seeing his customers dig into the cone paper bag to reach for the first hot oliebol, licking their fingers and laughing with family and friends. When I ask him if he ever thought of taking up another profession, he tells me that the thought just never crossed his mind, nor has it crossed that of his daughter, who is keen to carry on the family business.

Yohan from Gebakkraam Abel in Ghent is the fifth generation and ready to take over from his parents. He tells me there was no doubt in his mind to continue the tradition: "I was born between the oliebollen and the clouds of icing sugar, and I really looked up to my parents. I'm proud to carry it on." What he does worry about is that many towns and villages these days aren't fond of the kermis anymore. Until twenty years ago everyone looked forward to the hustle and bustle, but today more and more people have a "not in my backyard" mentality. The iconic Antwerp Sinksenfoor was pushed out of the heart of the city this way.

Gebakkraamen can set up shop on their own in town squares, as Abel has been doing for a long time in Ghent, but they all miss the other traders and mostly the color the kermis brings.

Kermis gastronomy is in their blood, just as it is for the many Flemish, Walloon, and Dutch kermis families. They are a breed of people who carry on an ancient trade and keep this culinary heritage alive.

Oliebollen 17th century

The earliest known Dutch recipe for *olykoek* appears in the book *De Verstandige Kok* (The Clever Cook) from 1667. A painting by Albert Cuyp of a woman holding a bowl of *oliebollen* from around 1652 shows oliebollen that look like those in the recipe in *De Verstandige Kok*.

The 17th-century recipe contains a lot of raisins and equal amounts of flour plus chopped apple. Today's oliebollen sold at the fair are usually made without any fruit added, though people at home often still add raisins, candied fruits, and apple. Adding the fruit and almonds to the batter makes the dough sweeter, as sugar was too costly to use. The result is a knobbly ball of fried dough, as seen in Cuyp's painting and the photograph opposite.

The author of the 17th-century recipe instructs to use very little oil (canola oil, to be precise): just over a quart, which isn't a lot. Eighteenth-century recipes recommend twice as much oil. A smaller amount of oil means you must adjust the size of the pot or of the balls, which cannot be too large or too round.

People who could not afford to use a lot of oil would make flat fritters, as seen in the painting by Hans Francken on page 66. Today in the United States, this type of batter pudding is known as a "Dutch baby."

Makes 20 oliebollen

4½ oz (125 g) blanched almonds

1 small apple, not too sweet

1 ¾ cups (225 g) all-purpose flour

2 ¼ tsp (7 g) instant dry yeast

pinch of ground cinnamon

pinch of ground ginger

1 clove, ground

pinch of salt

1 cup whole milk, tepid

1 medium egg yolk, beaten

2 Tbsp (25 g) unsalted butter, melted and cooled

8 oz (225 g) dark raisins

canola oil, vegetable oil, or lard, for deep-frying

confectioners' sugar, for dusting

Use a deep fryer or a deep heavy-bottomed saucepan.

Finely chop the almonds and do the same with the apple; cubes of just under ½ inch are fine.

Combine the flour, yeast, spices, and salt in a large bowl or the bowl of an electric mixer fitted with the whisk attachment. Pour in half of the milk, the egg yolk, and the butter and mix to combine. Now gradually add the rest of the milk until you get smooth batter that doesn't pour from a spoon like crêpe batter but is scoopable like cake batter. Fold in the raisins, almonds, and apple, then cover the bowl and set the batter aside to rest for 30 minutes.

Heat the oil to 350°F in a deep fryer or deep heavy-bottomed saucepan. The oil is the correct temperature when a cube of bread is added and turns golden brown in 60 seconds. Scoop nice balls of the batter using 2 tablespoons and let them carefully slide into the hot oil. Fry for 5–6 minutes until golden brown. Do not overcrowd the frying basket or pan: each time you add new batter the temperature lowers, which impacts the quality of the frying. Give each scoop of batter the chance to set slightly before adding another scoop of batter.

Transfer the cooked oliebollen to a tray lined with paper towels while you fry the rest, then pop them on a serving tray – or, if you want to go traditional, into a paper bag or paper cone – and dust generously with confectioners' sugar.

Oliebollen

From as soon as humans figured out you could cook something in scalding hot fat, people have fried food. And for as long as people have been frying dough, it has been connected to a celebration. We might take a full pot of fat or oil for granted these days, but in the past frying was a costly affair. Common people could not afford to use up that amount of fat or oil, so frying dough was connected to days when people came together to share; hence, *oliebollen,* or doughnuts, are connected to New Year's celebrations, Carnival, Mardi Gras, and village fairs, or *kermis.* This was a special treat, even though the fried dough was made of humble ingredients.

This recipe was developed with the help and approval of Gebakkraam Abel from Ghent. They bake my favorite oliebollen, so it was wonderful to have their assistance. They did mention that at home they never taste the same as from the kermis, since the atmosphere of the kermis and the paper cone they are served in are part of the experience, but also frying in extra-large kettles means the temperature of the oil doesn't drop as soon as you pop in the dough, which is essential to a perfectly fluffy oliebol.

While these fritters are usually eaten just as they are with sugar, the celebrated author Jan de Gouy of *De burgerskeuken en pasteibakkerij in ieders bereik,* published in 1924, suggests serving them hot or cold with a fruit or cream sauce. This reminds me of delicate cheese fritters I had in Hungary. In the carnival town of Aalst, oliebollen are often served covered with Flemish beef stew, resembling the dumplings served with stews in Eastern Europe. Carnivalists have told me it creates an excellent layer to welcome copious amounts of beer.

De Gouy finds it necessary to note that these fried dough balls are Flemish cuisine. In Flanders these days we often call them *smoutebollen,* after *smout,* the animal fat that was for a long time used to fry them. Although today most waffle palaces or *gebakkraamen* at the kermis are offering Spanish churros, de Gouy gives a recipe for "Beignets Seringues" in his book: batter piped into hot oil using a syringe – so can churros also be considered a traditional Belgian treat? In any case, if you visit Belgium or the Netherlands, don't pass on the opportunity to treat yourself to a large pointy paper bag with hot sugar-dusted oliebollen from a gebakkraam.

Makes 12 oliebollen

1 ⅔ cups (200 g) bread flour

1 Tbsp superfine sugar

1 tsp salt

2 ¼ tsp (7 g) instant dry yeast

¾ cup whole milk,
   at room temperature

5 Tbsp water

1 Tbsp melted butter or oil

2 qt oil or lard, for frying

confectioners' sugar, for dusting

Use a deep fryer or a deep heavy-bottomed saucepan.

Combine the flour, sugar, salt, and yeast in a large bowl or the bowl of an electric mixer fitted with the whisk attachment. Pour in the milk, the water, and the melted butter or oil and whisk until your batter is smooth. It should be wet and scoopable, but it shouldn't pour from a spoon like crêpe batter. Cover the bowl and set the batter aside to rest for 45 minutes.

Heat the oil to 350°F in a deep fryer or deep heavy-bottomed saucepan. The oil is the correct temperature when a cube of bread is added and turns golden brown in 60 seconds. Use an ice-cream scoop to make nice scoops of the batter and let them slide into the hot oil. Fry for 5–6 minutes on each side until golden brown: use your eyes (not the clock) to judge doneness, and don't leave the fryer unattended. Transfer to a tray lined with paper towels while you cook the remainder, then pop them on a serving tray – or, if you want to go traditional, put them into a paper bag or paper cone – and dust generously with confectioners' sugar. Eat them hot and with your hands: licking your fingers is essential.

Variation: Mix superfine sugar (I have a pod of vanilla in my jar of sugar) with a little cinnamon and use that instead of confectioners' sugar to dust the oliebollen. This is not traditional at all but very nice indeed!

THE CLEVER COOK

DUTCH AND BELGIAN COLONISTS OF AMERICA

In 1609 the English explorer Henry Hudson set sail from Amsterdam to look for a Northwest Passage to the Orient. On the payroll of the Dutch East India Company, he sailed his ship *Halve Maen* up the Hudson River, which was later named after him.

With the prospect of fertile arable land and a prosperous fur trade, the fundamentals of Dutch colonization had been laid.

While the first settlers are always referred to as Dutch, many were Walloons from what is now Belgium, though at that time it was known as the Southern Netherlands under Spanish rule. The northern Netherlands (now still known by that name) had broken off from the South after the fall of Antwerp.

The colonists, in need of land, persuaded the Native Americans to sell the island of Manhattan and paid the bargain price of sixty guilders for it. A letter dated 5 November 1626, from a deputy of the Dutch parliament, indicates the new settlers had farmed the area and successfully harvested wheat, rye, barley, oats, buckwheat, canary seed, small beans, and flax. It also mentions an abundance of fur and oak, and nut-wood.[19] They founded New Amsterdam on Manhattan Island, which became the capital of New Netherland in 1625.

Influential people were granted large pieces of land as a reward for bringing at least fifty families (or fifty colonists within four years) along with them to settle in New Netherland. These grants were called "patroonships," issued by the 1629 Charter of Freedoms and Exemptions of the Dutch West India Company.

The title of *patroon* – a landholder with manorial rights – came with powerful rights and privileges: they could create a whole society with its own town or village, its own local officials, and its own civil and criminal court. Settlers living in these patroonships were relieved of paying public taxes for ten years, but paid rent to the patroon instead. We can still see some of these patroonships in today's America. Dutch settler Jonas Bronck founded the Bronx. There is a 1930s mural at the Bronx County Courthouse depicting Bronck's arrival in the 17th century.

New Netherland came under English control in 1664, and New Amsterdam was renamed New York after Charles II of England granted the lands to his brother, the Duke of York. The Dutch Republic recaptured the city nine years later, renaming it "New Orange" only to lose it to the English again a year later through the Treaty of Westminster in 1674.

Although it wasn't just Dutch (and Walloon) people immigrating to America, they left the most evident mark. Their old customs married with a new culture they created in the years that followed. Experts on Dutch colonial food customs call it "New Netherlandish."

The settlers from the 17th-century Low Countries were used to a good quality of life. Thanks to the growing economies of Antwerp and Amsterdam, these regions had known a much earlier birth of consumerism, and with it a wealthy middle class. Even the poorer classes could afford good food. Everyone ate well in the Low Countries.

In *Descriptions of the New Netherlands*, published in 1655, the author writes a glowing report on the endeavors of his countrymen in the new colony. The new settlers planted fruit trees: "every kind that grew in the Netherlands' was brought to New Netherland – apples, pears, cherries, peaches, apricots, plums, almonds, persimmons, figs, redcurrants, gooseberries, cloves, and licorice trees, and quinces from England." Grapevines occurred naturally, and Germany, too, had sent vine cuttings to grow.

Pehr Kalm, the Finnish traveler who also wrote about England, wrote about the Dutch food customs in America in 1777. He noted that the food preparation methods were very different from those of the English, even though they had been ruling the area for eighty-five years. He said that the Dutch didn't drink coffee and noticed that they put a piece of sugar in their mouth and then drank their tea instead of putting the sugar in the tea. This is a custom that was still very much alive in the last century in the Netherlands. Kalm said that although they usually had bread and butter or bread and milk for breakfast, they occasionally had cheese at breakfast or dinner, not in slices but scraped or grated. Kalm also described a culture of eating salads, dressed with oil, vinegar, and salt and pepper, and describes coleslaw.

Even though the English took over the government of the area, they lived side by side with the Dutch, who were allowed to stay after the conflict. Kalm also wrote that there was a Dutch church and an English church in Albany, but that there was at that time no minister at the English church, and everyone understood Dutch, so they probably attended one of the two services held each Sunday. He also wrote that the grandest estates were the ones owned by those who descended from Dutch settlers.

The clever cook

The great 17th-century Dutch cookbook *De Verstandige Kok* (The Clever Cook) was, as part of a larger volume called *Het Vermakelijck Landtleven* (The Pleasurable Country Life), a prolific work in the Low Countries, published in Amsterdam, Antwerp, and Ghent. It provided a handbook of the pleasurable country life described in its title, in addition to cookery and preserving, sections on beekeeping, gardening, and medicine. Significantly, there are several copies of this book in libraries all over America, showing that the book and its influence and teachings were widespread.

The book takes recipes from several older works, many from the Flemish Carolus Battus: some forty recipes come from his *Cocboeck* of 1593 and a few come from his *Secreetboeck* of 1601. Battus had based many of his recipes on a manuscript from Ghent, for example, and there could have been even more sources that no longer exist.

The recipes in the *De Verstandige Kok* are for the bourgeoisie, not exclusively the royal table. The earliest known Dutch recipe for much-loved *olykoek* or *oliebollen* appears in the book, which enabled the fried dough recipe to travel to America.

In a recipe book from the Van Rensselaer family, one of the original Dutch patroons from 1785–1835, we find recipes for age-old important Dutch sweets, cookies, soft "wafuls," "pan cakes," and "oly cooks." The recipe for oliebollen contains a staggering twelve eggs for one pound of flour, butter, and sugar.

The Van Cortlandt family was another important family of settlers who left Dutch recipes, and even though the recipes were in English, they still had Dutch titles. Here too are "oliecooks" and recipes for "puffert," "bollebuysjes" (poffertjes), pancakes and waffles, and two different sorts of "honey cooke." The "honey cooke" is like *peperkoek*: one is a plain loaf cake and the other contains citron and orange peel. The Dutch words *koeckjens* and *koekjes* gave the Americans the word "cookie."

Washington Irving, writing as Diedrich Knickerbocker in his *A History of New York* in 1809, showed how Dutch customs were still very much alive:

> Sometimes the table was graced with immense apple-pies, or saucers full of preserved peaches and pears; but it was always sure to boast an enormous dish of balls of sweetened dough, fried in hog's fat, and called doughnuts, or olykoeks – a delicious kind of cake, at present scarce known in this city, except in genuine Dutch families.

While apple pie is very common all over Belgium, it is emblematic of Dutch culture. Signs outside restaurants all over the Netherlands will try to lure you in for *appeltaart en koffie* (with coffee).

In another chapter of his tome, Irving mentions the link between courting and gingerbread, but also oliebollen:

> Every love-sick maiden fondly crammed the pockets of her hero with gingerbread and doughnuts; many a copper ring was exchanged, and crooked sixpence broken, in pledge of eternal constancy: and there remain extant to this day some love verses written on that occasion, sufficiently crabbed and incomprehensible to confound the whole universe.

In "The Legend of Sleepy Hollow" from 1818, Irving describes a Dutch country tea table:

> Such heaped up platters of cakes of various and almost indescribable kinds, known only to experienced Dutch housewives! There was the doughty doughnut, the tender oly koek, and the crisp and crumbling cruller; sweet cakes and short cakes, ginger cakes and honey cakes, and the whole family of cakes. And then there were apple pies, and peach pies, and pumpkin pies; besides slices of ham and smoked beef; and moreover delectable dishes

*of preserved plums, and peaches, and pears, and quinces;
not to mention broiled shad and roasted chickens;
together with bowls of milk and cream, all mingled
higgledy-piggledy, pretty much as I have enumerated
them, with the motherly teapot sending up its clouds
of vapor from the midst – Heaven bless the mark!*

With this list is also one of the first references in print
for oliebollen being named doughnuts. One of the
first recipes in print for "Dough Nuts" appeared in *The
Frugal Housewife* by Susannah Carter, in 1803:

Dough Nuts.
*To one pound of flour, put one quarter of a pound of
butter, one quarter of a pound of sugar, and two spoonfuls
of yeast; mix them all together in warm milk or water, of
the thickness of bread, let it raise, and make them in what
form you please, boil your fat (consisting of hog's lard),
and put them in.*

Interestingly this exact recipe appeared in *The Art
of Cookery, Made Plain and Easy*, an iconic English
cookery book by Mrs Hannah Glasse, in a new edition
with modern improvements, published in 1805 under
"Several New Receipts Adapted to the American Mode
of Cooking."

The Frugal Housewife had been published in London
and Dublin in 1765. When it was first reprinted in
North America in 1772, there was no mention of
colonial cooking methods or ingredients. In the edition
of 1803, an "appendix containing several new receipts
adapted to the American mode of cooking" was added,
most likely to better compete with Amelia Simmons's
American Cookery (published in 1796). Simmons had,
interestingly, copied entire passages from *The Frugal
Housewife*'s earlier editions to create her book, which
was the first cookbook written by an American to be
published in America.

When did doughnuts get a hole?
The *Washington Post* published an article on 26 March
1916 stating, "The man who invented the hole in the
doughnut has been found." They interviewed Captain
Gregory, then 85, about how he came to the idea to
cut out the middle of a doughnut when he was about
16 years old.

*Well, sir, they used to fry all right around the edges,
but when you had the edges done the insides was all
raw dough. And the twisters used to sop up all the
grease just where they bent, and they were tough on the
digestion. . . . I took the cover off the ship's tin pepper box,
and I cut into the middle of that doughnut the first hole
ever seen by mortal eyes!*

When Gregory came home from sea he told his mother
about the hole he created in the doughnut. His mother
then made "several panfuls" and sent them to Rockland,
Maine, where everybody was delighted and never again
made doughnuts any other way. He thought about
producing a doughnut cutter, but someone beat him
to it. According to the *Encyclopedia of American Food
and Drink*, a housewares catalogue of 1870 shows a
doughnut cutter, including a corer.

By 1920 the doughnut with a hole had become a
standard. Herman and Minnie Seekamp introduced
Clyde's Delicious Donuts in 1920 and old photos
already show a hole in the doughnut.

In Belgium and the Netherlands, however, the doughnut
or oliebol remained a ball, and the ring-shaped version
traveled back from America to Europe as the doughnut.

Apple beignets

Apple beignets are sold at the *kermis* (fair) from waffle-palace wagons. Many people prefer them to *oliebollen* (doughnuts): they do get you a step closer to your "five a day," if you don't count the batter and fat. Using an apple with firm flesh will prevent the beignet from becoming soggy or falling apart. And have you ever wondered why your icing sugar tends to disappear seconds after you've dusted your baked goods, while in the shops and at the fair the sugar remains in place like a light shower of snow? They use a special icing sugar that doesn't melt. You can get it from specialist shops, but it isn't a must; plain confectioners' sugar does the job if dusted on seconds before serving.

Makes 28 apple beignets

6 medium-firm apples, such as Cox, pippin, Jonagold, Cortland, Granny Smith, or your favorite pie apple (a buttery texture, sweet with tart notes is what you need)

1 ⅔ cups (200 g) bread flour, plus extra for dusting

1 Tbsp superfine sugar

1 tsp salt

¾ cup whole milk, at room temperature

2 medium eggs, separated

1 Tbsp melted butter or oil

2 qt oil or lard, for deep-frying

confectioners' sugar, for dusting

Use a deep fryer or a deep heavy-bottomed saucepan.

Peel and core the apples and cut crosswise into ½-inch-thick slices.

Put the flour, sugar, and salt in a large bowl or the bowl of an electric mixer fitted with the whisk attachment. Add the milk, the egg yolks, and melted butter and whisk or mix until you get a smooth batter. Whisk the egg whites to stiff peaks and fold into the batter.

Heat the oil to 350°F in a deep fryer or deep heavy-bottomed saucepan. The oil is the correct temperature when a cube of bread is added and turns golden brown in 60 seconds. Dust the apple slices with a thin coating of flour, making sure no pockets of flour are stuck to the fruit. Using tongs, dip each slice in the batter so the apple is covered, then carefully lower the apple slices into the hot fat.

Fry the beignets for 5 minutes until golden brown, flipping them over halfway through the cooking time. Transfer to a baking sheet lined with paper towels while you fry the remaining apple slices. Serve on a serving plate, dusted generously with confectioners' sugar. Eat hot and with your hands; licking your fingers is essential.

Nonnevotten

Baked for Vastenavond, or Shrove Tuesday, in Dutch Limburg, these buns are made from a yeast dough, twisted into a ring or a knot shape and then fried and covered in cinnamon sugar. Today they are available from about a month before Carnival until Ash Wednesday.

The tale surrounding the origin of this bun dates back to 1676 when ring-shaped breads were offered to the French commanders who wanted to besiege the Limburg city of Sittard. Why you'd like to offer pastries to a leader of an army that is there to cause trouble is unclear to me.

The name translates to "nun's rags," and Sittard did have an order of Franciscan sisters between 1600 and 1700. The legend goes that they would fry up dough to give to people donating rags. As at the Carnival of Binche and the Krakelingenfeest of Geraardsbergen, oranges are thrown to the crowd at Sittard's carnival. It is very possible that the *krakeling* of Geraardsbergen and the *nonnevot* were once a very similar bun. In the iconic Flemish cookbook from the Farmers' Wives' Union, a ball-shaped fritter is titled *nonnevestjes*, which translates as "nun's vests."

Makes 14

4 cups (500 g) bread flour

¼ cup (55 g) superfine sugar

4 Tbsp (60 g) unsalted butter, softened

4 ¾ tsp (15 g) instant dry yeast

1 cup water

1 tsp salt

2 qt oil or lard, for deep-frying

For the cinnamon sugar

½ cup (100 g) superfine sugar

2 ½ Tbsp (20 g) ground cinnamon

Use a deep fryer or a deep heavy-bottomed saucepan.

Combine the flour, ¼ cup sugar, butter, and yeast in a large bowl or the bowl of an electric mixer fitted with a dough hook. Pour in half of the water and start kneading. When the liquid is completely absorbed, pour in the remaining water and knead for 5 minutes. Let the dough rest for 5 minutes.

Add the salt and knead for 10 minutes, scraping the dough off the dough hook and side of the bowl if needed, until it has come together in a smooth and elastic dough that is neither too dry nor terribly wet.

Cover the dough and set aside for 1 hour until it has doubled in size.

Briefly knead the dough and divide it into 14 equal pieces. Take a piece of dough and lightly flatten it on your work surface, then pull the outer parts in like a purse and gently squeeze together like a dumpling so that the dough can no longer split open while rising. Roll the dough into 18-inch strands, then knot as shown opposite.

Place the knots on a baking sheet, cover the sheet with a piece of cheese-cloth, and wrap it in a large plastic bag (I keep one especially for this purpose). Rest the knots for 15 minutes.

Toward the end of the resting time, heat the oil in a deep fryer or deep heavy-bottomed saucepan to 350°F. The oil is the correct temperature when a cube of bread is added and turns golden brown in 60 seconds.

In a bowl large enough to hold a knot, make cinnamon sugar by mixing the ½ cup sugar with the cinnamon. Line a tray with paper towels.

Working in batches, carefully lower the knots into the hot oil and fry until golden. Transfer each knot to the tray with paper towels to remove any excess oil, then transfer to the bowl of cinnamon sugar and coat all over. Eat them warm, preferably, like doughnuts.

Boules de Berlin

These fried dough balls filled with custard are also called *boules de l'Yser* or *Diksmuidse IJzerbollen* after the West Flanders town of Diksmuide. They renamed this treat after the First World War because the area was hit hard and no one needed reminding of the Germans.

While old cookery books reveal these were once eaten for Shrove Tuesday as *vastenavondkoekjes*, since at least the start of the 20th century they have been a seaside treat. They were sold by beach vendors dressed in white cotton suits and caps, carrying trays of *boules* on their heads and shouting, "*lekkere Berlijnse Bollen!*" ("tasty Berlin balls"). The sensation of pillowy dough in combination with fine sugar, custard, and sand is ingrained into the memory of many Belgians. In like manner, Portugal has the *bola de Berlim* and Italians enjoy their *bomboloni*.

Why Berlin?
In Germany, they have *Berliner Krapfen* and *Berliner Pfannkuchen* (which can be translated as pancake, though it actually means that the boule was fried in a pan),

which are made with the same kind of dough but filled with jam. Unlike the boules de Berlin, they are not halved and filled with pastry cream, but the jam is piped in as for a jam doughnut. Berliner Pfannkuchen are then finished off with fine sugar crystals, but boules de Berlin get a generous dusting of confectioners' sugar.

The first German recipe for a filled fried dough ball or beignet appeared, remarkably, in the cookbook *Kuchenmeisterei*, which was published in Nuremberg in 1485. There are several recipes for "Krapfen," usually filled with an apple or pear compote, although one recipe instructs to dust the beignets with sugar.

Today these boules de Berlin are most often halved, using the beautiful pale line around their middle that comes as a result of frying them, as a guide for the knife. They are then filled with a generous swirl of thick custard, but old cookery books usually gave three options: one with custard, one with jam, and one leaving them whole or adding raisins to the dough.

Makes 12 boules

4 cups (500 g) bread flour

¼ cup (55 g) superfine sugar

4 ¾ tsp (15 g) instant dry yeast

1 cup whole milk

1 tsp salt

4 Tbsp (60 g) butter, softened

2 qt oil or lard, for deep-frying

confectioners' sugar, for dusting

For the custard

9 medium egg yolks

6 Tbsp (75 g) superfine sugar

3 ½ Tbsp (40 g) custard powder, or
    5 Tbsp (40 g) cornstarch

3 cups whole milk

⅓ cup heavy cream (36–40% fat)

1 vanilla bean, split, or 1 bay leaf

A note on bay leaves
Before vanilla took over
our flavoring palate in the
19th century, bay was frequently
used along with cinnamon to flavor
custards. I adore bay leaf custard;
why not give it a go?

Use a deep fryer or a deep heavy-bottomed saucepan.

Combine the flour, sugar, and yeast in a large bowl or the bowl of an electric mixer fitted with the dough hook. Pour in half of the milk and start kneading. When the milk is completely absorbed, pour in the rest of the milk and knead for 5 minutes. Let the dough rest for 5 minutes.

Add the salt on one side and the soft butter in chunks on the other side and knead for 10 minutes, scraping the dough off the dough hook and side of the bowl if needed, until it has come together in a smooth and elastic dough that is neither too dry nor terribly wet.

Cover the dough and set aside for 1 hour until it has doubled in size.

Briefly knead the dough and divide it into 12 equal pieces. Take 1 piece of dough and lightly flatten it on your work surface, then pull the outer parts in like a purse and gently squeeze together like a dumpling so that the dough can no longer split open while rising. Turn the dough over so the squeezed ends are on the bottom. It should be nice and smooth on top: if not, flatten it out and start again.

Place each ball on a baking sheet, cover the sheet of balls with a piece of cheesecloth, and wrap it in a large plastic bag (I keep one especially for this purpose). Rest the balls for 30 minutes.

Toward the end of the resting time, heat the oil in a deep fryer or deep heavy-bottomed saucepan to 325°F. The oil is the correct temperature when a cube of bread is added and turns golden brown in 70 seconds.

Working in batches, carefully lower the dough balls into the hot oil and fry until golden. They should have a distinctive pale line around the middle. Put the cooked boules on a tray lined with paper towels while you cook the remainder, then set aside to cool completely.

Meanwhile, for the custard, have a large, shallow ovenproof dish ready. Whisk the egg yolks, sugar, and custard powder until creamy. In French culinary terms, you've now made a *ruban* (ribbon).

In a large saucepan, warm the milk and cream with the seeds of the vanilla bean. Remove from the heat and strain the milk if you want to get rid of the black vanilla seeds, or leave them in and show the world you used the real stuff. Add a tablespoon of the warm milk to the ruban and whisk well, then add the ruban to the warm milk, whisking constantly. Return the pan to the stove over low heat and whisk until the custard thickens, removing from the heat as soon as the mixture begins to give more resistance to whisking.

Immediately pour the hot custard into the cold ovenproof dish, then cover the top of the custard (not the dish) with a sheet of plastic wrap. The plastic wrap prevents the custard from forming a skin. Let the custard cool, then transfer to a piping (icing) bag to fill the cooled boules. Split the boules and pipe the cold custard onto the base, then replace the top. Finish with a dusting of confectioners' sugar.

VLAAI

After one of my late nights writing this book, I had the strangest dream. A large fair had arrived in town, but in contrast to that excitement, there was also a funeral. While around me there was a lot of hustle and bustle and people running around organizing funny hats for the festivities and coffins for the funeral, I stood in front of my house as though I wasn't aware of all the busyness surrounding me. I looked up, then rushed up the stairs to my bedroom to pick out my best dress, which for some reason was packed away in one of the many red suitcases in the cupboard. The dress too was red, of course, but shorter than I would normally feel comfortable to wear. I ran back down, in thick woollen socks and out into the street again, where an English friend helped me close the final buttons of my red dress, patting my shoulder. I looked ready for a feast, yet very inappropriately dressed for a funeral. But I had something else on my mind. I climbed up my house as though it was the most normal thing to do, and when I finally reached the top, I started tiling the roof with *vlaai*…

Sometimes dreams are hard to explain, but in this case I could perfectly trace the origin of all the details. The dream was a pudding made with all the ingredients I had used that day in my writing, plus a few other thoughts I had had on my mind that day. I had lamented being away from England, looked at a photo of a friend who had passed last Christmas, and I had talked about the connection between prune pie and prunes and brothels in Shakespearean London. But most importantly, my eyes had carefully scanned a painting by Pieter Bruegel called *Netherlandish Proverbs*.

It is a colorful collection portraying proverbs, most of them still used in modern Dutch. The most unassuming of scenes, though odd, depicts the proverb: "There the roof is tiled with *vlaaien*, (pies)" meaning that people are wealthy in that house. My roof is certainly not tiled with vlaaien, but I do feel very rich because I can sit here by the window of my beloved house (that looks nothing like the one in the dream), writing with the rays of sunshine giving much-needed warmth through the glass after a cold February, while I sip tepid tea. The next morning I added this story about my dream to the top of this

page and realized as I came to the end that although the dream had been a pudding of the day before, there was a message in that dream that I had come to realize after all: my roof is indeed tiled with vlaai.

The pie of the Low Countries: vlaai

A *vlaai* is a sweet pie or tart that usually contains fruit, rice pudding, or a mixture of bread or old buns soaked in milk and flavored with spices. The image of a vlaai with a lattice top is the most iconic depiction of a traditional vlaai, but they are also equally often made as an open pie or with a pastry lid. There are even vlaai with a crumble, sugar, or *schuim* (foam) top.

Could the type of pastry, maybe, define something as a vlaai? Sadly not, because although they most commonly have a yeast-raised pie dough originally made with sifted rye flour, they can also be made with a richer shortcrust pastry. Today they are usually only made partially with sifted rye flour or completely with white wheat flour. The older recipes don't even define the pastry. People would have used a sturdy dough of water and flour and maybe a little fat. Some pies wouldn't have had, and still today don't have, a crust at all.

Is vlaai a pie you exclusively find in the region of Limburg, where they are most closely related today? Again no, because vlaai was eaten not just in Limburg; the pie crosses the border of provinces as though a border had never been there, and even goes further into modern Flanders, the Netherlands, and Germany.

The only thing we can really say with certainty is that a pie made with cooked or baked fruit or a type of milk pudding or filling thickened with bread is a vlaai. And for it to be a *Limburgse vlaai* it should consist of only filling and no fancy toppings such as whipped cream.

Sixteenth-century paintings such as this one by Bruegel (a copy of one by his father) show two different vlaai, a dark brown one and a light-colored one. This doesn't mean that there were only two kinds of vlaai, but that the painter decided to pick two with the most contrasting tones. While the artists don't paint something that looks like today's fruit vlaai, the recipe books of that time do indeed have recipes for pies with fruits such as cherries, apples, pears, and prunes.

145

Vlaaien were an essential part of the *kermis*, or village fair, which often came to town around harvest (see page 128). Weddings and Carnival, too, prompted vlaai making. In Limburg every special occasion is paired with vlaai, even funeral meals. When the time for festivities came, the women of the family would make the pies from the fruit they had preserved from summer or autumn, or they'd use fresh fruit depending on the season. Uncooked vlaaien were placed on large wooden planks, some as long as six to ten feet, and carried to the communal oven or the village bakery to be cooked. Sometimes the women would bring the filling and the baker would use his own pie dough.

Vlaai is also sold from door to door by youth organizations and schools: this is called a *vlaaienslag*, freely translated to "pie battle." It is usually to raise funds for a feast or other activities. I went on a vlaaienslag as a child and felt it was a festive occasion to carry around stacks of vlaaien in the street.

As the Low Countries are in an apple, pear, and cherry-growing region, many pies were made with the fruit that was plentiful. Old varieties of these fruits, now sadly nearly all lost to time, were much more tart and benefitted from stewing and baking to sweeten them up.

Tart apples and pears were cooked down into a purée or dried in a cooling woodfired oven. This was a process that could take many days: after the bread was baked, the pears were packed onto the oven floor and left to dry out until they were wrinkly and dark. In the vernacular, these dried pears were called *bakkemuizen* (baked mice), so the pie became *bakkemoezevlaai*.

The pears were kept in crates, wicker baskets, or potato sacks and would last until the next harvest and possibly longer if need be. When needed for vlaai, they were washed or soaked, then cooked with sugar. The mixture was then passed through a sieve until it was *moes*, or purée.

The bakkemoezevlaai had disappeared in a coincidence of circumstances: the tart heirloom pear varieties it requires have been replaced with sweeter commercial crops in the landscape; there is no need to use up the falling heat of a wood-fired oven now that bakeries have modern ovens; and finally, people associated it with a time when fresh fruit was no longer available or when harvests had failed. This vlaai was the last one baked in the season, when all the apples, apricots, and cherries were used up, and the dried pears were all that was left.

In West Flanders, the *Avelgemse perentaart* is made with windfall cooking pears, stewed into a dark purée, which is then spiced with cloves, nutmeg, and cinnamon.

In Antwerp it is still traditional to eat prune vlaai for Ash Wednesday and no one really remembers why that is. The juicy theory is that in 16th-century London, brothels would place a dish of stewed prunes in the window. These establishments were known as "stews" or "stewhouses," because in medieval times bathing houses where you could stew yourself in hot water often offered a little more service than just a soak. But why then would these prunes be eaten on Ash Wednesday? If they were indeed associated with the desires of the flesh, eating them just before Lent could have a symbolic meaning of preparing for abstinence during Lent. These bathing houses, often highly luxurious, also existed all over Western Europe; in Dutch they were called "stoves." Looking at Netherlandish paintings of bathing houses from the 16th century, there is not any sight of pies or tarts, even though dining and bathing occurs frequently together. Dining tables, bath tubs, and beds were placed in one room. In the painting *Party in a Brothel* by the Brunswick monogrammist (c. 1540, held in the Rijksmuseum, Amsterdam), there are also no pies, but instead there is waffle making.

A word on vlaai tins

Vlaaien are almost all made in tins that have slanted sides, which means the base is smaller in diameter than the top. Measurements in bakeware shops always give you the size of the finished pie top, which can be confusing as the base of the vlaai is significantly smaller.

There isn't a standard vlaai size, as there are also the tiny *vlaaikes*, only a couple of inches wide, from the town of Lier in Flanders, as well as the *flamiche*, which is the largest vlaai with its fourteen-inch diameter. And the vlaai of East Flanders, which doesn't have a crust, is made in an earthenware dish. On some occasions tins with fluted rims are used.

If your tins are not quite the right size, don't panic: you can still use them. If they are larger you will simply have shallower filling; if they are smaller, you might have some filling left over...and you will almost always have pastry left over to play around with.

Vlaai – cherry or gooseberry

This is a simple *Limburgse vlaai*, traditionally made with the fruit that is plentiful in the region. It is utterly beautiful when made well and freshly baked, but can be equally disappointing and dry when bought from the supermarket. There is nowhere to hide with this fruit tart: you cannot cover it in fancy icing or impress with complicated piping techniques or a shiny mirror glaze. If you skimp on quality, you will pay the price in lack of flavor and pleasure.

I adore these vlaaien for their honesty: with no additional toppings they need to woo you with flavor. The fruit preserved in water can be bought in jars for home baking and in large tins for the bakery. The jars and tins are not an inferior product, just fruit that has been preserved immediately after harvest to become vlaai filling, the way our grandmothers used to do it. The only difference is that the fruit is usually no longer local, but still not from too far away. The advantage is that the freshest fruit has been used. Buy fresh fruit if you can get it and start from scratch, but if you can get hold of a good-quality preserved fruit in water, use it.

Traditional fruit fillings are cherry, gooseberry, and apricot. In Belgium and the Netherlands, *noordkrieken* (sour cherries) are used, but you can use sweet cherries too and adjust the sugar content according to your taste. We call it *kriekentaart*, and the earliest recipe I found came out of a medieval manuscript from the area of Ghent.

Makes 1 tart with a lattice top

For the filling

1 ½ lb (700 g) jarred unsweetened
   cherries or gooseberries,
   including their liquid

2 Tbsp potato starch
   or cornstarch

¼ cup (50 g) sugar, or to taste

milk, for brushing

For the pastry

4 cups (500 g) bread flour

14 Tbsp (200 g) unsalted butter,
   softened

¼ cup (50 g) superfine sugar

3 ¼ tsp (10 g) instant dry yeast

1 tsp salt

¾ cup water

Note: Vlaai is often finished by scattering non-melting sugar crystals over the top before baking. These are available from specialty baking supply stores.

Use an 11-inch top diameter x 9-inch base diameter x 1¼-inch depth pie tin, greased and floured.

For the filling, drain the cherries or gooseberries and keep the juice. Whisk the potato starch with a little of the juice until all the flour pockets are dissolved.

Transfer the drained liquid with the potato starch mixture and the sugar to a saucepan over medium heat and simmer until it thickens. Remove from the heat and add the cherries or gooseberries, then set aside to cool. Adding the fruit at the end will prevent it from going too soft.

For the pastry, combine the flour, butter, sugar, yeast, and salt in a large bowl or the bowl of an electric mixer fitted with the dough hook. Pour in the water and knead for 10 minutes until the dough is smooth. Cover the bowl and leave to rest for 1 hour or overnight in the fridge.

Preheat the oven to 350°F. Do not use the fan setting. Halve the pastry and shape it into balls. Roll out one ball as thinly as you can manage, then lay it over the greased and floured tin, pressing it into the base, leaving the excess pastry.

Roll out the second ball to ⅛ inch thick and cut strips for the lattice. Because we make so many vlaaien in Belgium, we have special lattice stamps here!

Pierce the pastry in the tin all over with a fork, then spoon in the filling. Wet the rim of the tart, arrange the lattice strips on top, and cut away the excess pastry. Brush the pastry all over with a little milk.

Transfer the vlaai to the middle of your oven and bake for 30–35 minutes until the pastry is golden brown.

You will have leftover pastry, which you can use to make small jam tarts, or you can double the filling and make more of this vlaai. Alternatively you could make one more large vlaai that does not need a lattice top, such as the Potsuikervlaai on page 153.

Bakkemoezevlaai

At the bakery, after the bread was baked, tart and unripe pears were stuffed onto the oven floor of a cooling wood-fired oven and dried until they were wrinkly and dark (*bakkemuizen*). The pears were then soaked and stewed until they ended up as a luscious dark pear purée with great depth of flavor.

The only bakery that still makes *vlaai* with traditional bakkemuizen is Knapen in Flemish Limburg. The baker, Jack, seeks out heirloom pear varieties and dries all the pears in his modern oven as it cools, but as these are modern ovens, the cooling time is moments not hours. It takes Jack three weeks to fully dry them this way, but he tells me he can store the dried pears for a year.

When I'm baking or cooking in the oven every day, I'll pop pears on a tray and, every evening when I turn off the oven, I put in the tray with pears and leave them until morning. I do this over a few weeks until they are dry and wrinkly and appear not to have any moisture left. For the sake of ease and because I really want you to bake and experience this vlaai, I'm giving you a method to do this in three days. Remember, once your oven is at temperature, it stops using electricity, only using energy from time to time to keep warm.

This recipe is excellent to use up pears from a long-forgotten tree in your garden or neighborhood; pears that appear to not have any juice at all; unripe windfall pears; pears you discard because they don't give any satisfying flesh but only seem to suck up all the moisture in your mouth. These pears give nothing to you raw, but will reward you with an intense flavor when you give them time and warmth.

Makes 1 vlaai

For the filling

12 small unripe or tart pears, whole

2 Tbsp (25 g) sugar

¼ tsp ground cinnamon

For the pastry

2 cups (250 g) bread flour

7 Tbsp (100 g) unsalted butter, softened

2 Tbsp (25 g) superfine sugar

2 ¼ tsp (7 g) instant dry yeast

½ tsp salt

6 Tbsp water

Use an 11-inch top diameter x 9-inch base diameter x 1¼-inch depth pie tin, greased and floured. Start a day ahead of baking.

For the filling, dry the pears in the oven for 6 hours a day at 160°F for 6 days, or 12 hours a day for 3 days, not removing them after the oven is turned off. Alternatively use the long method I describe above.

The day before you want to bake, put the dried pears into a saucepan and add just enough boiled water to cover them.

For the pastry, combine the flour, butter, sugar, yeast, and salt in a large bowl or the bowl of an electric mixer fitted with the dough hook. Pour in the water and knead for 10 minutes until the dough is smooth. Cover the bowl and leave to rest for 1 hour or overnight in the fridge.

Refresh the water in the saucepan of pears and cook over medium heat for 30–45 minutes until the pears are softened. Remove from the heat, drain (reserving cooking water), and set aside until the pears are cool enough to handle. Purée the pears by pressing them through a sieve, discarding the solids. Transfer the purée to a saucepan and bring to a boil with the saved water, the sugar, and the cinnamon. Simmer for 5 minutes, then turn off the heat and set aside for the beautiful chocolate-like purée to cool.

Preheat the oven to 350°F. Do not use the fan setting.

When the dough has risen, knock out the air and roll out the dough as thin as you can, then lay it over the greased and floured tin, press into the base, and cut away the excess. Pierce the base all over with a fork, then spoon in the purée. Use a fork to decorate the surface as seen in the photograph opposite.

Place the vlaai in the middle of the oven and bake for 25 minutes until the pastry is browned. Let cool before serving and prepare to be charmed.

Potsuikervlaai

This sugar and custard tart has an excellent velvet-like mouthfeel with the sandy sugar topping as a contrast. One of our contestants on *Bake Off* in Flanders was from the Flemish Limburg region, where vlaai are most popular today. Four years later I found myself by chance in the bakery where she buys her favorite vlaai and I talked to the baker. After I tasted it, it is now a firm favorite in our house too.

The *potsuiker* in the name translates to "bowl of sugar," which is rather interesting as *potsuyckere* was used as the name for sugar scraped from solid sugar loaves (cones) in 15th-century cookery texts. In *Een notabel boecxken van cokeryen*, the first printed cookery book in Dutch, I found *saenvladen*, a flan-like custard tart (without a crust) sweetened with potsuyckere. The recipe right before it in the same book is *gouwieren*, a cheese and egg bake – it's unclear if it has a crust or not – topped with egg yolks and sugar. After it is baked, potsuyckere is added on top. Maybe a reader thought adding sugar on top of a baked pie was a good idea from reading the first recipe and added it to the second. The flan got a crust, the sugar was mixed with some butter and flour *ét voila*, you have a potsuikervlaai. Could it be this easy? Sometimes it is, but we cannot say for sure. What is sure, is that this vlaai does not appear in 17th-, 18th-, or 19th-century cookbooks.

Serves 4–6 people

For the pastry

2 cups (250 g) bread flour

7 Tbsp (100 g) unsalted butter, softened

2 Tbsp (25 g) superfine sugar

2 ¼ tsp (7 g) instant dry yeast

½ tsp salt

6 Tbsp water

For the sugar-crumb topping

3½ Tbsp (50 g) butter, softened

¾ cup (90 g) all-purpose flour

½ cup (90 g) soft light brown sugar

For the custard

6 medium egg yolks

6 Tbsp (80 g) superfine sugar

2 Tbsp (25 g) custard powder, or 3 Tbsp (25 g) cornstarch

2 cups whole milk

3½ Tbsp heavy cream (36–40% fat)

1 vanilla bean, split, or 1 bay leaf

Use an 11-inch top diameter x 9-inch base diameter x 1¼-inch depth pie tin, greased and floured.

For the pastry, combine the flour, butter, sugar, yeast, and salt in a large bowl or the bowl of an electric mixer fitted with the dough hook. Pour in the water and knead for 10 minutes until the dough is smooth. Cover the bowl and leave to rest for 1 hour or overnight in the fridge.

For the sugar-crumb topping, rub the butter into the flour and sugar until the mixture is crumbly, then keep in the fridge until needed.

Make the custard according to the instructions on page 143.

While the custard cools, preheat the oven to 350°F. Do not use the fan setting.

When the pastry has risen, knock out the air and roll out the pastry as thin as you can, then lay it over the greased and floured tin. Press it into the base and cut away the excess pastry. Pierce the base all over with a fork, then spoon the custard into the tart. Get the sugar crumb topping out of the fridge and sprinkle it over the custard.

Bake in the middle of the oven for 30–35 minutes until the pastry is browned. Set aside to cool completely before serving.

Variation: This vlaai can also be topped with meringue instead of the sugar mixture.

Pruimenvlaai for the coming of Lent

In my birth town of Antwerp we eat *pruimenvlaai* (prune tart) on Ash Wednesday. It is the last day of Carnival, the day before Lent, and the day when Catholics receive a black ash cross on their forehead as a sign of penance. Many people claim that the prune tart is connected to Ash Wednesday because the prunes are black. Others say prune tart was considered a poor man's food, so it was suitable to eat before Lent. Prunes, however, have never been a poor man's food and, as common as the ingredient might seem today, it is hardly cheap.

Pruimenvlaai appears often in cookery books throughout the centuries. Like all other vlaaien, they were a treat for festive occasions, and the imminent arrival of forty days of fasting called for one last splurge. As I mentioned in the introduction to vlaai (see page 147), prunes were also believed to have a cleansing and protective property, which could be another reason people ate them on the day before Lent.

Whatever our ancestors believed, this tradition is still firmly rooted in the city of Antwerp. And this is one of my favorite vlaaien. When I was growing up, our local bakery had a couple of them each Sunday, and my mother would often bring back a slice for me. I'd put it on a plate on the dining table and have just a forkful at a time so that I could enjoy it for the whole day.

Plums

Prunes are dried plums and, in the time of wood-fired bakery ovens, unripe plums were dried in the falling heat of the oven, just as the pears for the *bakkemoezevlaai* on page 151. This was done as a means to store fruit, but also because some fruits just didn't ripen enough for them to be nice to eat raw. The process of slow drying gave them the sweetness the lack of sun during our short summers couldn't. The same happened with apricots.

The origin of this recipe

A village bakery where I used to hang out at as a sixteen-year-old, when friends were partying next door, made the best prune tarts. But let me tell you about that bakery first. One evening when I came by, the milk had just come from the farm and I was given a glass. Up until that moment, being a city girl, I had never tasted raw milk, although I was a big milk drinker. I remember I was quite stunned by the flavor and texture, somewhere between milk and cream, leaving me with greasy lips.

I could taste the animal connection, which was a stark contrast to the anonymous, watery, tasteless skimmed milk we had at home.

It must have been a sign that I would become who I am today, that a bakery enticed me more than a party. What happened in that bakery at night felt like magic. The process of creating bread and buns from flour, water, and whatever else was needed too was magic. Once you entered the back door of the bakery, a different world opened. The scent of yeast leavening dough and bread baking was like the scent of life itself. I wanted to stay there all night and be part of it.

When I started baking properly, meaning no more endless variations on the few recipes I had, the bakery owner, whose name is Ils, gave me her recipe for prune tart. We have stayed in touch: it helps when you both have red hair (it creates a strong bond) and you love baking. So here is the recipe it evolved into.

While other fruit vlaaien are made with a yeast dough, in Antwerp the prune pie is made with a shortcrust pastry, highlighting the importance of this vlaai. In old English cookery books this type of pastry was called paste royal because of its richness. You are more than welcome to use yeast dough as for the other vlaaien, as they do in Dutch and Flemish Limburg and also in the Belgian community in Wisconsin where they keep vlaai alive in their "Belgian pie" culture (see page 190).

Abrikozenvlaai

Dried apricot vlaai is made in the same way as prune tart by soaking and then cooking the dried apricots. Just omit the spices for the apricot version.

Pruimenvlaai and abrikozenvlaai

Serves 4–6 people

For pruimenvlaai (prune vlaai) filling

1 lb (500 g) prunes (dried plums), pitted

1 tsp lemon juice

1 cinnamon stick

1 rosemary sprig

1 Tbsp dark brown sugar

pinch of ground cinnamon

For the pastry

2 cups (250 g) all-purpose flour

⅔ cup (125 g) superfine sugar

pinch of salt

pinch of ground cinnamon

pinch of baking powder

½ cup (125 g) unsalted butter, cubed

1 medium egg + 1 egg yolk

2 Tbsp milk, for brushing

For abrikozenvlaai (dried apricot vlaai) filling variation

1 lb (500 g) dried apricots, pitted

1 tsp lemon juice

1 Tbsp white sugar

Use an 11-inch top diameter x 10-inch base diameter x 1¼-inch depth pie tin, greased and floured.

For the pruimenvlaai filling, soak the prunes in water overnight with the lemon juice, cinnamon stick, and rosemary. For the abrikozenvlaai filling, soak the dried apricots in water overnight with the lemon juice.

Dtrain the prunes or apricots and reserve ¾ cup of the soaking water. Put the prunes or apricots and reserved water in a medium saucepan over low heat. Add the sugar (and, for the pruimenvlaai, the cinnamon) and bring to a simmer.

Simmer for 15 minutes until the fruit is soft. Allow the fruit to cool in the liquid, then purée the fruit with the liquid in a blender or food processor. If the purée is too runny at this point, you can put it back in the saucepan over low heat to reduce it a bit further. If you do this, let it cool again before further use. It will become more solid when it has cooled. The consistency should be very thick, not runny; when stirring through the fruit, the base of the saucepan should be visible.

To make the pastry, combine the flour, sugar, salt, cinnamon, baking powder, and butter in a food processor. Pulse for 8 seconds or until the mixture resembles breadcrumbs. Add the egg and egg yolk and pulse again until the dough forms a ball in the bowl. Remove from the bowl and knead briefly.

Wrap the pastry in plastic wrap and put it in the fridge to rest for 30 minutes.

Preheat the oven to 325°F. Do not use the fan setting. Briefly knead the pastry until smooth, then roll out to about 1⁄16 inch thick. Lay the pastry greased and floured and let it sink into the tin. Use a ball of leftover dough to gently push the pastry into the sides of the tin. Cut away the excess pastry and knead it back together into a smooth ball again.

Cut a piece of parchment paper just ever so slightly larger than the tin. Roll out the leftover pastry and cut out ½-inch-wide strips. Create a lattice on the paper and set it aside.

Scoop the fruit filling into the tart and brush the rim of the pastry with milk. Slide or flip the lattice top carefully onto the tart, adjust where needed, and crimp the edges of the strips into the rim, cutting away excess pastry.

Place the vlaai in the middle of the oven and bake for 35–40 minutes until the pastry has a golden color. Allow to cool completely before serving. In bakeries, this tart is usually finished off by brushing it all over with thinned apricot jam so it is very shiny, but I am not a fan of the sticky mess and the sweetness it adds.

This tart keeps for a few days when stored in a cool, dry place.

Oost Vlaamse vlaai

For thirteen years I lived in East Flanders, where this East Flemish *vlaai* is traditional. In contrast to the *vlaaien* on previous pages, it is not made in a crust, but in an earthenware dish. At our local market there was a trader who sold only these vlaaien: the table was laid out with a yellow tablecloth, and large, traditional heavy earthenware vlaai dishes were lined up in three rows. You then bought a wedge by weight.

The baked vlaai is solid with a slight wobble, a sunken middle, a beautiful dark brown color and sheen, and a spiced scent. The crusty edges are the best part.

I found an early example of this vlaai in the *Cocboeck* by Carolus Battus (1593). The recipe titled "Appelvlaeye" (apple vlaai) is made like the *Oost Vlaamse vaai* with *peperkoek* (pepper cake), spices, milk, and eggs but also includes apples, which are cooked to a pulp.

Gentse mastellen (see page 80) and *peperkoek* (see page 226) are traditional ingredients, but as housewives often had to make do with what they had, many recipes also contain other buns, cookies, and rusks, even plain bread; as long as you stick to the quantities you can swap with what you have. This vlaai is also known as *Aalsterse vlaai* from the carnival city of Aalst.

In Antwerp bakeries make the same vlaai but call it bread pudding. They make it to use up any unsold bread. The bread pudding is turned out of its dish and then covered in chocolate icing; usually raisins are added, or raisin bread is used.

This recipe is based on one given to me by someone who found it in their grandmother's notebook. It is, however, exactly the same recipe as the one in *Ons Kookboek*, published a few years after the Second World War. Like other vlaai, this one was also baked after the bread, using residual heat in the baker's oven.

Makes 8–12 portions

7 oz (200 g) Peperkoek (page 226)

1 qt whole milk

¼ cup (30 g) all-purpose flour

1 ¼ cups (250 g) brown sugar

9 oz (250 g) Gentse Mastel (page 80), or use plain buns plus an extra tsp of cinnamon

1 tsp ground cinnamon

1 tsp ground mace

butter, for greasing

2–3 Tbsp (25 g) candied peel

2–3 medium eggs

2 Tbsp appelstroop, beet syrup, golden syrup, or honey

pinch of salt

Use a 9½-inch diameter and 2½-inch deep ovenproof dish, or any 2-quart oven dish. Start 2 days ahead of serving.

Soak the peperkoek in enough just-boiled water to cover it.

Whisk 2 tablespoons of the milk with the flour. In a small saucepan, bring the remaining milk to a boil with the sugar and the buns, torn to shreds. When the buns have thickened the milk, add the milk and flour mixture and the soaked peperkoek and return to a boil, then remove the pan from the heat, stir in the spices, and let the mixture cool and rest overnight.

Preheat the oven to 350°F. Do not use the fan setting.

Butter the ovenproof dish and finely chop the candied peel. Add the eggs, syrup, chopped peel, and salt to the mixture and stir well to combine. Transfer the mixture to the ovenproof dish.

Place the dish on the bottom rack of the oven and bake for 1½ hours. The vlaai is ready when it comes away from the sides and the middle springs back when you carefully press the flat of your hand into the top. The vlaai will still have a gentle wobble in the middle, which will set once cooled.

When cooled, cover with a kitchen towel and set aside to rest overnight. The next day the top will have a lovely sheen and a nice crack all around the rim, and the middle will have sunk a little.

Traditionally this vlaai is sliced while still in the dish and not turned out.

Lierse vlaaike

Lierse vlaaike is a small spiced pie from the town of Lier, near Antwerp. Until recently, it wasn't sold anywhere outside Lier, which made it a rare treat. The vlaaikes are made from a sturdy pastry, rolled paper-thin, and filled with a sweet spiced mixture thickened by breadcrumbs.

The nature of these vlaaikes tells me they are based on an old recipe, but Lierse vlaaike only appears in print in the 19th century. The vlaaikes were immortalized by the writer Felix Timmermans in his story "In the Royal Vlaai," published in 1928. He writes that they are the size of an inkpot and were sold for the price of 50 cents a dozen. The classic size is 2¼ inches wide, but I made this recipe in standard small tart tins. It still looks like an inkpot.

A baker told me that in the old days the pastry for these vlaaikes was made simply of flour and water, shaped into rings and then left to dry out for up to a month. This is a practice that no longer happens. From 1999 all bakers in Lier use a standardized recipe approved by the "Order of the Liers Vlaaike." The ingredients are not a guarded secret, as they have been published in the newspaper and in other publications of the town of Lier; the method, however, was never shared.

The ingredient list was shared in the publication *Liers Vlaaike*, but contains essential typos in that it used centiliters instead of milliliters, and 750 centiliters equals a whopping 7.5 liters (2 gallons) to just 220 grams (2 ¾ cups) of breadcrumbs. The corrected and edited recipe you will find below, and the method is my own. As the original ingredient *kandijsiroop*, a syrup made from dark brown beet sugar, is not easy to get outside Belgium, I've used brown sugar instead.

Makes 16 vlaaikes

For the pastry

5 Tbsp (75 g) unsalted butter
   or lard, softened

½ cup water

2 ⅓ cups (275 g) bread flour

pinch of salt

For the filling

2 ¾ cup (220 g) stale *pistolet* (see page 76) or *beschuit* (see page 94) crumbs or fine breadcrumbs

1 ⅔ cups whole milk

3 ¾ cups (750 g) brown sugar

1 Tbsp ground cinnamon

½ Tbsp ground coriander

½ Tbsp ground cloves

½ Tbsp ground nutmeg

6 Tbsp (50 g) all-purpose flour

Use several small pie tins or rings, 3 inches top diameter x 1¼-inch depth, or use muffin tins of the approximate size, greased and floured.

For the pastry, melt the butter in the water in a small saucepan over low heat. Put the flour and salt in a bowl or the bowl of an electric mixer fitted with the dough hook, then pour in the butter mixture. Knead for 5 minutes until it comes together and is smooth. Cover and set aside while you make the filling.

Grate your stale pistolet or beschuit or any other type of bread you have. Store-bought breadcrumbs should be avoided as they are too dry and sandy.

In a large saucepan, warm the milk with the sugar until it is completely dissolved. Add the spices and the flour and finally the breadcrumbs. Set aside to rest for an hour while you prep your tins.

Grease and flour your pie tins, rings, or muffin tins. Roll out the dough on a floured work surface as thinly as you can manage; ¹⁄₁₆ inch is great. Use a 4-inch cutter to cut out discs for the pastry cases. Place a pastry disc in a tin and use the tips of your fingers to mold it into shape and press it up against the rim. By doing this you are also making the pastry case even thinner. Prick the base of each tart casing all over with a fork.

Scoop or pipe the filling into the tins and level the top using the back of a spoon. Put the tins on a large baking sheet. Preheat the oven to 350°F. Do not use the fan setting. When the oven is hot enough, bake the vlaaikes in the middle of the oven for 20 minutes until the filling has set and puffed up but the pastry is still pale.

After cooling, keep the vlaaikes in an airtight container or they will become rock-hard.

Mattentaart

The *mattentaart* is a cheese curd pie that is connected to the town of Geraardsbergen in East Flanders. The town is also famous for its *krakelingenfeest* (see page 114).

The meaning of the "mat" in mattentaart is explained in the 14th-century colloquium *De Bouc vanden Ambachten*, a manuscript written in conversational style in both Middle French and Middle Dutch and thus acting as an exercise book to learn the language. Phrases in the book explain the different crafts, animals, and, particularly interesting for my research, the common food of that time. The middle French *maton* is translated as *wronghele* (curd cheese), and, because French was the language of the elite, the word maton remained in place in *tart de maton*, which later became mattentaart.

Quite remarkably there is a recipe for these pies in *Een notabel boecxken van cokeryen*, the first printed cookbook in the Dutch language, published in Brussels around 1510. Like most historical cookbooks it has taken recipes from other sources, in this case *Le Viandier* from about 1490. In turn, later cookbooks and manuscripts have taken recipes from this "notable book of cookery." The recipe in this book mixes curd cheese with eggs and butter and flavors the whole with sage. The filling is baked into a crust and the result is then finished off with more butter.

A 16th-century manuscript from Ghent, which was a source for the important 17th-century Dutch cookbook *De Verstandige Kok*, features a recipe that just mixes the curd cheese, egg yolks, flour, and butter, baked in pastry, with no flavorings. This doesn't mean a clever cook wouldn't add them.

In 1612, Antonius Magirus (who scholars think was most likely from Antwerp in Brabant) published a recipe for a pie titled "Toerte van nates ende ander materie" (tart of "maton" and other stuff: "nates" is the same as maton). The recipes from this cookbook, *Koock-boeck oft familieren Keuken-boeck*, one of only two Dutch language cookbooks from the 17th century (printed in Leuven and Antwerp), are largely taken and translated from an Italian cookbook from 1570 – Bartolomeo Scappi's *Opera dell'arte de cucinare* – but also from the aforementioned "notable book of cookery."

The recipe for this early mattentaart is like many other recipes taken from Scappi, and if we look closely, we can see it in some of the words used. Apart from nates, he calls for *recotten* (ricotta; the Italian cheese made from whey) and *mostacciolen* (*mostaccioli*, almond cookies similar to amaretti). Another clue is the use of pine nuts (*pingelen*), which are widely used in Italian baking, even today. The pine nuts have disappeared from this recipe as it further evolved through time, and the almond cookies were swapped for almond flour.

In another 17th-century cookery text, a manuscript called *Brabants kookboek*, is a recipe for "toerte van Natten." Here the curd cheese is mixed with egg yolks, sugar, cinnamon, and musk (nutmeg), then boiled. When cooled down, the mixture is baked into a crust.

In the 18th century the landscape of cookbooks moves from (current) Belgium to the Netherlands. Fast-forward to the 19th century, when a socialist newspaper[20] from 1896 linked mattentaart to Brabant, giving a recipe for "Brabantse mattentaarten."

However, two years later the same newspaper moves the pie to another region in reports on a *kermis* (fairground) in Nederbrakel, just over six miles from Geraardsbergen, where the people enjoyed a typical Nederbrakel mattentaart.

Mattentaarten were not a regional treat until the first two decades of the 20th century, when the need for regionalization, prompted by the increase of tourism, made restaurants and bakeries promote dishes and products with a regional character. In a photo from the main street in Geraardsbergen dated 1912 you can make out a sign on a bakery that says "Ancienne Maison Morre: spécialité de tartes à maton."

The first time a mattentaart recipe is published as "Geraardsbergse Mattentaart" is in 1929 in the magazine *De Boerin* (The Female Farmer). The recipe uses puff pastry on the base and as a top, and the filling is made with curd cheese, almonds, a little salt, rum (optional), and whipped egg whites. This is still how the pie is made today, although rum is usually swapped for a splash of almond extract.

It was not until I was writing this book that I made my first trip to Geraardsbergen to research the pies at the source. Artisan bakery Broodhuis still makes the mattentaart to the traditional recipe with cheese straight from the farm, adding a little almond flour to the mix. The recipe is a secret, of course, but third-generation baker Jakob Druwé did tell me how to make it. Their secret recipe dates from the establishing of the bakery in 1890.

Makes 6 pies (see photograph on page 165)

For the curd cheese

3 qt fresh whole milk

1 qt buttermilk

1 tsp fresh lemon juice

For the quick puff pastry

or use 21 oz (600 g) ready-made all-butter puff pastry

1 cup (240 g) unsalted butter, cut into cubes no larger than ½ inch and frozen for 30 minutes

2 cups (240 g) all-purpose flour, plus extra for dusting

½ tsp sea salt

½ cup chilled water

1 beaten egg, for egg wash

For the filling

1 lb (500 g) curd cheese (see above)

4 medium eggs, separated

¾ cup (75 g) fine almond flour

1 tsp cornstarch

½ tsp baking powder

1 ¼ cups (250 g) superfine sugar

Use 3½- to 4-inch tart tins. Start a day ahead of baking if making cheese from scratch.

If making the cheese, start the day before. Place a clean piece of cheesecloth in a colander over a large bowl. Bring the milk to a boil in a large saucepan, then remove it from the heat and stir in the buttermilk and lemon juice in three large swirls. Set aside to rest for 30 minutes until cheese curds have started to form. (If nothing happens, then your milk isn't suitable. UHT milk does not work.) Carefully pour the mixture into the colander and drain the cheese over the bowl overnight (keep the whey for making pancakes). The recipe usually makes a little more cheese than you need for these tarts, so store any excess cheese in a container in the fridge for up to 2 days. If your milk makes less cheese, you can make up the difference with a little ricotta.

Make the pastry according to the method on page 215. Wrap in plastic wrap and store in the fridge until ready to bake. This pastry also freezes well.

The next day, pass the curd cheese mixture through a wire sieve into a large bowl and measure out 1 lb (500 g). Add the egg yolks to the cheese and combine well using a rubber spatula.

Preheat the oven to 450°F. Do not use the fan setting.

On a floured work surface, roll out the pastry to ¹⁄₁₆ inch thick.

Fold the almond flour and cornstarch into the cheese mixture and, right at the end, add the baking powder. Whisk the egg whites and sugar to stiff peaks as for meringue, then fold that into the cheese mixture.

Use half the pastry to line the pie tins and prick each base with a fork 3 times. Scoop the cheese filling into the pastry-lined tins, brush the rim of the pastry with egg wash, then lay the remaining pastry over the filling of each pie. Cut away excess pastry and crimp the edges all around tightly to secure the lid. You may need to gather offcuts and reroll the pastry to make the final 2 pies. Use a pair of scissors to cut a cross in the top of each pie, then brush all over with egg wash.

Transfer the pie tins to a baking sheet and bake for 20–25 minutes until they are golden, the surface has puffed up and cracked, and the filling is a golden yellow with a golden-brown blush. They will often tear at the sides, as the filling can be volatile.

Let the tarts cool, but eat them within 2 days or freeze and thaw overnight in the fridge.

Mattentaarten

Doornikse appeltaart

I discovered this recipe for apple pie connected to the city of Doornik (Tournai) in a cookery manuscript from Ghent; it was then copied into the *Cocboeck* published in 1593 by Carolus Battus, who also shared a recipe for an apple pie "in the Wallon fashion." Both these recipes in their turn were then reproduced in *De Verstandigen Kock* (The Clever Cook), which was published first in Amsterdam in 1667, but had several editions published in Antwerp, and editions in Ghent and Brussels. This cookbook traveled to America with many settlers from the Low Countries in the 17th century, as is shown by the many copies held in libraries there.

Although today Doornik is a Walloon town not far from the French border, in the 5th century it was the capital of the Frankish Empire. In the 15th century it was part of the Duchy of Flanders under French rule and an important center of the wool trade. In 1513, the English, under Henry VIII, conquered Doornik, which makes it the only Low Country town that was ever under English rule. So the town was indeed important enough to have a tart connected to it. Yet this recipe is completely forgotten about; in fact, it only appears in these three texts.

In the 1950s edition of *Ons Kookboek* from the Farmers' Wives' Union is a recipe for "Luikse Appeltaart," which is almost identical, with almond macaroons added to the mix and the cinnamon moving from the filling to the crust. This is my recipe based on the 16th-century recipes for Doornikse appeltaart.

Serves 4–6 people

For the shortcrust pastry

1 ½ cups (180 g) bread flour

2 Tbsp (20 g) confectioners' sugar

pinch of salt

7 Tbsp (100 g) unsalted butter, chilled

1 medium egg yolk

1 Tbsp cold water

For the filling

¾ lb (350 g) Cox, pippin, Granny Smith, or other slightly tart dessert apples

scant ½ cup (60 g) confectioners' sugar

½ cup (110 g) butter, melted

5 medium egg yolks + 1 whole egg

1 tsp ground cinnamon

1 Tbsp rice flour

Use an 11-inch top diameter x 9-inch base diameter x 1¼-inch depth pie plate or tin, greased and floured.

For the pastry, combine the flour, sugar, salt, and butter in a food processor fitted with the blade attachment. Pulse for 8 seconds or until the mixture resembles breadcrumbs. Add the egg yolk and water and pulse again until the dough forms a ball in the bowl. Remove from the bowl and knead briefly.

Wrap the pastry in plastic wrap and let it rest in the refrigerator for 30 minutes.

For the filling, slice the apples into rounds and then into thirds. You need 8 oz (225 g) of chopped apple.

Add the confectioners' sugar to the melted butter and beat until smooth. Add the egg yolks and the egg and beat well, then stir in the cinnamon. Set the filling aside to rest while preheating the oven to 350°F. Do not use the fan setting. Grease and flour the pie plate or tin.

Briefly knead the pastry until smooth, then pat it into a round disc and roll it out on a floured work surface to a thickness of ⅛ inch. Lay the pastry in the greased and floured pie plate or tin. Trim off excess pastry.

Coat the apple slices in the rice flour and arrange in the pie plate or tin. Stir the filling well, then pour it over the apple slices and gently shake the tart so the filling can get all around the apples.

Place the tart in the middle of the oven and turn down the heat to 325°F. Bake for 40 minutes until the filling is set, then increase the oven temperature to 350°F and bake for an additional 10 minutes until the pastry is golden brown and the filling golden.

Tarte au sucre brun, blanc, ou blond

This tart is also called *tarte à la cassonade*, and *tarte de Paveû* after the pavers of Waterloo because the pavers' wives used to make this pie for their husbands and the village *kermis* (fairgrounds). The tart came into existence when sugar production switched from cane to beet sugar and sugar became inexpensive and plentiful.

In 1863 the Raffinerie Nationale de Sucre Indigène et Exotique was founded in Waterloo, which brought sugar and sugar beet production to the region; however, legends claim that not one grain of sugar ever left this refinery. It had started out as a sugarcane refinery, but its location was too far from water for production to be possible, so it went bankrupt. The *sucrerie* then became a sugar beet refinery, only to go bankrupt before production even started. Yet the pavers' wives seemed to have access to brown sugar to create their sugary tart.

This tart uses the brown *kandij* sugar favored by Belgians, but there is also an identical version using light brown sugar and one with white sugar. You can decide which sugar to use, and most bakeries in Brussels and areas in Wallonia will offer all three versions: *tarte au sucre brun*, *blanc*, or *blond* (see page 26).

Makes 2 small tarts

For the pastry

2 cups (250 g) bread flour

¼ cup (50 g) superfine sugar

7 Tbsp (100 g) unsalted butter, softened

2 ¼ tsp (7 g) instant dry yeast

1 medium egg

2 ¾ fl oz whole milk or water, at room temperature (tepid in winter)

pinch of salt

For the filling

1 cup plus 2 Tbsp (240 g) dark brown or light brown sugar, or 1 ¼ cups (240 g) white sugar

2 medium eggs, beaten

7 Tbsp pouring cream (30% fat)

3½ Tbsp (50 g) butter, chilled and cubed

Use two pie plates or small pie tins, each 8½-inch top diameter x 8-inch base diameter x 1-inch depth, greased and floured.

For the pastry, combine the flour, sugar, soft butter, and yeast in a large bowl or the bowl of an electric mixer fitted with the dough hook. Add the egg and half the milk or water and start kneading. When the liquid is completely absorbed, add the remaining milk or water and knead for 5 minutes. Let the dough rest for 5 minutes.

Add the salt and knead for a further 10 minutes, scraping the dough off the dough hook and side of the bowl if needed, until it comes together in a smooth and elastic dough that is neither too dry nor terribly wet. Cover and leave to rest for 30 minutes.

Divide the dough in half and roll out into rounds. Lay a round over the base of each greased and floured tin and use your thumbs to push it into the edges. Use a fork to prick the bottom of the pastry all over. Cut away any excess pastry and set aside.

For the filling, cover each tart case with half of the sugar in an even layer.

Mix the beaten egg with the cream and pour it over the sugar in a spiral. It's not the intention to cover the entire thing, as the liquid will spread out, leaving some bits runny after baking. Dot all over with cubes of butter. Let the tarts rest for 10 minutes before baking so that the dough rises and the sugar absorbs the egg and the cream. If you like, use the offcuts of the pastry to decorate the rim of the pie.

Preheat the oven to 350°F. Do not use the fan setting. Bake the tarts in the middle of the oven for 20 minutes until the pastry is brown.

Serve lukewarm or at room temperature; it is best on the day of baking. If you want to eat it the next day, warm the pie in a hot oven until the sugar becomes runny again.

Tarte au stofé de Wavre

Stofé means fromage blanc or white cheese in Walloon, a cheese that typically resembles full-fat quark. The crust of this tart is first covered with a thin layer of applesauce, then the cheese mixture, flavored with macaroons and almond, is scooped on top. In the past, bitter almonds were used, but these are now considered poisonous and the alternative – apricot kernels – can be hard to find.

The *tarte au stofé* is eaten during the *Jeu de Jean et Alice*, a musical and folkloric event that has taken place in Wavre every five years since 1954. It isn't known when the tart was invented, but many similar recipes appear in Dutch cookery books from the 16th century onward.

The Confrérie au Stofé de Wavre has kindly shared their recipe with me: you find my adaptation below.

Makes 1 tart

For the pastry

2 cups (250 g) bread flour

3 Tbsp (40 g) superfine sugar

7 Tbsp (100 g) unsalted butter, softened

2 ¼ tsp (7 g) instant dry yeast

1 medium egg

2 ¾ fl oz whole milk or water, at room temperature (tepid in winter)

pinch of salt

For the filling

2 Tbsp (25 g) unsalted butter

¼ cup (25 g) crushed macaroons or amaretti cookies

⅜ oz (10 g) crushed apricot kernels* with ⅛ tsp rosewater, or use 1 tsp bitter almond extract

8 oz (250 g) fromage blanc or full-fat quark

3 medium eggs, separated

¼ cup (60 g) crème fraîche

½ cup (100 g) superfine sugar

1 cup (150 g) smooth apple compote

Use an 11-inch top diameter x 10-inch base diameter x 1¼-inch depth tart tin, greased and floured.

Make the pastry according to the instructions on page 169 and set aside to rest.

For the filling, melt the butter and let it cool. Crush the macaroons finely using a mortar and pestle.

Blanch the apricot kernels, if using, and remove the skins. Crush them to a paste using a mortar and pestle with the rosewater, which will prevent them from becoming oily.

In a large bowl, combine the cheese, the egg yolks, the crème fraîche, melted butter, macaroons, and the apricot kernels or almond extract. Fold everything together with a spatula without blending perfectly. Apparently the joy of this tart is finding some intact bits of fromage blanc.

Preheat the oven to 400°F. Do not use the fan setting.

Roll out the dough thinly and line the greased and floured tart tin. Pierce all over the base with a fork.

Beat the egg whites with the sugar until stiff and fold into the filling as gently as possible, so as not to lose too much air. Spread a thin layer of apple compote over the base. Spoon the filling evenly over the apple compote and level the top using the back of a tablespoon.

Bake the pie in the middle of the oven for 20–30 minutes until the pastry is nicely browned and the filling is puffed up and browned with slightly golden clouds in the middle. The filling will collapse, resulting in delightful wrinkles around the edge. Let cool on a wire rack.

*An important note on apricot kernels
They are a glorious product, but they should never be eaten raw and should always be used in the quantities supplied in the recipes. Apply a label to the jar of apricot kernels saying, "do not eat raw" to prevent hungry housemates or children from snacking on them. The raw kernels can make you very sick when you eat too many.

Tarte du Lothier

The *tarte du Lothier* is a tart from Genappe in Walloon Brabant with a rice semolina filling flavored with bitter almonds on top of an apricot purée. It is one of the local tarts I discovered about my country while I was doing research for this book. The Confrérie du Lothier has kindly shared their recipe with me: my adaptation, below, is much less sweet.

Makes 3 tarts

For the filling

⅜ oz (10 g) crushed apricot kernels (see note on page 170) with ⅛ tsp rosewater, or use ½ tsp bitter almond extract

1 qt whole milk

¾ cup (150 g) superfine sugar

1 cup (150 g) rice semolina

2 ¾ cups (400 g) apricot jam

5 medium egg yolks

8 medium egg whites

For the pastry

4 cups (500 g) bread flour

14 Tbsp (200 g) unsalted butter, softened

6 Tbsp (80 g) superfine sugar

3 ¼ tsp (10 g) instant dry yeast

2 tsp salt

⅔ cup water

Use three 8½-inch top diameter x 8-inch base diameter x 1-inch depth tart tins, greased and floured.

For the filling, blanch the apricot kernels, if using, and remove the skins. Crush them using a mortar and pestle with the rosewater, which will prevent them from becoming oily.

In a small saucepan, combine the milk, the apricot kernels or the almond extract, and the sugar and bring to a boil, then pour in the rice semolina and simmer for 7 minutes, stirring constantly. Transfer the mixture to a large bowl and cover the top of the mixture with plastic wrap to prevent a skin from forming. Set aside until needed.

Make the pastry following the instructions on page 169.

Preheat the oven to 425°F. Do not use the fan setting.

Roll out the dough thinly and line greased and floured tart tins, then pierce each base all over with a fork. Spread a thin layer of jam (about 5 tablespoons) over the base of the pastry in each tin.

Whisk the egg yolks into the semolina mixture. Beat the egg whites to stiff peaks and fold them into the filling as gently as possible, so as not to lose too much air.

Spoon the filling over the jam and smooth the top using the back of a tablespoon.

Bake the tarts in the middle of the oven for 25–30 minutes until the pastry and the filling are nicely golden brown, with slightly browner patches. The filling will puff up and then fall, resulting in a wrinkle around the edge.

This tart freezes wonderfully well – just thaw overnight in the fridge and take it out of the fridge 30 minutes before serving. By making 3 tarts, it also provides you with the opportunity to give one or two to loved ones or hungry colleagues.

Vaution de Verviers

The *vaution,* or *vôtion* in Wallonia, is a sugar tart from Verviers. It is basically a huge cinnamon bun, but instead of rolling the layered pastry, you stack it. Linguists think the name comes from *vôte*, which means "pancake" in Walloon: five discs of enriched yeast dough are stacked, with sugar, cinnamon, and butter between them to create a syrup that seeps through the dough. Vaution is related to the *tart au sucre* (see page 169), but its architecture is completely different. It is preferably eaten lukewarm and is popular during the Liège fair.

Makes 1 large tart

For the pastry

8 ⅓ cups (1 kg) bread flour

¼ cup (50 g) light brown sugar

1 cup + 5 Tbsp (300 g) unsalted butter, softened

6 ½ tsp (20 g) instant dry yeast

2 medium eggs

1 ⅔ cups whole milk

4 tsp salt

1 beaten egg, for egg wash

2 Tbsp confectioners' sugar, for dusting

For the filling

1 ½ cups (300 g) superfine sugar

½ cup (100 g) dark brown sugar

1 Tbsp ground cinnamon

10 Tbsp (150 g) unsalted butter, chilled

Use a 12–12¾ inch enamel pie plate or tin, greased and floured.

For the pastry, combine the flour, sugar, butter, and yeast in a large bowl or the bowl of an electric mixer fitted with a dough hook. Add the eggs and half of the milk and start kneading. When the liquid is completely absorbed, pour in the rest of the milk and knead for 5 minutes. Let the dough rest for 5 minutes, then add the salt and knead for 10 minutes until it has come together in a smooth and elastic dough that is neither too dry nor terribly wet.

Divide the dough into two 15-oz (415-g) pieces and three 12-oz (350-g) pieces and shape into neat balls. Cover the dough with a kitchen towel and set aside for 1 hour until it has almost doubled in size.

Meanwhile, for the filling, mix the sugars and cinnamon together and chop the butter into 20 cubes.

When ready to assemble the tart, roll out one of the larger dough balls until it is as wide as the greased and floured pie tin and around ⅛ inch thick, and lay it in the tin. Roll out one of the smaller balls and, if you have space for them, roll out the other balls too.

Preheat the oven to 350°F. Do not use the fan setting.

Scatter 3 tablespoons of the sugar mixture over the base dough, leaving ¾ inch clear around the edge of the dough, then dot with 5 cubes of butter. Brush the edge with the egg wash, then lay a smaller disc of dough on top of the filling. Repeat with the sugar mixture (this time all the way to the edge) and another 5 cubes of butter, offsetting the butter from the positions in the layer below. Lay another of the smaller discs of dough over the top and do the same. Repeat with the third small disc of dough and the remaining sugar mixture and butter. Lay the other large disc over the stack and secure it to the base layer around the edge, crimping the pastry together as neatly as you can using either a folding technique or a fork or pastry stamp. Brush all over the top with the egg wash, then sift the confectioners' sugar over the top.

Bake on the second rack (just under the middle) of the oven for 30–35 minutes until golden brown with white patches from the confectioners' sugar.

This tart is best served when still a little warm, but is also good at room temperature. Slice it in large wedges. The next day you can reheat pieces in a hot oven, or on a rack on top of a toaster.

Mastelles ~ tarte au sucre

Mastelles are the small version of a *tarte au sucre* that look a little like focaccia with the indents of the fingers. I prefer the small version, because I am used to buying them on trips to Dinant. It is rather confusing that these pastries are called this because *mastel* in Flemish is a whole different bake (see the *Gentse mastel* on page 80) and so is the *tarte au sucre* on page 169. In Wallonia, these other mastel buns are used in the *tart au mastele* in Ath. Although the names are similar (differing mainly in the number of Ls), the flavors are quite different, so the similar names are a puzzle that even my collection of historical cookery books can't help me figure out. A recipe from 1903 in *Manuel de cuisine et de pâtisserie par Madame Barella* doesn't give quantities, but the method reveals these pastries. Madame Barella was the headmistress of a girls' school in Brussels: it looks like the girls weren't short of sweet treats.

When making mastelles at home, the same pastry makes both mastelles and the *gozettes* on the facing page (photograph on pages 178–179). But you can also just make the mastelles: it's up to you!

Makes 12 small mastelles or 1 large one

For the pastry

4 cups (500 g) bread flour

2 Tbsp (25 g) superfine sugar

5 Tbsp (70 g) unsalted butter, softened

4 ¾ tsp (15 g) instant dry yeast

1 medium egg

1 ¼ cups whole milk, at room temperature

1 tsp fine sea salt

1 beaten egg + 2 Tbsp milk, for egg wash

For the topping

½ cup (120 g) unsalted butter, softened

⅓ cup heavy cream (36–40% fat)

1 ½ cups (175 g) confectioners' sugar

For th pastry, combine the flour, sugar, soft butter, and yeast in a large bowl or the bowl of an electric mixer fitted with the dough hook. Add the egg and half of the milk and start kneading. When the liquid is completely absorbed, pour in the rest of the milk and knead for 5 minutes. Let the dough rest for 5 minutes.

Add the salt and knead for a further 10 minutes until it has come together in a smooth and elastic dough that is neither too dry nor terribly wet. Cover the dough and set aside for 1 hour until it has doubled in size.

Preheat the oven to 425°F. Do not use the fan setting. Line a baking sheet with parchment paper.

For the topping, cut the butter into ¾-inch cubes and pour the cream into a jug.

When the dough has risen, knock out the air and divide it into 12 balls. Roll out the balls into ¼-inch-thick ovals and transfer them to the prepared baking sheet. Pierce all over with a fork to prevent the pastry from rising during baking.

Brush the pastry all over with the egg wash, then divide the confectioners' sugar over each tart, leaving a clear space the width of a finger around the edges. Finish off by placing 2 cubes of butter in the center of each mastelle.

Bake for 15 minutes until the pastry is golden brown and the top pale but blistered, then remove from the oven, brush all over with the cream, and set aside to rest on the sheet for 5 minutes. Transfer to a wire rack to cool.

These pastries can easily be revived the next day in a hot oven or your toaster.

Gozette à la crème and appelflap

Gozettes are known all over Belgium; in Flanders they used to use leftover *vlaai* pastry, but these days they use puff pastry, while in Wallonia they use enriched dough for their gozettes or *gozâ*. They can be filled with apple compote to make *appelflappen*, or with cherries, apricot, or – my favorite – custard cream. We always buy *gozettes à la crème* when we visit Dinant, where a bakery sells the best *flamiche, mastelles,* and gozettes, which makes a perfect lunch and dessert by the river Meuse. Appelflappen are eaten for New Year's in the Netherlands (made with puff pastry), while in Belgium they have become an everyday treat sold at every bakery.

This is the same pastry as for *mastelles* (opposite), so you can make half gozettes or appelflappen and half mastelles, should you wish. See pages 178–179 for the photograph.

Makes 12 gozettes or appelflappen

For the custard filling

9 medium egg yolks

6 Tbsp (75 g) superfine sugar

3 Tbsp (40 g) custard powder, or 5 Tbsp (40 g) cornstarch

3 cups whole milk

⅓ cup heavy cream (36–40% fat)

1 vanilla bean, split, or 1 bay leaf

For the pastry

4 cups (500 g) bread flour

2 Tbsp (25 g) superfine sugar

5 Tbsp (70 g) unsalted butter, softened

4 ¾ tsp (15 g) instant dry yeast

1 medium egg

1 ¼ cups whole milk, at room temperature

1 tsp fine sea salt

milk, for brushing

confectioners' sugar, for dusting

For appelflappen

1 jar apple compote

For the custard filling, have a large shallow ovenproof dish ready.

Whisk the egg yolks, sugar, and custard powder until creamy, then set aside. In French culinary terms, you've now made a *ruban* (ribbon).

In a large saucepan, warm the milk and cream with the seeds of the vanilla bean. Strain the milk if you want to get rid of the black vanilla seeds or leave them in and show the world you used the real stuff. Add a tablespoon of the warm milk to the ruban and whisk well, then add the ruban to the warm milk while constantly whisking. Return the pan to low heat and whisk until the custard thickens, turning off the heat as soon as the mixture appears to give more resistance to whisking it.

Immediately pour the hot custard into the cold ovenproof dish and cover the top of the custard (not the dish) with a sheet of plastic wrap. The plastic wrap prevents the custard from forming a skin. Sadly I have not found an alternative that is not plastic: a lid doesn't work because the condensation between the lid and custard will make it wet. Let the custard cool and then transfer to a piping bag.

To make the pastry, follow the instructions as for the mastelles, opposite. Toward the end of the resting time, preheat the oven to 425°F. Do not use the fan setting. Line a baking sheet with parchment paper.

When the dough has risen, knock out the air and divide it into 12 balls. Roll out the balls into ¼-inch-thick ovals and transfer them to the prepared baking sheet.

Now fold all the ovals in half, without pressing the pastry (when making appelflappen, add 2 tablespoons of apple compote to each one before you fold and omit the custard). Brush all over the top with the milk, then transfer the sheet to the middle of the oven. Bake for 15 minutes until the pastry is just golden brown and let cool on a wire rack.

When cool, cut open the buns that you're filling with cream for gozettes à la crème on the seam created by folding the dough, making sure the halves remain attached along the straight side, then pipe the custard into the buns. Appelflappen need nothing more than to cool. Dust both the appelflappen and the gozettes generously with confectioners' sugar to serve.

Gozettes à la crème and mastelles (tartes au sucre)

Rijstevlaai ~ tarte au riz

Rijstevlaai, tarte au riz, blanke Doreye, or *tarte blanche* in Wallonia, from Liège, is a *vlaai* filled with rice pudding. In Verviers in Wallonia the tart is preserved by the Seigneurie de la Vèrvî-riz.

There are first references to this tart in a cookbook from 1604: Lancelot de Casteau, master cook of three Prince-Bishops of Liège, published an ancestor of the rice tart in his *Ouverture de Cuisine*. While today the rice pie is always flavored with vanilla, this is a modern development as vanilla wasn't available in the 17th century. Lancelot suggests cinnamon and rosewater, which you should definitely try. A cookbook from 1917 titled *Le Coin de la Ménagère par Tante Colinette* also uses cinnamon and even adds broth. Both recipes use rice that has been cooked some time before baking, rather than using it straightaway. This does indeed improve the texture of the rice.

Lancelot instructs to finish the tarts like the others in his chapter, which means adding a lattice top. Today this vlaai is never made with a lattice top as the cooked rice looks very agreeable, although it might not have been fancy enough for Prince-Bishops of Liège in the zeitgeist of the early 1600s.

There are two main differences between a Flemish/Dutch rijstevlaai and a tarte au riz from Wallonia: the first adds custard to the finished rice pudding while the latter just adds eggs, the Liège rice tart whisking the egg white to stiff peaks. The Walloon version is therefore lighter than the Flemish/Dutch version. In Verviers they used to add crushed almond macaroons to the rice. The best rice tart I've ever had came from a bakery in a little town in Ostbelgien. I've attempted to recreate it below. In a good rice tart the filling isn't very solid, but barely keeping together.

Makes 1 large tart

For the rice pudding

1 ½ qt whole milk

⅛ tsp *each* of ground cinnamon and rosewater, or 1 vanilla bean, split

¾ cup (140 g) pudding rice or risotto rice

2 medium eggs + 1 egg yolk

¼ cup (50 g) superfine sugar

1 ½ Tbsp (20 g) unsalted butter, melted

1 Tbsp confectioners' sugar

For the pastry

2 cups (250 g) bread flour

7 Tbsp (100 g) unsalted butter, softened

2 Tbsp (25 g) superfine sugar

2 ¼ tsp (7 g) instant dry yeast

½ tsp salt

6 Tbsp water

Use an 11-inch top diameter x 10-inch base diameter x 1¼-inch depth tart tin, greased and floured. Start a day ahead of baking.

To prepare the rice for the rice pudding, 1 day ahead, simmer the milk with the cinnamon and rosewater or the vanilla bean and the rice in a saucepan over low heat, covered, for 40 minutes, stirring occasionally. When the rice is tender, uncover the pan and remove from the heat. Set aside to cool slightly, remove the vanilla bean if you used it, then cover the rice and keep it in the fridge overnight.

The next day, remove the rice from the fridge 1 hour before cooking. Make the pastry according to the instructions on page 169.

While the dough is rising, to make the rice pudding, beat the 2 eggs with the superfine sugar until creamy, as though you are making custard. Stir the egg mixture into the saucepan with the rice and add the butter. Return the pan to the stove over low heat. Simmer for 20 minutes until it thickens, stirring constantly, then remove the pan from the heat and stir occasionally until the pudding has cooled down.

Preheat the oven to 400°F. Do not use the fan setting.

When the dough has risen, knock out the air and roll out the dough as thin as you can, then place it over the greased and floured tin, press into the base, and cut away the excess pastry. Pierce the bottom all over with a fork, then spoon the rice pudding into the tart, reserving 2 tablespoons of the mixture. Mix the extra egg yolk and the confectioners' sugar with the reserved rice pudding and spread that on top of the vlaai, leveling the top using a pastry brush. You will have a little pastry and filling left over; enough to make 2 small tarts.

Bake the tart in the middle of the oven for 40–45 minutes until golden brown with pale flecks. Set aside to cool before serving.

Two tarts, one "boulette" of cheese

The *tarte al djote* from Nivelles and the *flamiche de Dinant* (recipes on the following pages) are two of the most important (savory) cheese tarts of Wallonia. They are both made with a *boulette* cheese (or *bètchéye* in Walloon) from the region. This cheese is made by mixing raw skimmed milk into fermented curds, leaving it to coagulate. Its texture is dry and crumbly and unlike any other cheese I've had the pleasure to taste. You can see the version used for flamiche (the *Romedenne*) in the photograph opposite. The complete process of making the cheese is a closely guarded secret, so much so that when creameries cease to produce, knowledge is not being passed on for fear of people stealing the recipe. I cannot stress enough that placing too much importance on the secrecy of a recipe will ultimately mean it will be forever lost.

The tarte al djote

The tarte al djote is a cheese, egg, and chard tart from Nivelles, a town in Walloon Brabant, located south of Brussels. The rather rustic tart has its origins in medieval times, and although many old texts mention cheese tarts and cheese tarts with green leafy vegetables, there is no mention of the name "d'jote," which is perfectly normal in culinary history, as people only felt the need to name every single dish much later.

The composition of the tart tells me it was meant for special occasions when one could afford to use a large amount of eggs, butter, and cheese.

Le Viandier de Taillevent, one of the earliest French cookbooks from the late 13th or very early 14th century, gives a recipe for a "Tortes de harbe, fromaige, et oeuf." Using parsley, mint, chard, spinach, lettuce, marjoram, basil, and wild thyme, eggs and cheese, but no butter, the pie is then seasoned with ground ginger, cinnamon, and long pepper. The 14th-century English cookbook, *The Forme of Cury*, gives a recipe for a similar tart, adding onion, herbs (not specifying) and green cheese – which is a mature cheese – eggs, butter and a seasoning of saffron, salt, currants, and "powdour douce" (a medieval spice blend). Both these medieval recipes look a lot like our tarte al djote; only the spices are missing in the tart today. In the 16th century, a manuscript from Ghent gave a recipe for a chervil tart with cheese, butter dotted all around and added after baking, before serving.

The latter – adding butter on top of the baked tart – is exactly what is done before serving the tarte al djote, while adding knobs of butter before baking is part of the procedure of the flamiche. Chard is the main green in the recipe, in addition to onion and parsley.

If you live in an area where chard is harder to find, I find the leaf of bok choy is very similar, and chervil creates a very delicate flavor.

In a 16th-century manuscript cookbook from Antwerp there appears a "Warmoestoerte" made with a handful of *warmoes* and chervil mixed with fresh cheese, eggs, and breadcrumbs. The Dutch word for chard, "warmoes" appears in several centuries-old recipes for tarts; in this context and at this time, warmoes could mean a variety of green leafy vegetables rather than just chard. This shows how we can project our modern language on old texts and be mistaken. Language is ever evolving. It is therefore possible that our tarte al djote was indeed made with a variety of green leafy vegetables at some point. *Jottes* is an old French dialect word for this slightly bitter vegetable.

The only thing we know for sure is that its current recipe was in existence in 1918, when the Restaurant des Alliés in Nivelles was advertised as "the oldest house recognized for delicious al djote tarts," serving them "*bî tchaude, bî blète, queèl bûre déglète*" (very hot, with chard, and dripping butter) in the old Walloon language. In Nivelles bakeries you can also get a version without vegetables: *tarte al djote blanc*, or *tarte macayance* after the cheese mixture. Seasoned tarte al djote makers leave the cheese out at room temperature to become *à point*, which means "a little sweaty."

Flamiche de Dinant

The flamiche de Dinant is a relative of the tarte al djote and similar medieval tarts, made with a yeast dough and filled with typical strong local Romedenne cheese, eggs, and butter. In Northern France they make a version of this tart adding leek to the mix.

The local legend about the origin of the flamiche tells us the story of a girl from a Romedenne farm who walked to Dinant to sell her wares at the market. But on her way the poor girl fell, leaving everything in her wicker basket unsellable; the eggs broken and mixed with the

fresh cheese and the soft butter. To save the produce she ran to the bakery and asked for a piece of bread dough from which she made a pie crust, in it went the cheese, the eggs, and the butter, and what came out of the oven was flamiche!

The Confrérie Royale des Quarteniers de la Flamiche Dinantaise was created in 1956 in honor of the flamiche, which is celebrated on the first weekend of September at the Braderie de Dinant.

The etymology of the tarte al djote is easiest to explain as djote means chard, but the origin of flamiche is much more obscure. "Flamiche" has a resemblance to the Alsace *flammkuchen* (pizza) and *flambé*; "flam" meaning flame. Gaston Clément claims in his 1950s *De Raadsman in de Kookkunst* that in times of wood-fired ovens the flamiche was indeed made flat like a flammkuchen.

I know that it might be hard to source the boulette cheese for these tarts, but since they are both descended from centuries-old recipes where the cheese wasn't

specified and cooks knew best which cheese to use for the recipe, it is totally fine to swap the traditional cheese for shredded mature Cheddar or Gouda, or a similar cheese local to you, if you think it will work better. In northern France where they make flamiche with leek, they use *maroilles*, a cow's milk cheese made in the region of Picardy.

Both the tarte al djote and the flamiche should be eaten hot or lukewarm and are best accompanied, according to locals, by a glass of Burgundy wine.

Tarte al djote

Makes 4 individual tarts

For the pastry

4 cups (500 g) all-purpose flour

½ cup (125 g) salted butter, softened

3 ½ tsp (11 g) instant dry yeast

2 tsp salt

2 medium eggs

½ cup whole milk

For the filling

14 oz (400 g) cheese (see page 183)

5 Tbsp (75 g) salted butter, plus extra butter, for serving

1 medium egg, plus 1 egg yolk

½ tsp ground white pepper

pinch of salt

1 ¼ oz (35 g) Swiss chard, leaves only, finely chopped

2 medium shallots, finely chopped

⅓ cup (20 g) finely chopped flat-leaf parsley leaves

Use 4 pie tins, 8-inch top diameter x 7-inch base diameter x 1-inch depth, greased and floured.

To make the pastry, combine the flour, butter, yeast, and salt in a large bowl or the bowl of an electric mixer fitted with a dough hook and knead until you get a coarse mixture. Add the eggs and milk and knead for 10 minutes until the dough is smooth. Cover the bowl and set aside to rest for 30 minutes or overnight in the fridge.

For the filling, crumble or shred the cheese and leave it out to get "sweaty."

Meanwhile, melt the butter in a saucepan over low heat and brown it (beurre noisette). Set aside to cool so that the butter doesn't cook the eggs.

Mix the cheese with the cooled melted butter, the egg, egg yolk, pepper, and salt. Fold the chard, shallots, and parsley through and set aside.

Preheat the oven to 400°F. Do not use the fan setting.

When the dough has risen, knock out the air, divide in 4, and roll out all 4 pieces of dough as thin as you can. Lay the dough rounds over the greased and floured tins, press into the base, and cut away the excess pastry. Pierce the bases all over with a fork.

Spoon in filling to just under ½ inch deep in each pastry-lined tin.

Place the tarts on a baking sheet, place on the lowest rack of the oven, and bake for 20 minutes until the crust has a blush. Transfer to a wire rack and set aside to rest for 5 minutes for the cheese to coagulate so you can safely remove the tart from the tin.

Serve warm, with a knob of extra butter on top to melt. Pair with a full-bodied red wine (Burgundy is traditional) or a dark monastery beer.

The next day you can reheat the tarts in a 400°F oven for 10 minutes.

The baked tarts freeze incredibly well: just thaw in the fridge and reheat.

Flamiche de Dinant

I have a postcard from the 1970s with a retro-looking scene of a *flamiche* surrounded by a plate of the traditional Romedenne cheese, a bottle of Burgundy, and a carved wooden mold for making *couque de Dinant* (see page 243). On the back is a recipe for making flamiche that is exactly what a woman in bakery Defossez in Dinant generously taught me last year. It isn't very complicated at all, but the secret lies in how you handle the filling. Whisk it all together and it will not be a flamiche: carefully dotting the butter and cheese over the base and then pouring over the eggs whole will indeed create the perfect flamiche. The amount of pepper might startle you, but is essential to cut through the richness of the cheese. If you do not like things peppery or your cheese isn't very pungent, put in half the pepper. I enjoy how the pepper kicks you in the face and leaves the back of your throat all tingly while your lips, in contrast, are greasy from the richness of the filling.

The citadel town of Dinant in Wallonia has a very special place in my heart. I must have been around six or seven years old when all the children in my class at school were loaded into a bus for a special trip to the French-language part of our country. To us kids it felt like we were going on a proper holiday abroad; I mean, they spoke a language different from ours, and there were cliffs and hills, while Flanders is flat. My first glimpse of Dinant was the view you see on the next page. The 13th-century cathedral with its unique onion-shaped tower, the cliff crowned with the citadel towering over the town, and the colorful houses on the quay of the river Meuse. I bought a couque de Dinant for my mother that day, splashing all my spending money on it. I didn't see the flamiche; I think the couque spoke more to the imagination of a child. I discovered this rich cheese tart only when I took my husband to Dinant for his first visit.

Makes 2 large tarts

For the pastry

4 cups (500 g) bread flour

1 ½ Tbsp (20 g) salted butter, softened

3 ½ tsp (11 g) instant dry yeast

1 ⅓ cups whole milk, lukewarm

2 tsp salt

For the filling

14–18 oz (400–500 g) strong cheese (see page 183)

1 cup (250 g) unsalted butter, cold

18 medium eggs

2 tsp freshly ground black pepper

½ tsp salt

Use two 11-inch top diameter x 9-inch base diameter x 1¼-inch depth pie tins, greased and floured.

For the pastry, combine the flour, butter, yeast, and salt in a large bowl or the bowl of an electric mixer fitted with the dough hook. Pour in the milk and knead for 10 minutes until the dough is smooth. Cover the bowl and set aside to rest for 1 hour.

Preheat the oven to 425°F. Do not use the fan setting.

Roll out the dough until it is just larger than your greased and floured tart tin. Lay the dough on top and use your thumb to press the dough into the tin. Trim any excess dough with a knife.

For the filling, crumble or shred the cheese and set aside. Cut the cold butter into small (about ½-inch) cubes and dot over the base of the tart. Arrange the cheese evenly around the butter. Break the eggs into a large bowl, add the pepper and salt, and stir gently without whisking to keep most of the eggs whole: this will create a crater effect with the chunks of butter when the pie bakes. Pour the eggs into the tart.

Bake the tart on the bottom rack of the oven for 35–40 minutes until golden brown with pale flecks.

Serve warm with a full-bodied red wine (Burgundy is traditional) or a dark monastery beer.

The next day you can reheat the tart in a 375°F oven for 10 minutes.

AMERICAN BELGIAN PIE

**"'Simple Simon met a pieman going to the fair …'
A modern simple Simon might be going to a kermis
and he would most likely meet a Belgian housewife
who had just finished making a batch of Belgian
pies. This is kermis time in Door County …"
So starts an article in *The Door County Advocate*,
dated 9 October 1969.**

It is rather remarkable to discover a Belgian community
in Wisconsin, USA. They celebrate Belgian traditions
and foodways and hold annual *kermis* (fairs) for which
they bake Belgian pies in great numbers. They even live
in towns they named after their Belgian counterparts.

From 1623, Belgian–Walloon Huguenots were the first
group of European settlers in Manhattan, New Jersey,
Delaware, Connecticut, and Pennsylvania,[21] led by Jessé
de Forest, a Reformed Protestant Christian in search of
a life free from persecution.

Fast-forward to the mid-19th century: Belgium is a
young country on the verge of the Great Depression.
Arable land is scarce, the population ever growing,
work underpaid, and Flemish- and French-speaking
working-class Belgians live in dire circumstances with
few prospects of a better life.

While a number of Flemish people immigrated to
America, tired of the language discrimination they faced
in Belgium and in search for a better life in general,
most of these immigrants were from Wallonia, the
French-speaking part of Belgium. Flemish people moved
to different areas than their Walloon neighbors and
founded several Dutch-language newspapers, of which
the *Gazette van Detroit* is most notable, as it existed
from 1914 to as recently as 2018.

Antwerp was the largest port for immigration to
America, with the Red Star Line ships connecting the
port with the United States and Canada. There is an
Antwerp in New York and Ohio, Hoboken in New
Jersey, Ghent in Minnesota, Liège in Missouri, Charleroi
in Pennsylvania, but the state with the most Belgian
namesake towns is Wisconsin: with Brussels, Namur,
Rosiere, Walhain, and Luxembourg.

Today Wisconsin and Michigan have the largest Belgian
American communities, and it started with just a couple
of Walloon families who founded a community in 1856.
They cleared the land and built homes and lives for their
kin. To the eyes of a Belgian it is strange to see a road
sign for a Belgian town in an American landscape, but
in the towns themselves many citizens attempt to live
a life they think of as a Belgian way of life. In 1858 the
first "kermis" was held in Rosiere, kicking off a tradition
of an annual harvest fair. Just like in their homeland,
vlaaien are baked for kermis; they call them Belgian pies.
They do not look like the pies in Belgium, as they have
developed differently, but to the Belgians of Wisconsin
these are the pies of "the old country."

To find out more about American Belgian culinary
traditions, I read the cookery notebook of Margaret
Draize, from Wisconsin. Margaret was born in 1927
and was asked by her friends and family to write down
all that she knew from her grandparents and parents
and note down the recipes to become a handbook for
the Belgian Americans in the region. She gives recipes
for many sweet and savory dishes that I recognize to be
Belgian, but also many that had already evolved in the
States, which I cannot link to Belgium. Researching
further, I have to conclude that there is no greater
love for Belgian cuisine than the love these Belgian
Americans have for theirs. Maybe it is because they are
far from home and nostalgically yearning for it, and in
Belgium we have grown to covet the exotic so that we no
longer see the beauty of our *peperkoek* and pie.

On the journey of this book I have tried to become a
tourist in my own country, looking on with wonder to
truly see what is there. Reading the words of Belgian
Americans about Belgian culture has helped me to open
my eyes further.

I talked to Gina Guth, one of the people teaching
Belgian pie making in her cookery school, keeping
the heritage alive in Wisconsin. Her great-great-
grandmother was a first-generation emigrant from
Belgium. Her mother, Jean, baked so many pies they
often took over the house, and every horizontal surface
was covered in pies.

Gina knows these Belgian pies don't look like the pies
in Belgium today but describes them beautifully as
"a snapshot of a time gone by, a relic of a hardscrabble
immigrant's life, when folks made food with what they

had on hand, and with a nod to familiar flavors and techniques." Walloons took their favorite recipes to heart as they kept hold of their heritage, and this style of pie, completely lost in Belgium in this form, remained alive in Belgian American families.

Gina sent me an article entitled "Keeping the Kermiss" from the *Milwaukee Journal* from 1970, where her mother is seen arranging a couple of dozen Belgian pies on wooden shelves. It reads that it's kermis time and pies aren't made by the dozens, but by the hundreds. As they were made for kermis, Belgian pies were traditionally always made en masse, never just one as we would expect from modern recipes.

Just like in Belgian and Dutch Limburg, where pies were also made in large quantities for kermis, these pies were baked in outdoor wood-fired ovens. The bread was baked weekly, and the pies were baked in the falling heat after the bread was finished.

That is why, in the 1990s, the Belgian pie was disappearing, as people didn't know what to do with the generous recipes from their grandmothers. That generosity was bestowed on me when Gina shared her

knowledge and taught me Belgian pie making over the internet at a time when travel was restricted.

The recipe you find here for the dough and the toppings is hers, adapted by me for an international audience, to hopefully live on in this book for future generations of Belgian pie makers.

The pies are eaten handheld, rather than on a plate with knife and fork, just like the way vlaaien are traditionally eaten in Belgian and Dutch Limburg – holding the crust and supporting the tip with your pinky finger, like a slice of pizza. Gina says that Grandma Jean's pies were noted for their thin crust and thick filling.

Belgian pie

The recipe for the cheese topping from Jean Guth, Gina's mother, uses a mixture of dry and creamy cottage cheese. Dry cottage cheese is not easy to find, so Gina takes small-curd (minimum 4 percent milk fat) creamy cottage cheese, rinses off the cream, then squeezes out the moisture in a cloth to obtain dry cheese curds. If cottage cheese is hard to get where you are, there is a recipe for making curd cheese on page 163.

Traditional fillings that Gina teaches in her school are prune, raisin, apple, cherry, and rice. Apart from the raisin, these are also traditional fillings for Belgian and Dutch pies, but the cheese topping is typical only of Belgian pies in the United States.

As Gina goes about creating her dough differently from the way I do it, I have given you my method below. There is no "best method" (although some would disagree) apart from the method you feel most comfortable with. For Gina it is important to continue the traditional method of mixing the dough; if you want to learn how, she gives classes in her cookery school and online.

Makes 4 pies

For the pastry

6 Tbsp (85 g) heavy cream
(36–40% fat)

3 Tbsp water

3 ½ cups (410 g) all-purpose flour

½ cup (120 g) unsalted butter,
softened

2 medium eggs

⅓ cup (65 g) superfine sugar

2 tsp instant dry yeast

¼ tsp salt

Use four 8-inch top diameter x 7-inch base diameter x 1-inch depth pie tins, greased and floured.

Warm the cream over medium heat until a skin forms on the top, but do not let it boil, then turn off the heat, add the water, and let cool. In a large bowl or the bowl of an electric mixer fitted with the dough hook, combine the flour, soft butter, eggs, sugar, and yeast. Knead until incorporated, then add the cream and water mixture and knead for 5 minutes. At this point the dough looks more like cake batter than pie dough.

Now add the salt and knead for a further 5 minutes until the dough comes together into a soft ball. Cover the bowl and leave to rest for 1 hour until doubled in size.

Meanwhile, make the cheese topping and one or two of the fillings opposite.

Grease the pie tins with butter or lard, then flour them. Divide the dough into 4 balls and place into the pie tins. This dough should not and cannot be rolled out. Just use the palm of your hand to press the dough flat, then use your fingers to push it into shape, like for a pan pizza. The dough should be pushed out to the edge of the base, not up the sides.

Rest the pastry for 5 minutes, covered with a kitchen towel, while you preheat the oven to 350°F. Do not use the fan setting.

Scoop the filling on top, leaving a rim of ½ inch around the edge of the pastry. Then scoop the cheese topping on top, leaving a rim of about ¾ inch of the fruit filling visible all around.

Gina's instructions for traditional ovens with top and bottom heat (which is for me the only way for baking) are to start by baking the pies on the second rack from the bottom. When the crust is golden brown on the bottom after about 10 minutes, transfer the pies to the top rack. Bake for about 5–8 minutes until the pie crust is pale golden brown. Transfer to a wire rack and leave to cool, or carefully take them out of the tins and cool them on a wire rack. Or, when making 40 pies, cool them on kitchen towels, as the Belgian American mothers would have done.

For the cheese topping

1 ½ lb (680 g) small-curd cottage cheese (minimum 4% milk fat)

4 tsp sugar

2 medium egg yolks

Divide the cottage cheese in half. Rinse half in a strainer under running water until all the cream is rinsed off. Place the rinsed cheese in a piece of cheesecloth and gently but firmly squeeze the moisture out, discarding the liquid.

In a food processor, mix together the dry curd with the remaining half of the moist small-curd cottage cheese. Add the sugar and egg yolks to the cheese mixture and blend just until the texture is somewhat grainy instead of smooth. If it is too smooth it will run off the pie. Keep it cold until ready to top your pies.

For prune filling (for 2 pies)

6 oz (170 g) pitted prunes (dried plums)

½ cup (125 g) applesauce (optional, for milder prune taste)

Soak the prunes in water overnight.

Strain the prunes. In a medium saucepan, bring the prunes and applesauce to a simmer over low heat. Simmer for 15 minutes until the fruit is soft.

Allow the fruit to cool in the liquid, then purée the fruit and the liquid in a blender or food processor. If the purée is too runny at this point, you can put it back in the saucepan over low heat to reduce it a bit further. If you do this, let it cool again before further use. It will become more solid when it has cooled. The consistency should be very thick, not runny; when stirring through the prunes, the base of the saucepan should be visible.

For cherry filling (for 2 pies)

10 oz (280 g) tart cherries, fresh, canned, or frozen, pitted and drained if needed (reserve the juice if draining)

⅓ cup (70 g) superfine sugar

2 Tbsp cornstarch

pinch of salt

6 Tbsp (90 g) cherry cooking liquid, drained juice, or water

Cook the cherries (if using fresh or frozen) until soft but not breaking up, and measure out part of the cooking liquid for the sauce.

In a saucepan, combine the sugar, cornstarch, and salt. Gradually add the cherry cooking liquid or juice and stir until smooth. Cook, whisking, until thickened. This will take a long time to thicken. Gina uses Door County cherry pie filling, which is locally made from Door cherries.

SAVORING GOLDEN AGE ART

Dutch and Flemish still-life paintings of the Golden Age show products of the foreign trade that made the nation's fortunes during their period of glory. They are case studies of 16th-century material culture. They were painted when the Southern Netherlands (current Belgium) and Italy were the centers of art and culture in Western Europe: an extraordinary moment in the history of art in Europe.

Although most frequently referred to as the "Dutch masters," the style of painting originated in Flanders in what is now Belgium. At that time the area was part of the Spanish Netherlands (1556–1714). Pieter Aertsen (1508–1575) and Joachim Beuckelaer (c. 1535–1575), both residents of Antwerp, were two of the first to paint kitchen and market scenes portrayed as still life. Beuckelaer learned the style of market and kitchen scenes from Aertsen, who was his uncle, and certainly pioneered the style in the Low Countries.

The first artist to paint a still life of food as a table setting in a way that makes you feel part of the painting as a guest was Clara Peeters (1594–c. 1657), born and trained in Antwerp. Her earliest known painting dates from 1607. Osias Beert (c. 1580–1623), also from Antwerp, followed with a distinctively similar style. It is generally assumed that Floris Van Dyck (c. 1575–1651) from Haarlem was inspired by Peeters. Pieter Claesz (1597–1661), also from Antwerp, painted in a similar style to Peeters and Beert but preferred dramatic pies to stacks of cheeses or confectionery, and Willem Claesz. Heda (1594–1680) from Haarlem again followed from the late 1620s in his own style.

I grew up with a still-life table scene hanging in our living room across from where I had my place at the dinner table. It was not of the artistry of Clara Peeters, Osias Beert, or any of the other aforementioned artists, but nonetheless it intrigued me. Food and tableware had to be important and relevant to be painted with such care.

Clara Peeters first showed herself in a diary I had in which every day had a different work of art. It was printed on thin paper, and the book was tattered fairly

quickly, but for the first years of my life, that was my only book with art, and I spent a lot of time just flipping the pages and studying the artwork, looking for windows into the past and its customs. I loved history and mythology, and wanted to go to art school when I grew up, which I did after much resistance from my parents. It was much later that I discovered that Clara Peeters had lived in the same district in Antwerp where I grew up. While before I had been drawn only to her art, now I also felt a deeper connection to her. She was my neighbor in another century; she was highly skilled, influential, and also celebrated; a woman in a time when prospects for women were incredibly limited.

Her work was commissioned by the Spanish art collector the Marquis of Leganés, whom Rubens described as one of the greatest connoisseurs of art in the world. From as early as 1666, two of her works were registered in the royal collection of Madrid.

Clara's paintings and the artwork of the other artists of the same period are a study of material culture in the 17th century. They are a window into the past, but not to a realistic table setting. Dutch cheeses weren't stacked high in whole or half wheels on the table; they were there, at every meal, praised for their health benefits, but in smaller wedges. But as the rest of the items in the scenes of these painters were so opulent, the cheese had to be in a prominent position as the equal of the precious glasswork made in Antwerp "à la façon de Venice," spices from afar, pricey sugar comfits, dainty pastries and letter cookies, porcelain from China, exotic shells, and silver from Antwerp and Nuremberg.

While it is often assumed these paintings were pointing out excess, I believe they were a celebration of all the treasures the Southern and northern Netherlands had to offer: revered cheeses and butter and all the luxurious commodities that arrived in the port of Antwerp; the trade links; and craftsmanship in the stoneware, silverware, and glassware. Herring, the gold mine of the Dutch economy, features often in the paintings by Netherlandish artists. This was a display of wealth, this was "the best of," this was artistic patriotism. A 17th-century advertisement for the region. The newly founded Dutch republic needed a PR campaign.

CLARA PEETERS (1594–c. 1657): *Table with a cloth, salt cellar, gilt tazza, pie, jug, porcelain dish with olives, and roast fowl*, 1611.

Yet several of the painters of still life were from Flanders, in particular Antwerp. Were these paintings a statement to show "better together" in a United Netherlands, free of Spanish rule? Was it a statement of religion? Most of the Flemish painters of food still life are assumed to be Catholic, while the religion in the northern Netherlands was Protestant, which generally condemned frivolity.

Or was there enough allegorical meaning in the painting to excuse its luxury and turn it into a statement against indulgence? Stacked cheeses showing excess; *zuivel op zuivel is voer voor de duivel* ("dairy on dairy is considered the devil's food"), so butter on top of cheese is also excessive. Wine and bread are Eucharistic symbols, while walnuts stand for the suffering of Christ.

Artistic playfulness

Artists didn't only have an eye for the aesthetic or the allegorical. They also had the playful insight to use letter cookies to spell out their names or initials. Or they engraved them onto knives. Clara Peeters appears in

reflection in several items in her paintings. These works of art might have been painted by request, but the artists often found ways to include themselves in the story. It motivates the spectator of the painting to search for clues, making the art interactive.

Food features prominently in the still-life paintings of the 17th century; they give us a unique insight into material culture and, with regard to the history of food, the shapes and forms of luxurious sweets, cookies, pretzels, and breads. But it is not in the still-life paintings but in the genre paintings that we find out more about food customs and traditions and the politics surrounding those traditions.

Sebastiaan Vrancx shows us, in his *An Allegory of Winter* (1608; held in a private collection), a snowy landscape with a *duivekater* or *vollaard* festive loaf in the foreground, waffles, pancakes, and fine white buns next to winter vegetables, nuts, a stack of clothes, and a Carnival mask.

Hans Francken's *Winter still life with pancakes, waffles and duivekater* (see page 66), from the same period, also shows an array of festive winter bakes, yet here the food is the main affair. There is no landscape apart from a landscape of baking. Waffles, vollaard, or duivekater, fine white buns, letter cookies, syrup, *peperkoek* or *hylickmaker*, fritters, nuts and citrus, apples and medlars. Food must have mattered: specific foods for specific occasions mattered enough to paint them so vividly, boldly, like they were everything to people – a light in a dark period of the year; the prospect of feasting and giving bakes to loved ones. This is not different from the pictures of festive Christmas or Easter tables on social media today. The food is emblematic of the occasion.

Jan Steen (1628–1679), very much as Bruegel had a century before, shows us which foods are linked with feasts. In one of Steen's many Twelfth Night paintings I spot waffles, and for the last fifty years or so in Belgium it has become the custom to have a *galette des rois* on Epiphany, as in France.

Steen also painted two versions of the much-loved Low Country feast of Saint Nicholas, showing which bakes were associated with the feast. After the Dutch Revolt in 1572–1648, it was forbidden to express the Catholic faith, let alone venerate a Catholic saint. Because the feast would be full of Catholic symbolism, which was based on pagan customs, Protestants tried to abolish the Sinterklaas feast.

But the Saint Nicholas feast was rooted too deeply into the culture of Belgium and the Netherlands, and people, in the Netherlands especially, revolted against the banning of the Saint Nicholas markets and the selling of Saint Nicholas peperkoek.

In the most famous of Steen's two paintings (see page 207), we see all the iconography that represents Saint Nicholas, but not the holy man himself. There is a shoe in the foreground representing the custom of children placing their shoe in front of the fireplace to receive gifts. To the left there is a basketful of traditional Saint Nicholas bakes: a long heavy peperkoek (see page 226), waffles, sweet buns, fruit, and nuts. A large duivekater (see page 75) is leaning against the small

table full of treats, on which is a single rolled *oublie* waffle (see page 46), sugar comfits, and a coin stuck into an apple. There are oranges on the floor. The little girl in the foreground holds a doll dressed in ecclesiastical robes and she also holds a bucket full of treats. The baby in the background holds a Saint Nicholas–shaped cake, a *klaaskoek* (see page 216), while she and other children look up the chimney for a glimpse of the good old man. On the left, a boy is crying because his shoe was left empty; he must know what he has done wrong to be left wanting like this.

The food in this painting is significant as it became synonymous with the feast. People could tell from the selection of sweet treats that this is the feast of Saint Nicholas without seeing the saint or knowing the name of the painting. Interestingly, today, more than 350 years later, we can still look at this painting and recognize the culinary symbolism. The combination of peperkoek, shaped cakes and bread, oranges, and sweets is a clear mark of the feast even today.

Anarchy in art

Baking, giving, and devouring these cakes, sweets, and gingerbread koek can be seen as a form of protest, a way to consume the forbidden feast, like eating the body of Christ at Communion makes you part of a community. Painting these feasts during this time could have been dangerous to those who wielded the brush and paint. Protestants never managed to eradicate the feast of Saint Nicholas, and it became an emblem of the Counter-Reformation.

OSIAS BEERT (c. 1580–1623): *Dishes with Oysters, Fruit, and Wine*, c. 1620/1625, National Gallery of Art, USA. Clockwise from top left: à la façon de Venise wine glassware; a bowl of dried fruit and nuts with a beschuit on top; chestnuts; quince paste; a bowl of red and white letter cookies mixed with other sweet bakes (possibly Portuguese spice cookies); oysters; and, in the center, a bowl of mixed comfits and sweets.

Letter cookies

In 17th-century banqueting still-life paintings from the Low Countries, you often see beautifully formed letter cookies. They are usually depicted in a light and darker reddish color. Gold and silver leaf was often laid on these cookies for the artist to play with. The letters lie there, as part of an array of festive treats, fruits, and nuts, their gilding glistening and luring us into the painting. Peter Binoit (1590–1632) painted what is the most enticing heap of letters in his work *Still life with letter pastry* (c. 1615, held in the Groninger Museum) and, if you look closely, they spell his name. This shows that letter cookies were a playful thing, an icebreaker to aid the dinner conversation of the well-to-do. People could look for their initials, swap them with one another, and then dip them in sweet spiced wine.

The earliest recipe for these delicate letter cookies I have discovered in a manuscript from Antwerp dated to around 1580, but, as is common with recipes this old, it is not very detailed. While the letter-shaped cookies appear very often in Netherlandic still-life paintings of the 17th century, they do not appear as frequently in cookery books as in the 18th century, and they disappear altogether in the 19th century. They might have vanished from cookbooks but during Saint Nicholas children still receive letter cookies. They are of course no longer embellished with gold or silver and hold a more educational function, in addition to being a treat.

As you look closely at the letters in paintings like the one by Osias Beert on page 197, the letters are clearly shaped in a mold. While I was eager to use my antique wooden letter mold for the pictures in this book, I want you to know you can shape your cookies free-form or use cookie cutters too.

This recipe is adapted from an 18th-century conversational cookery book called *t'Zaamenspraak tusschen een mevrouw, banket-bakker en confiturier* ("Conversation between a lady, confectioner, and jam maker"). It instructs to use water, but I have interpreted this as rosewater; the seasoning is cloves, but cinnamon is used in other recipes and far more agreeable. In many paintings, the white letters appear to have a thin layer of sugar icing, but this wasn't confirmed in any historical recipe. It could have been the artists who took some license here.

Makes several letters

1 ¾ cups (225 g) confectioners' sugar

4 oz (110 g) blanched almonds

½ tsp rosewater

4 Tbsp (60 g) unsalted butter, melted and cooled

1 medium egg

1 tsp ground cloves or cinnamon

1 ½ cups (175 g) all-purpose flour

rice flour, for dusting

Start the evening before you want to bake. Put the sugar, blanched almonds, and rosewater in a food processor and pulse until the mixture is coarsely chopped. Add the butter, egg, and cloves or cinnamon and pulse until you get a paste. If the mixture does not become a paste, add a splash of water; the texture depends on how much moisture your almonds have.

Finally work in the flour, bit by bit, until fully incorporated. Then remove the dough from the food processor and knead until smooth. Put the dough in an airtight container and set aside to rest overnight.

Preheat the oven to 350°F. Do not use the fan setting. Knead your dough to make it supple. Dust a work surface with rice flour and roll out the dough to ½-inch thickness. Cut out or shape letters and lay them on a baking sheet lined with parchment paper.

Bake for 5–7 minutes in the middle of the oven. These cookies should be only very lightly colored.

To make red letters
Divide the dough in two and color one half red with a natural food coloring or a historical one, such as red saunders (a type of sandalwood, which was dissolved in alcohol to yield a natural red-brown color) or cochineal, made from dried cochineal bugs (if you think that sounds gross, remember – it could be in your red lipstick).

Spice cookies

This is a rather intriguing story: In some 17th-century still-life paintings a pastry can be spotted alongside letter cookies and marzipans. It is pale, perhaps the size of a TimTam or Bourbon cookie, and thick like a tiny cushion, but sometimes it is in the shape of a letter or circle (look closely at the letter cookies in the painting by Osias Beert on page 197 and then turn to the next page for a photograph of these cookies). Its delicate white surface is slit with sharp cuts revealing the dark brown filling. I wondered for a long time what these were as there were no clues in 16th-, 17th- or 18th-century recipe collections from the Low Country region. At one point I thought the artist must have taken artistic liberties, but then I found that these sweets appear in works by different Netherlandish artists, not just one. A clue came when I spotted them in the art of Juan Van der Hamen (1596–1631), the son of a Flemish courtier in Madrid and a half-Spanish, half-Flemish mother. He was inspired by Flemish still-life painters, so he could have copied the sweets. Or did he know them from his time in Spain? Could they be Spanish?

I discovered pastries in the Azores, an island group off Portugal, that look exactly like those seen in the paintings. Their name today: *espécies de São Jorge*, or *bolashas de espece*, which translates simply to spice cookies. They are connected to the island of São Jorge in the Azores and are only rarely found in mainland Portugal. I found a very similar recipe in a Portuguese cookbook published in 1680.

But what is the Portugese–Flemish connection? The Portuguese had been trading sugar and ivory in Bruges as early as the 15th century; by 1501 they had moved their market for the colonial spice trade to Antwerp. Antwerp was the place where everything happened when it came to trade, finances, modern thinking, and art.

A wealthy Flemish merchant named Willem Van der Haegen – known in Portuguese as Guilherme da Silveira (although there is a debate about his name) – established several settlements in the Azores, including in Topo, São Jorge, in 1480. He established wheat growing and woad (blue) dye plantations, and he also brought with him, from Flanders, a culture for making cheese that the Flemish are still credited for today. The archipelago became known as New Flanders or the Flemish Islands.

Ships laden with spices from India made stops in the Azores, providing the most important ingredients for these pastries. Adding the spices to breadcrumbs and making a paste is something we see frequently in culinary history and this is no different. The filling resembles that of *Lierse vlaaikes* (see page 160).

With a direct link to Antwerp, these pastries could have either originated in Antwerp using spices that were transported by Portuguese ships, or they originated in the kitchens of wealthy colonists in the Azores and traveled to Antwerp where they were welcomed with interest from the large number of Antwerpian still-life painters mentioned in this book. For artists so visually focused, these pastries must have been a delight to paint.

We will probably never know for sure, as written sources of that period are scarce since mutinous Spanish soldiers burnt the city archives during the brutal sack of Antwerp in 1576. These pastries survive only in art.

Intriguingly, they are known of in California by people of Portuguese descent who settled there from São Jorge. There is even a Holy Ghost fiesta in San Jose, where these cookies are auctioned off for charity; and at Christmas, too, these pastries grace the table.

These pastries are part of the artistic history of the heart of the Low Countries, so I wanted to include a recipe for them. As the Antwerpian artists were inspired by these intricate pastries in their work, I am inspired by their art more than four hundred years later.

**Makes 17 pastries
(photograph on pages 202–203)**

For the filling

1 cup (110 g) dried breadcrumbs or beschuit crumbs (see page 94), or use fresh crumbs, toasted and then measured

½ tsp ground cinnamon

¼ tsp ground nutmeg

¼ tsp ground aniseed

⅛ tsp ground cloves

⅛ tsp ground allspice

⅛ tsp ground long pepper (or the peppercorns you have)

finely grated zest of ½ lemon

2 Tbsp (30 g) unsalted butter

7 Tbsp water

½ cup (110 g) superfine sugar

For the pastry

2 ½ cups (300 g) bread flour

1 Tbsp superfine sugar

½ tsp salt

1 Tbsp (15 g) lard or unsalted butter, softened

1 medium egg

6 Tbsp water

For the filling, start the evening before you want to bake. If using fresh breadcrumbs, toast them lightly in a hot pan or oven and allow to cool. Put the crumbs, spices, and lemon zest in a large bowl and stir to combine.

In a small saucepan, melt the butter into the water, then add the sugar and simmer until dissolved. Pour the hot mixture into the crumbs and stir with a wooden spoon or spatula until the mixture comes together. If your breadcrumbs are really dry, they will take up more moisture, resulting in a dry and crumbly mess. If so, add a splash of water and knead to bring it together. When cool, cover and set aside to rest overnight or for a few hours.

For the pastry, combine the flour, sugar, salt, and lard or butter in a food processor and pulse for a few seconds. Add the egg and the water and pulse for a few minutes until the pastry forms a ball. Knead for 1 minute by hand then cover the supple pastry and rest it for an hour in the fridge for the gluten to develop.

Meanwhile, knead the filling, divide into 17 portions, and shape each one into a tiny sausage 5–6 inches long and the thickness of a pinky finger (¼–½ inch).

Preheat the oven to 325°F. Do not use the fan setting. Line a baking sheet with parchment paper.

Take the pastry out of the fridge and roll it out thinly in batches, using a pasta machine if you have one (roll to thickness 4). Lay the pastry on a clean surface and place the sausages of filling mixture on top, keeping a two-finger space between them, and use a sharp knife to cut through the pastry between the sausages to make individual pastries.

Use a fluted ravioli cutter or a plain knife to cut short lines in the spaces beside the filling, then roll the pastry around the filling and crimp tightly to close. Cut away excess pastry, then bend the cookies carefully into the shape of a crescent moon with the fold on the inside. This will create a nice pattern on the outside if you've used a fluted ravioli cutter. Now pull the ends together and close into a circle. Use your finger to make an indent between the cuts to force the filling to bulge out a little as it bakes.

Transfer the cookies to the baking sheet and bake in the middle of the oven for 20 minutes until lightly golden, then transfer to a wire rack to cool. Keep in an airtight container.

Variation: To make a pillow shape, place small blobs of filling on a sheet of pastry. On another sheet of pastry add 3 cuts to the top with a sharp knife or a ravioli cutter to get the pattern. Let the cut sheet of pastry sink over the filling and press your fingers all around as though you are making ravioli. Then use a knife or ravioli cutter to cut all around each cookie for a nice finish. If you're feeling extra creative, try and make a letter, as seen in the photograph on the following pages, although this is more fiddly.

THE FEAST OF SAINT NICHOLAS

We all want to believe in fairy tales. We want it to be true that there is a long-bearded man, wise with age, riding his gray-and-white horse high in the winter sky over our very rooftops. We remember the time when we believed it, a reassuring time when anything was possible. On the night of the fifth of December, we hopefully put our shoe by the fireplace with a letter for the Saint, a beer for his sidekick, and a carrot for the horse. In bed we listened for a sound so that we could catch a glimpse of the old man, but every year we fell asleep before the grandfather of all arrived at our door. The next morning, it was magical to find the neatly wrapped gifts by the chimney, left with care next to our shoe, and the rest of the room full of *speculaas*, *kruidnoten*, chocolate figurines and letter cookies, oranges and mandarins, scattered as though they were thrown around in haste. The combination of scents of the aforementioned treats created the perfume of the moment that remains vividly locked into my memory.

Sinterklaas, Santa Claus, Santa, Father Christmas, Père Noël—whatever you call the old man who visits children with gifts during December, they can all be traced back to a single figure in history and folklore: Saint Nicholas.

Saint Nicholas was a bishop of ancient Greek Myra who lived between the third and the fourth century. The exact year of his birth and death are unknown, and the first surviving mention of him dates from two hundred years after his death when the Byzantine emperor Theodosius II, who ruled from 401 to 450 CE, ordered the building of the Church of Saint Nicholas in Myra.

The "marriage maker"

He was a wealthy man, but gave away all of his inherited wealth, using part of it for dowries to save three impoverished maidens. Nicholas threw bags of gold through the window of the house, though in later stories he used the chimney to bring his gifts, foreshadowing the traditional story that Sinterklaas or his helpers come down the chimney with presents. This is also how he got to be called the "marriage maker," prompting the custom of creating a *peperkoek* with the same name.

The three resurrected children

Nicholas performed numerous miracles during his life, but the most famous of all his deeds was the story of the resurrected children that appeared in late medieval times. The legend tells how, in one story a village butcher, in another tale an innkeeper, snatched children, murdered them, chopped them up, and placed their remains in curing barrels to sell them off as food. Nicholas supposedly visited the area, which was crippled by a terrible famine, to bring relief to the hungry. But he could see right through what the butcher or innkeeper had done and saved the dead children, resurrecting them by making the sign of the cross.

Because of its symbolic and morbid nature, this story started to dominate the other miracles the saint had supposedly performed. It was repeated in stained-glass windows, wall paintings, and in a significant book called *Les Grandes Heures d'Anne de Bretagne*, created between 1503 and 1508. The opulent illustration in the book shows Saint Nicholas resurrecting the three butchered children who are standing in a curing barrel. This would become the most iconic depiction of Saint Nicholas, and people came to understand that he was the patron saint of children. In Belgium and the Netherlands, *koekplanken* (gingerbread molds) were carved with the scene of the bishop and the three resurrected children in a barrel. Chocolate figurines, too, depicted this scene (as pictured opposite).

A banned feast

With the Reformation and the rising Puritanism in the 17th century, the veneration of saints such as Saint Nicholas was strongly discouraged as idolatry and superstition. In England, there was a ban on Christmas rites, Father Christmas, and everything connected to the feast, enforced by the Puritan government. In the Netherlands, it was the Saint Nicholas festivities that the new Protestant religion wanted to eradicate. Saint Nicholas, then a feast for adults too, was outlawed during this period, and the traditional Saint Nicholas markets full of stalls selling gingerbread and other sweet treats were banned. This led to a great revolt in the towns of Dordrecht and Amsterdam, where people weren't going to give up their favorite festivity of the year and the sweet bakes connected to it; especially since Saint Nicholas is the patron saint of Amsterdam.

The different guises of the saint

Sinterklaas has been an ever-evolving feast from its inception. It is molded by society's changes and therefore the saint has taken on several forms over time.

Early depictions of Sinterklaas depict him as a holy man, but Sinterklaas hasn't always been portrayed as a saint. The poet Jan van Gijsen mentions a Sinterklaas figure in Amsterdam in 1720 dressed as a jester; an 18th-century *centsprent* (the forerunner of the comic strip: see an example on page 209) in the Fries Museum at Leeuwarden also depicts this harlequin figure. A 16th-century illustration held in the Stadtbibliothek Nürnberg shows a jester throwing nuts to children while seated on his horse for the Schembartlauf. This places the gift-giving figure at Carnival, similar to Sintegreef (see page 127) in Belgium, who is also sometimes portrayed with a jester's hat.

In a Dutch illustration from around 1761–1804, held in the Rijksmuseum in Amsterdam, Sinterklaas is depicted as a beardless younger man dressed in civilian clothing and a tricorne hat rather than ecclesiastical robes and mitre. His sidekick was a captain-like figure.

We don't know if people viewed Sinterklaas this way at this point in time, but the text accompanying the engraving does outline what the feast is all about:

Saint Nicholas plays the boss, with children and with man; how many long for this "klaas." His helper looks like a captain, tasked to search out sweet children and bad. The latter he brings the rod; the former another book to study. Children who are obedient to their parents he shall honour with cake, "banket" and sweets, or a doll to play with. Children, learn with diligence and use your books so Saint Nicholas will visit you with favor.

Another engraving of Sinterklaas from around 1814–1830 shows that such engravings were reused as a cost-effective way to create imagery. According to the Rijksmuseum, the source engraving is a 16th-century portrait of Emperor Charles V, altered for the purpose.

Jan Steen's Sinterklaas feast

In the famous 17th-century painting *The Feast of Saint Nicholas* by Jan Steen (on the page opposite), we see all the iconography – especially the sweet treats connected to the feast – that represents Sinterklaas, but the holy man himself is absent. Here a family is gathered by the chimney on Sinterklaas morning: we know it is morning because there is daylight coming through the window. In the Netherlands, Sinterklaas would more often come on the evening of the fifth of December – called *pakjesavond* – while in the area of current Belgium and Germany the custom is that Sinterklaas traveled under the blanket of night, over the rooftops with his horse, while the children slept. There is peperkoek or a *klaaskoek* (see page 216) formed into the Saint's silhouette, held tightly by the baby who is looking up the chimney with her brothers to catch a glimpse of the revered and generous saint.

In the foreground on the left is a shallow wicker basket full of treats: waffles, sweet buns, apples, nuts, loaf peperkoek (see page 226) decorated with almonds, and a thinner honey cake, possibly *taai-taai* (see page 251) or *hylickmaker* (see page 231). On the floor two oranges or mandarins (clementines) guide our eyes to an impressive *duivekater* loaf (see page 75). The layer of egg wash on the loaf glistens in the light that illuminates the scene. It leans against a stool, on which sits a blushing apple pierced with a coin, a large wafer or *oublie* (see page 46), a rolled-up thin waffle (*nieuwjaarsrolletje*, see page 48), a letter cookie (see page 198), sugar comfits, a paper bag with nuts, and what looks like sugar work in the shape of bacon that we call *spek*. The little girl in the center holds a doll dressed as a religious figure; on her arm is a bucket with treats and a small rooster-shaped loaf on a stick (*haantje op een stekje*).

The custom of placing a shoe by the chimney to await the gift-giver's arrival is hinted at, with the presence of the shoes in the painting. A boy is crying because his shoe remained empty, apart from a few twigs. The twigs represent the *roe* or rod used for disciplining children. A children's Sinterklaas songs goes: "If you've been good you get treats, if you've been bad you get the rod."

The painting is a reminder of the traditional way to celebrate the Sinterklaas feast. Steen was a storyteller and, if you look at his oeuvre, he must have loved baked goods – both in daily life and also for feasts and festivals.

Although this painting was made as a private commission, it was sold as early as 1743 and could have been on public display from then, so that people could see it and be reminded of the traditions. Art influenced by life, perhaps embellished here and there, then in turn influencing life.

While Sinterklaas used to be a rather rowdy affair with the Saint Nicholas fairs and feasts in the street, this

JAN HAVICKZ. STEEN *The Feast of Saint Nicholas* (1665–1668) with peperkoek, hylikmacker, waffles, oublies, duivekater, fruit, buns, sugar comfits, and a "haantje op een stekje" – a little rooster on a stick.

painting shows that the feast had started to move to the family home, where it is celebrated to this day.

From the late 19th century, the arrival parade of the saint in large cities and villages became a fixture. Seated on his gray-white horse, he arrived from sunnier parts bringing the sun in the shape of oranges and mandarins, *speculaas* (see page 252), *pepernoten* (see page 211), and *kruidnoten* (see page 213). These festive bakes were made with warming spices, and were thrown into the crowd for the children to catch and tuck into their sacks and the pockets of winter coats.

The horse on which Sinterklaas – and also Saint Martin and the Sintegreef – rides can be linked to Wodan's eight-legged magical horse, Sleipnir. In Horst, in Dutch Limburg, it is the horse that was celebrated on its own[22] in the form of a large horse-shaped loaf. It is also part of Andean culture, where *pan caballo* (horse bread) is baked as an offering for All Saints' Day. Bakes shaped into human figures, babies, and animals refer to the pre-Christian sacrificial bread.

For us children, the big arrival parade ahead of the feast meant that we had to be extra good, because Saint Nicholas would be very near and we didn't want to wake up and find out from the contents of our shoes that the letter to the saint wasn't collected, the carrot remained untouched by the horse, and the beer was unopened.

I absolutely adored the feast of Sinterklaas and the warmth and joy it brought to school and our house on Sinterklaas morning: the floor bedecked with speculaas, kruidnoten, marzipan fruit and mandarins plus the occasional chocolate figurine (for show, as none of us were crazy about chocolate). I especially savor the memory of the scent of orange and mandarin flesh and peel, spices, and chocolate: this combination takes me into a state of nostalgia for my childhood.

Pepernoten

Both *pepernoten* (spiced nuts) and the *kruidnoten* on the next page are so-called *strooigoed* (tossing goods): sweet treats distributed at festivals by either Saint Nicholas, Sintegreef, or other characters – tossed into the crowd for children to catch and collect in their sweets bag.

Pepernoten are small cakes made of *taai-taai* (see page 251) dough, which translates to "chewy-chewy." The dough is very tough, and the baked result has a delightfully chewy texture. They are part of the *peperkoek* (see page 226) family – hence the pepper in the name referring to an old word for spices – and even though today they are primarily a Dutch treat, in Flanders 18th- and 19th-century sources mention them in combination with the celebrations of the Sintegreef (see page 127).

We have just one store to thank for keeping these pepernoten alive in Belgium: a Dutch store called Hema, which celebrates Sinterklaas every year with decorations and food. I adore it.

The joy of these small cakes is in that they are baked packed together in a tin, like people on an underground train on Monday morning. And when they are baked, you tear them apart so that they all have corn-on-the-cob-like indents, revealing their pale interior in contrast to the golden-brown blush on the top and bottom. I can hardly ever stop myself from having a handful instead of just one or two of these chewy little nuggets. The chewier they are the more I want them.

Makes 70 tiny cookies

⅔ cup (200 g) runny honey

3½ oz (100 g) light brown sugar

1 tsp ground aniseed

2 ⅓ cups (280 g) white rye flour

1 tsp baking soda

pinch of salt

vegetable oil, for coating

Use an 8-inch round tin (you can use a square tin if you don't have a round one). Make the dough 3 days before baking.

In a saucepan over low heat, warm the honey, sugar, and aniseed. When the liquid just appears to move inward (not bubble) around the edges, remove from the heat (if you have a confectionary thermometer, it should be 176°F).

Put the flour, baking soda, and salt in a large bowl and mix well. Make a well, pour in the hot honey mixture, and stir with a sturdy wooden spoon. (I use a Scottish porridge stick – a spurtle.) When the dough is cool enough to handle, knead into a supple yet sturdy dough. The mixture will appear crumbly at first but will eventually come together. Let the dough rest, covered, in a cool place for a minimum of 3 days.

On the day of baking.
Preheat the oven to 350°F. Do not use the fan setting. Meanwhile, knead the dough, which will be very tough.

Have a bowl of oil ready and lightly grease the tin. The easiest way to make the small balls even is to roll out the dough into a sausage the thickness of your finger. Chop off one piece and weigh it: it should be ¼ oz (8 g). Now use the nugget as a template to chop the rest of the dough.

Roll the nuggets into balls, coat lightly with the oil, which will give a sheen, and arrange them in the tin all snug together. While they bake they will expand and press into one another.

Bake for 20 minutes until golden. To eat, warm or cold, tear them apart, revealing the paler sides where they hugged together. Keep in an airtight container for up to 3 weeks.

Kruidnoten

Kruidnoten (*Pfeffernüsse* in German) means spiced nuts: these are tiny brittle *speculaas* cookies only a little larger than a hazelnut. At Saint Nicholas festivities these small cookies are thrown into the crowd by Saint Nicholas's helpers during the arrival parades, though in recent years, because of health concerns, only wrapped sweets and mandarins (clementines) or oranges are thrown. Kruidnoten are now left on school desks, or in the house around the fireplace on Saint Nicholas morning, where they won't get dirty. Throwing these cookies in dark corners of the room is linked to a pagan custom of evicting evil from the darkness.

These cookies were introduced to America via the translation of an important German cookbook: *German National Cookery for American Kitchens*, by Henriette Davidis-Holle, published in 1904. Today they are most popular in Belgium and the Netherlands. They are sold in large bags, plain or covered in a layer of white, milk, or dark chocolate. I absolutely adored these and used to snack on them at Saint Nicholas time; walking back and forth to the cupboard with a handful of cookies. The trick to creating the best kruidnoten is putting just the right amount of salt in them. This is crucial to make them addictive.

Makes 176 tiny cookies: you can halve the recipe, but you will regret doing so as these are very good and eat like peanuts.

14 Tbsp (190 g) unsalted butter, softened

1 cup + 2 Tbsp (225 g) dark brown sugar

1 tsp sea salt

4 tsp Speculaas Spice (see below)

3 Tbsp buttermilk (or milk with 1 tsp of lemon juice whisked in)

3 ½ cups (420 g) all-purpose flour or white rye flour

2 tsp baking soda

Speculaas Spice
(makes more than you need, but keeps very well in a jar in a dark place)

2 Tbsp ground cinnamon

½ tsp ground cloves

¼ tsp *each* of ground ginger, nutmeg, coriander, allspice, mace, cardamom, long pepper (or the peppercorns you have)

Start a day ahead of baking.

A day before you plan to bake, make the dough. Cream the butter with the brown sugar and the salt. Creaming cuts little air pockets into the fat, which is why this step is important and is best achieved with an electric mixer. The mixture has to appear lighter in color than when you first started to beat it, and it will also become creamier as you go, hence "creaming."

Add the spices and the buttermilk and combine well. Blend the flour with the baking soda and add it to the dough. Knead until well combined, which can take a while; don't be alarmed if the dough seems dry and crumbly, it will come together into a smooth yet sturdy dough by kneading with your hands – you can use a mixer for the butter and sugar, but for this part you need elbow grease. Place in a covered bowl and set aside in a cool place (not your fridge) overnight.

On the day of baking, preheat the oven to 325°F. Do not use the fan setting. Line a baking sheet with parchment paper.

Knead the rested dough to make it supple. If it is crumbly or dry, this means your sugar or flour were very dry, but just knead and it will come together. When making tiny cookies like these they really should be all the same size, or some will burn when baking. Weigh out ⅛ oz (5 g) chunks of dough and roll into balls. Place the balls on the baking sheet: they will not expand a lot during baking, so you can fit a lot of them on one sheet.

Bake for 18–20 minutes. As the dough is brown, it's hard to give a cue, but I find that they are best when the cookies are a darker brown around the edges on the bottom.

When kept in an airtight cookie tin these kruidnoten keep for 3 weeks, so when baked at Saint Nicholas you will have the last ones by Christmas.

Banketletter

Banketletter is a letter made out of pastry and filled with almond paste. It is a traditional treat for Saint Nicholas celebrations and usually sold in easy-to-shape letters such as O, I, M or – my favorite and very apt for the festivities – the letter S. The reason these letters are made for Saint Nicholas is because making bread or cookies in the shape of letters always had an educational function, and Saint Nicholas is a children's feast. There are examples of gingerbread molds from Germany with the alphabet, and in Italy the letter pasta in soup, too, had an aim to tickle children's brains without it being too obvious.

For Christmas and New Year's you see this same confection shaped into a circle to create a wreath and decorated with bright red candied cherries, green angelica, and other candied fruits, depending on the bakery. The custom is in decline in Belgium, but still in full swing in the Netherlands.

The earliest recipe for banketletter I was able to track down appears in the *Volmaakte Grondbeginselen der Keukenkunde* (Perfect Fundamentals of Cuisine) published in 1758. It uses a "fine pastry," though today puff pastry has become the norm. I use my quick puff pastry, as it gives a much more satisfying result than using ready-made.

Makes 2 large letters or 1 letter and 1 Christmas wreath

For the almond filling

1 lb (500 g) blanched almonds (or use almond meal and omit the chopping step)

2 cups (400 g) superfine sugar

½ tsp rosewater

3 medium eggs

finely grated zest of 1 lemon

For the quick puff pastry

2 cups (240 g) all-purpose flour

½ tsp sea salt

1 cup (240 g) unsalted butter, cut into cubes no larger than ½ inch and frozen for 30 minutes

½ cup chilled water

flour, for dusting

1 beaten egg yolk (reserved from filling, if not used) + 1 Tbsp milk, for egg wash

nuts and candied fruit, for decorating (optional)

To make the almond filling, start at least 1 day before. (This filling can also be used for almond-stuffed *speculaas*; see page 236.)

Put the blanched almonds, sugar, and rosewater in a food processor and pulse until the mixture is coarsely chopped. Add the first 2 eggs and the lemon zest and pulse until you get a paste. If the mixture does not become a paste, separate the third egg yolk from the white, add the white, and pulse. Usually you don't need the entire third egg – it depends on how much moisture the almonds have. You want a sticky, pliable paste. If you have the egg yolk left over, reserve it to use with 1 tablespoon of milk for the egg wash.

For the pastry, combine the flour and salt in the bowl of a food processor fitted with the blade attachment. Take the butter from the freezer and toss the butter in the flour so that the butter is coated with flour. This will prevent sticking.

Pulse the mixture twice for 1 second. Add half of the cold water and pulse 3 times, then add the rest of the water and pulse 6 times.

Dust your work surface with flour and take the dough out of the bowl. Push the dough flat with your hands, but do not knead it – the small chunks of butter that are visible in the dough must be preserved and should create a marbled effect.

Dust the dough with flour and pat it flat into a rectangle with a rolling pin. Fold in one-third of the dough toward the center, then fold in one-third from the opposite end (as though you were folding a piece of paper), pat it down lightly with the rolling pin, and then fold it in thirds again, but in the opposite direction. Repeat once, then wrap the dough in plastic wrap and let it rest for at least 30 minutes in the refrigerator. Repeat the folding and chilling step 3 times.

Preheat the oven to 425°F. Do not use the fan setting. Line a baking sheet with parchment paper. Whisk the egg yolk and milk to make egg wash.

On a sheet of floured parchment paper, roll out half of the dough to a 28 x 4–inch rectangle. Arrange half of the almond filling in a 24-inch sausage in the center of the rectangle. Fold the bottom side of the pastry over the filling using the paper to help roll, and brush with the egg wash. Brush the top side of the pastry and use the paper to roll the sausage further and crimp together all around, making sure the ends are tucked in neatly. Now carefully shape into a letter or a circle and lay it on the baking sheet, with the seam-side down. Brush with the egg wash and leave as it is, or decorate with nuts or candied fruit, if you like. Do the same for the second letter or wreath. Freeze any leftover almond filling for later use.

Bake in the middle of the oven for 45 minutes until the top is firm and the sides form wrinkles. Let cool on the sheet on a wire rack.

Mantepeirden and klaaskoeken

In a magazine from 1879,[15] a correspondent writes that on Saint Martin (which falls on 11 November) he was visited by singing boys carrying lanterns made of carved beets. The song mentioned the baking of waffles and the eating of *koek* (cake).

That koek is not *peperkoek* (pepper cake) this time but *mantepeird*, translated as "man on horse," depicting Saint Martin on a horse in sweet enriched bread dough. It is a custom from coastal West Vlaanderen, where Sint Maarten or Sintemette completely replaces Sinterklaas. In the past, children would carry the bread on a stick in Sint Maarten parades. The custom of mantepeirden blends with *klaaskoeken* (for Sinterklaas) in some regions, with the bread shaped as a naïve figure with a mitre instead.

While Saint Nicholas has some pagan links in its customs, Saint Martin goes all out with parades of children carrying carved-out beets and paper lanterns. There are also large bonfires to mark the start of winter.

Other names for these breads are *klaaspeirden* and *mikkemannen* or *buikman* in Limburg and Dutch Brabant, where they are also often made with a small white stick baked into the bread. The custom is also known in Germany, where they can go by many different names depending on the region: *Stoeteman*, *Wekkeman*, *Weckman*, *Weggekèl*, *Sevensman*, *Piepespringer*, *Stutenkerl*, *Hefekerl*, and *Männele* (which is also the name for this little pipe-smoking bread man in Alsace, France, though usually made without the pipes, which are only for sale in Germany). In Luxembourg they are known as *boxemännchen*.

Makes several small loaves

4 cups (500 g) bread flour, plus extra for dusting

¼ cup (50 g) superfine sugar

3 ¼ tsp (10 g) instant dry yeast

1 cup whole milk, at room temperature

2 medium eggs

2 tsp salt

5 Tbsp (75 g) unsalted butter, softened

1 egg yolk + 1 Tbsp milk, for egg wash

Combine the flour, sugar, and yeast in a large bowl or the bowl of an electric mixer fitted with a dough hook. Pour in half of the milk and the eggs and start kneading. When the liquid is completely absorbed, pour in the rest of the milk and knead for 5 minutes. Let the dough rest for 5 minutes.

Add the salt on one side and the butter in chunks on the other side and knead for 10 minutes, scraping the dough off the dough hook and side of the bowl if needed, until it has come together in a smooth and elastic dough that is neither too dry nor terribly wet.

Cover the dough and set aside for 1 hour until it has doubled in size.

Knock the air out of the dough, flatten into roughly a square, fold the ends in, and pat back down to the size it was before. Now roll out on a floured surface to ½-inch thickness, then cut out the shape of a man with a mitre or a man on a horse. You can make a template – it doesn't have to be perfect – then cut around the template. Lay the shaped loaves on a baking sheet with ample room for them to rise. Cover and set aside to rise again for 1 hour.

Preheat the oven to 400°F. Do not use the fan setting. Brush the top of the loaf with the egg and milk mixture and bake for 12–15 minutes until the loaves are golden brown. Let cool on a wire rack.

217

SWEET TOOTH

In medieval times, sugar was used as sparingly as spices due to its high price. It was also believed to have medicinal properties, and it was used as a means to sell and serve medicine. Sweets, jams, and fruit cheeses find their origins in the apothecary's shop.

From the 16th century onward, sugar consumption was rising, not due to greater consumption per person – as sugar remained a luxury product until the 18th century – but because of the rapid population growth.

The 17th century saw a rise in sugar consumption, not for baking but for sweetening new drinks, such as hot chocolate, tea, and coffee. Sugar was still scarce, which is why sweet recipes continue to use honey as a sweetener up until the 18th century.

In the 17th-century health book *De Borgerlyke Tafel* (The Civil Table), Steven Blankaart writes that, "the whiter the sugar, the healthier" because it takes away all the acid in our body. But he also warns that, in large quantities, sugar is harmful.

Sugar had different grades according to how refined it was. Raw sugar or molasses arrived in the sugar refinery, where it was boiled to a syrup. That syrup was then purified, and the number of times the sugar went through that process yielded different qualities of sugar: highly refined white sugar loaves or cones, second-grade (less white) sugar loaves, and syrup – or *stroop* as we call it – which was the cheapest form and most widely used by common people.

Melado, or molasses, is the darkest stroop; unlike highly refined white sugars, molasses contains many vitamins.

> Among other things, they [America] have brought us
> so much sugar, so that it is now in every kitchen,
> and it is devoured with such greed; while it was
> previously only to be found in the Apothecary,
> and preserved only for the sick, so to speak;
> so that it is now used almost always for food,
> while beforehand only taken as medicine.

Abraham Ortelius

Entry for "America" in *Theatrum orbis terrarum*, the first modern atlas, published in Antwerp, 1571.

Stroop was originally made from cane sugar, though for the past 150 years or so it has been derived from sugar beets. It seeped into *peperkoek* and other honey cakes when honey became too expensive. It was smeared onto bread, between two halves of a waffle, and poured over pancakes and waffles. It is to the Dutch and Belgians what golden syrup is to British culture and maple syrup to American culture. The stroop was kept in earthenware stroop jars, of which many have been found in archaeological excavations.

The Dutch like a lighter stroop (*schenkstroop*), while the Belgians prefer a very dark and dense stroop produced exclusively by sugar refinery Candico in Antwerp (see page 26).

At the end of the 19th century and in the early 1900s, a lot of beet sugar factories in Limburg switched from producing sugar to beet stroop. The new steam cookers and hydraulic presses powered by electricity made the work less intensive, and stroop could be made on an industrial scale.

Soon producers started mixing beet stroop with fruit stroop, creating *rinse stroop*. In 2011, a consumer association noted that most industrially produced versions of this type of *appelstroop* contain only 30 percent fruit. Therefore, it is interesting that they can market this stroop as apple syrup when sugar beet makes up 70 percent of the content. There is a movement for change, so that some large-scale producers now also offer a 100 percent fruit option.

Apple and pear stroop

Another traditional source for sweetness was, and still is, apple and pear stroop, made with 100 percent fruit since medieval times in the Pays de Herve in Wallonia, Belgian and Dutch Limburg, and the German Rhineland. Before the industrial revolution and the switch from tall fruit trees to the more manageable dwarf trees, fruit harvests included a high proportion of windfalls. Those windfalls would go into the copper kettle steaming away in a barn by the orchard with a wood fire pit underneath.

The production was situated in monasteries and in farms, places that had access to the fruit and the means to keep a fire going for hours on end to produce the stroop. After hours of cooking, a thick, black "moreish" stroop that is buttery rather than syrupy is the result, which is why in English it is often called apple butter. At home, too, people would cook down the fruit from their trees as a way to preserve it. Every family will have both of these stroops in their larder; the latter – while used in baking and in stews – is usually eaten smeared generously onto bread.

THE LOW COUNTRIES' GINGERBREAD

For centuries, the craving for sweetness was satisfied with honey. First wild honey, but later beekeeping became part of everyday rural life. That one would knead honey and flour into a dough for cake is a natural and logical evolution.

The *Lebzelter* (the "medar," or honey processor) processed the honey and made some into honey cakes and some into mead, then turned the honeycombs into beeswax for ornaments and candles. For centuries these three were connected. Honey-cake making was usually done in monasteries, where bees were kept and the monks were in need of church candles and, of course, were partial to mead. A painting in a Nuremberg manuscript from 1520 depicts a monk baking honey cakes.

Peperkoek and *speculaas* are the Low Countries' gingerbread. They evolved from those cakes made simply with honey and flour. They exist in three main styles: the kind that is printed with a carved wooden mold, the free-form kind that requires no tool per se, and the cake that is baked into loaves (either free-form or in a wooden frame; now usually metal). The free-form and loaf cake are the oldest, as the printed cake needed a material culture of carved molds to exist. While they are all peperkoek, the variations had different names through time: there is *honigkoek* (honey cake), *cruyd koek, zoetekoek, lijfkoek, hylickmaker,* simply *koek, liefcoecken, taai-taai, pepernoten* or *peperbollen, Lebkuchen, Printen, Pfefferküchen,* and *speculatie* or *speculaas.*

In medieval times, every important city in the Low Countries and parts of Germany had its own koek, *koekebakkers* (bakeries), and often even a koekebakkers' guild. Places of pilgrimage, too, had a koek culture because there was a need for beeswax church candles (and mead) in those places of worship, and therefore it created a sales market for the Lebzelter.

Ghent used to be famous for its koek, but it is now forgotten. A legend says that Philip the Good, Duke of Burgundy and Earl of Flanders, was presented with a gift of peperkoek on his arrival in Ghent in 1452. Philip, being French, had rehearsed a speech in Dutch, especially for the occasion. He loved the peperkoek so much that he took the baker who made it back to

Detail of *The Feast of Saint Nicholas,* by Jan Steen (see page 207) with peperkoek loaf, hylickmaker, waffles, and white bread buns.

Paris to teach the French how to do it. Wouldn't it be fabulous if peperkoek or *pain d'épice* were invented in this low land? Only...in 1452 Philip, who did indeed give a speech in Dutch, declared war on Ghent. So it seems unlikely the angry townspeople would have gifted him precious peperkoek at a time he was threatening Ghent with high taxes on other essentials.

Munich in Germany was so proud of the excellent quality of their Lebkuchen that they fixed its ingredients in an ordinance as early as 1474. It is because they kept standards for their Lebkuchen ingredients so high that it became too expensive to produce and sell, and Nuremberg overtook Munich as the capital of Lebkuchen production for most of Germany.

Today only a few cities or regions remain that have a distinctive koek culture. The specialized peperkoek shops and peperkoek market stalls have all but disappeared from our streets, but many bakers still make their own koek, especially in Friesland. Of the specialized koek shops, there is Bussink in Deventer, Holland, still selling *Deventer koek* and one in Den Bosch selling *Bossche koek* holding on to this tradition.

East Flanders is home to two of the largest peperkoek bakeries in Europe. Dinant in Wallonia still has a couple of bakeries selling their rock-hard *couque de Dinant* (see page 243). In Germany there is Lebkuchen Schmidt in Nuremberg and, in Aachen, Nobis Printen Bäckerei has been baking Lebkuchen since 1858. The theory is that copper craftsmen from Dinant immigrated to Aachen in the Golden Age, bringing their couque with them.

"City of cake"
Deventer has the nickname *koekstad* in the Netherlands. Koek has been baked in Deventer since at least 1417, and its history is remarkably well documented in the town archives. A 15th-century ordinance outlines in detail the weight and appearance of the large and small Deventer loaf honey cakes: they must be long and narrow and weigh three and two pounds respectively. The ordinance also stipulated that no one outside of Deventer was allowed to bake this honey cake.

The koek bakers' guild supervised compliance with the ordinance, and new koek bakers had to swear an oath to honor it. The ordinance on the making of the cake was amended in 1534, 1544, and 1557. The cakes are provided with the mark of the cookie baker and the city eagle. In 1593 there were thirteen koek bakers connected to the guild; by 1637, the city had twnety-five bakers. The spices for making Deventer koek are outlined in a manuscript from 1477 written by Reyner Oesterhusen, who was a doctor from Deventer.[23]

While "koek" is the origin of the American English word "cookie," koek in the Dutch language area doesn't mean cookie exclusively; it means loaf peperkoek, printed peperkoek, or *gebildbrot* (specially shaped celebratory loaves).

Peperkoek rivalry
The town's museum holds a silver guild cup dated 1659, inscribed with a poem that starts with the words: "Deventer koek is highly praised throughout Holland."

Deventer was an important town from the early Middle Ages because of its location by the IJssel river that made it a part of the Hanseatic League. Towns with a connection to the water or trade routes generally have a rich koek culture. In an attempt to bypass the Deventer koek bakers, the city of Amsterdam even decided to draw up guidelines for the size and weight of the koek that could be sold in Amsterdam. The Deventer koek did not meet the weight, according to those new rules of course, so it was for a time banned in Amsterdam, which allowed the Amsterdam koek bakers to make more profit. Deventer sent an envoy, and the koek issue and the feud between the towns over koek was eventually solved. Amsterdammers loved koek so much they were even dubbed "koek eaters" in the 16th century because of their sweet tooth.

Koek and the rites of passage
Peperkoek was part of every celebration and, in particular, for the rites of passage. Koek was there for courtship when a girl came of age, for weddings, and to mourn the dead. Suitors bought a koek for their love at the annual fair or Carnival festivities, and koeken were split and eaten at weddings to wish a long and happy life. Children looked eagerly at the neat piles of koek in the display window of the koek bakeries or market stalls. On the eve of All Souls' Day the people baked koek; for Lost Monday the children would receive koek; employers treated their workers to koek and beer for New Year's. An account in a magazine from 1879 tells me that the two last customs were dwindling at that time, but it was replaced by simply giving workers and children a koek they could take home. I remember my dad bringing home a loaf of peperkoek, as a gift from work, around Christmas. My mother remembers the baker carrying thick heart-shaped peperkoek around at Christmastime, on his bread rounds.

Koek was often eaten with beer, which is also mentioned in the lyrics of a lullaby as *koeken en brouw*.[15] We must remember that before tea, coffee, and hot chocolate came to our shores in the 17th century, these spiced cakes were enjoyed with beer and with either spiced or sweet wine as part of a banqueting course, a sweet course after the meal, meant to aid digestion. This is something we witness in the *banketjes* still-life paintings from the Flemish and Dutch Golden Age (see page 194) and also in some of the genre paintings.

The pepper in *peperkoek*
The "pepper" in peperkoek means a mixture of spices, including pepper, though pepper isn't always used in old recipes. Ginger, when used, is used sparingly so that it

forms a supporting flavor in harmony with cinnamon, cloves, allspice, nutmeg, and mace. Because ginger isn't our main flavoring on the Continent, we do not call these bakes "gingerbread." We also never used actual bread as an ingredient, which was a practice in England for early gingerbread.

Spicing varies between cinnamon as the prominent flavor, cloves in older recipes, and aniseed in the Netherlands and Germany. Honey and (rye) flour were the main ingredients before sugar imports made the use of sugar syrup in cheaper versions possible. Brown sugar made the dough darker and the flavor more rounded. When times, tastes, and fashions changed, the tough printed peperkoek got butter as an ingredient, and speculatie or speculaas was born. It didn't replace the older-style koek, though, as taai-taai is still very tough (taai translates as tough or chewy) and the couque de Dinant is still the same as it was a thousand years ago, using just honey and flour.

Koek for medicinal purposes

Cakes made with honey and flour are as old as bread, but recipes appeared only when people started to write them down, first in medical texts and later in manuscripts devoted solely to cooking. The aforementioned manuscript noting the spices for peperkoek, written by the doctor of Deventer, was one such medical text, and it is also the first written reference to the word "peperkoek." For peperkoek to appear in a work like that shows it would have been around for a while, to make it common enough to use in this context.

Een notabel boecxken van cokeryen (A notable book of cookery), the oldest printed cookbook in the Dutch language, dated 1510–14, published in Brussels, gives a recipe for *liefcoecken*, to be used in other recipes as an ingredient. The koek is made simply with honey, flour, and spices, made into any shape the cook desires.

In a 16th-century manuscript from Ghent, there is a recipe for kruidkoek: it contains honey, pepper, nutmeg, ginger, cloves, and saffron. Flour is not in the ingredient list but is most likely omitted because the owner of the handwritten cookery book knew that part by heart, while the ratios for honey and spices might have been easier to forget.

Peperkoek is mentioned in a 17th-century Dutch-to-French dictionary, *Schat-kamer, der nederduytische en*

A shop window display with honey cakes, in Dinant.

francoysche tale begrypende (A treasury of understanding the Dutch and French languages), by Caspar Van den Ende. The entry for peperkoek gives the following translation: *Pain d'épice, Gâteau poivre.*

Peperkoek recipes are rare in early cookbooks because the cakes were usually bought from the koekebakker and not baked at home. This is the same reason that we don't commonly find recipes for everyday bread in early cookbooks.

If a mention of the koek can be found in early cookery books, it will often appear under its earliest names: *kruidkoekjes, liefkoek, liefkoek,* and *lyfkoeck.* And usually, it appears as an ingredient to use in other dishes. A venison sauce made with peperkoek often occurs in old cookery texts. Adding koek to stews is something we still do today in Belgium and the Netherlands.

In *Het secreet-boek vol heerlijke konsten* (1694), a book with recipes for medicines and confectionery by Carolus Battus, there is a recipe for "Peper-koecxkens" (see page 230) and "Kruyt-koecxkens," which are small shaped spiced cakes. The first contains cinnamon, grains of paradise or melegueta pepper, ginger, nutmeg, and pepper, in that order; the kruyt-koecxkens omit the pepper, grains of paradise, and cinnamon but add cloves. Both recipes contain honey, while the peper-koecxkens recipe also has an equal measure of sugar but doesn't contain the wine the kruyt-koecxkens has. One recipe clearly says to use wheat while the other says "fine flour," so we can conclude this recipe is for the upper class who can afford the first-grade bolted wheat. Battus instructs to use half rye and half wheat in one of his earlier books: *Eenige uytnemende excelente Secreten van Koockerijen*. These recipes are given alongside marzipan and quince confection (marmalade), highlighting again how sweet recipes were connected to the wellbeing of people. Apothecaries' shops must have looked like sweetshops in those days.

The marriage maker

In the 18th century, peperkoek got an intriguing name: *hylickmaker*. A recipe published in the *De Volmaakte Hollandse Keuken-meid* (The Perfect Dutch Kitchenmaid) contains flour, brown sugar, honey, cloves, nutmeg, and cinnamon in equal measure, candied citron, dried orange peel, and potash. Potash is an old-style leavening agent made by burning the wood from oak and beech, dissolving the ash in water, and evaporating the filtered solution until you get a soluble salt that gives bakes a rise when it comes in contact with an acid. Potash consists of potassium carbonate and potassium salts such as potassium chloride and potassium sulfate. While some chemists will still sell potash or potassium, sodium bicarbonate (baking soda) can be used instead. Baking powder, on the other hand, cannot be used, as the dough has to rest.

This 18th-century recipe is for a loaf peperkoek, and the method has evolved to one that is still used today for traditional peperkoek in bakeries, boiling the honey and sugar and then adding the rest of the ingredients. In these instructions, it was not made clear to let the dough rest yet, but this doesn't mean that they didn't let the dough mature, only that it was considered common knowledge, so didn't need to be explained.

The title is significant because hylickmaker means "marriage maker." This shows the custom of giving a peperkoek to a lover in courtship, and the marriage maker also symbolizes Saint Nicholas (see page 205), who, apart from resurrecting the three children, also gave dowries to girls, making their marriage possible. Saint Nicholas was also referred to as the *Goed Heiligman*, which can be translated to holy man or marriage maker.

Some regions require a girl to walk around on the village *kermis*, or fairground, with the peperkoek in her hands or bound to her wrist with a ribbon. In other regions the young man visits the girl at home on the last day of the fair; the peperkoek stayed in the house, and if he gets a slice of the koek he gave a week or two before, the girl agrees to the marriage. But if he gets the whole koek, this means she declines.

When the koek is printed in a wooden mold, it usually resembles a human figure, either a lady or a man, called "the lovers." If the girl breaks off the head, she agrees to the marriage; if she breaks off the figure's feet and gives them to the young man, he should take his leave. The connection between a marriage proposal and peperkoek was still alive at the start of the 20th century, but as all manners and etiquette have changed, the hylickmaker – peperkoek as a love letter – has become obsolete.

Koek as entertainment

At the village fair, koek is also used as entertainment. The practice of *Capfen Koecken* is illustrated on a wood or stone print depicting all the entertainment and food of the village fair. This was a practice for which either the hard edges of the koek were used, or a tough loaf koek was baked especially. A special little axe was then used to try to chop the koek in half. If you couldn't do it, you had to pay for the koek; if you did it, bystanders had to pay.

Another more recent koek-related competition at village fairs was hanging buttered slices of koek from a tree or stick and trying to be the first to eat the dangling slice while your hands were tied behind your back, which often resulted in your face being covered in butter. This was also often done by couples who were courting.

Gilding peperkoek with real gold was a popular pastime for families in the 18th and 19th centuries when winter celebrations became a family activity.

Loaf peperkoek

The loaf peperkoek (see the photograph opposite), is also called honingkoek, *ontbijtkoek* (breakfast cake), *kandijkoek* (kandij cake), *kermiskoek* (fair cake), *zoetekoek* (sweet cake), *kruidkoek* (spiced cake), or *sukkadekoek* (citron cake): these are a few common names with some variation in the recipes for Low Country loaf gingerbread.

In Belgium and the Netherlands this is a loaf every household would have in the pantry, because its long shelf life meant you could always benefit from it. As a child I grew up eating it for breakfast (hence the name ontbijtkoek) or as a midmorning or afternoon snack spread generously with butter (sadly at our house this meant margarine). It is used to thicken and flavor meat sauces and stews and as an ingredient for vlaai (see page 158) and for making new peperkoek.

Peperkoek monopoly

Like the dark rye bread, koek baking eventually moved from the bakery to the factory, and those factories eagerly and greedily bought up all the small koek bakers until only a handful of large koek factories remained. The peperkoek disappeared from our high streets and moved into the more industrial areas. Many koekbakkers disappeared during the Second World War when they were forced to entirely or partly swap their manufacturing to *beschuit* (rusks). The same happened in Aachen in Germany to the Lebkuchen bakeries. Lokeren in Flanders used to have a koekbakker in the town center, too, but luckily the actual bakery, De Vreese, still exists outside of town in a larger factory still owned by the fifth generation of the De Vreese family. (Although as I am writing this, another peperkoek factory, Vondemolen, has put an offer in to buy De Vreese, which would give it a peperkoek monopoly in Belgium.)

The koek was taken for granted as sugar became cheap and it replaced honey. After all, it is the expensive treats we usually celebrate the most so, for the past thirty years, this kind of cake is no longer a special treat. Yet it is still part of everyday life: koek is always there in the back of a Dutch or Belgian larder because it keeps for months. Is there no bread? Koek is always good. Going somewhere? Quickly grab a slice of koek on the way out. A sinking feeling in the afternoon? A slice of koek with a good layer of butter will help.

At Christmastime, loaf peperkoek suddenly gets some of its celebratory nature back when it is sold shaped like a heart and decorated with sugar icing. Speculaas printed in various shapes and sizes is still considered festive, as are the Lebkuchen in Germany, where they too come to the foreground between Saint Nicholas and New Year's.

But changes in prosperity, religion, and the political and economic landscape can influence the importance we bestow on food items. The celebrated koek – once treasured like the most expensive chocolate or caviar today; glistening with real gold leaf, the koek that appears in Golden Age paintings; the koek around which rules and regulations were formed akin to those governing the baking of bread and the brewing of beer; the koek that provoked feuds between cities and rivalry between the town's koekbakers – that koek, or the importance given to it in our culture, is sadly no more.

Loaf peperkoek

ONTBIJTKOEK

Peperkoek

Although it had been a product uniquely baked by registered *koekbakkers*, around the beginning of the 20th cenury, recipes for loaf *peperkoek* (pepper cake) of different types start to appear in textbooks used in the bakery school. In a book from 1927, there are eight recipes for this type of koek, and while these recipes are very similar, there are a few differences: bakeries would usually have offered a couple of options. All recipes use (sifted) rye flour – there is no discussion there – but honey is used in many of the recipes, while sugar syrup is used in others, either along with honey or alone. The early recipes for koek would have used just honey, but as this became expensive and sugar prices fell, sugar seeped into the koek. This doesn't mean the koek became a lower-quality product, indeed not: adding sugar or grape sugar (glucose) and sugar syrup improved the texture of the koek. Glucose is widely used in baking and candymaking to prevent crystallization of the sugar, keeping the end result moist.

Six of the eight recipes use water, while two use a combination of water and milk. Half of the recipes use old or leftover koek as an ingredient. A spice mix especially developed for this koek, known in other countries as mixed spice or pumpkin pie spice, is used in all the recipes but one. Cinnamon as an extra flavoring on top of the spice mix occurs in just one recipe, and the same goes for ginger. Then there is one recipe using mixed candied fruit and one using strips of candied orange. Apart from the above, rising agents such as potash and sodium carbonate are used.

Traditional koek method
The method of koek making in the traditional way is lengthy but worth it. *Kantkoek* – offcuts of the outer edges that are drier and baked to a darker color – or stale koek is blended with large amounts of honey. This is brought to the boiling point and left until the stale koek is all soft, then rye flour is added to the mixture and it is kneaded to a mother dough.

The mother dough rests or ripens in metal troughs for at least one week, though professional peperkoek bakers leave it to rest for months. The enzymes will now break down the starch. This is called "*teren*" in Dutch peperkoek terms, which translates to "digesting."

After the dough has rested, the final set of ingredients is added: these are the flavorings, such as spices, more honey or other liquids, dried or candied fruits, and pearl (nib) or candy sugar. The dough is then kneaded to a supple yet sturdy dough. In the olden days bakers kneaded the dough by slinging it around a hook on the wall. They were also helped by kneading machines powered by horsepower. Needless to say this is a dough that is hard to work by hand, and it needs a powerful mixer to do the job for you. This is why I have developed this recipe for you. The end result yields the typical mouthfeel of the koek, which gives some resistance when you bit into it.

In large koek bakeries more than one cake is baked at the same time in large – originally wooden, but now metal – frames, though De Vreese–Van Loo koek bakers still use a wooden frame for their artisanal version. They also advised me on how my dough should feel and warned me against boiling the honey.

After baking, the koek is left to rest a while: a freshly baked peperkoek is like a freshly baked English parkin... it's not yet at its best. After resting, the peperkoek is cut into loaves of a distinctive shape.

Master koek makers were experts in blending different honeys to obtain the unique flavor in their koek. But honey is expensive, so it makes sense that sugar took over. As sugar does improve the end product, it is in the recipe here.

The combination of *appelstroop* and honey yields a dark koek, while using all honey (or with a portion of golden syrup) gives you the color that is traditional to this bake; however, I find the appelstroop – which appears in home recipes for this koek – gives a wonderful depth of flavor. But I realize that while I can just run out for a jar, it is not readily available elsewhere in the world. So using all honey or honey plus golden or glucose syrup could be the easiest option for you. I advise against using blackstrap molasses or even regular molasses because it is far too powerful in flavor.

Makes 1 or 2 peperkoek
(see the photograph on
page 225)

¾ cup (250 g) runny honey

1 ¼ cups (400 g) sugar beet syrup,
   appelstroop, glucose syrup,
   golden syrup, or runny honey

½ cup (100 g) superfine sugar

5 cups (600 g) white rye flour
   or spelt flour if you can't get rye

2 Tbsp ground cinnamon

1 tsp *each* of ground nutmeg,
   ground ginger, ground coriander,
   ground cardamom, ground long
   pepper or black peppercorns,
   ground cloves*

½ tsp ground aniseed

pinch of salt

¾ cup buttermilk (or milk with
   2 Tbsp lemon juice)

2 tsp baking soda

Coffee creamer or milk,
   for coating the spoon

1 cup (200 g) pearl sugar
   (nib sugar) – large nibs are best,
   but small is fine too (optional)

* If you do not have all these
spices you can use 5 Tbsp (30 g)
pumpkin pie spice instead.

**Use an 8-inch square tin or a 9 x 5–inch loaf tin, greased and lined
with parchment paper. Start a day ahead of baking.**

In a large saucepan, combine the honey and sugar beet syrup (or substitute)
and the sugar. Warm over low heat, making sure it doesn't boil. When the
liquid just appears to form bubbles, remove from the heat (if you have
a sugar thermometer, it should be 175°F). Boiling the honey gives it a
bitter flavor.

Tip in half of the flour and stir, then add the spices and salt and stir. When
the flour is fully incorporated, add the buttermilk, then the rest of the flour
mixed with the baking soda. Use elbow grease to mix the dough together,
making sure no flour pockets remain.

Scoop the batter into the prepared tin in blobs, then even it out by dipping
a tablespoon in coffee creamer or milk and using the back of the spoon to
push the dough down. This will prevent the spoon from sticking to the
batter. The milk will give the top of the peperkoek a nice sheen after baking.

Cover the tin and set aside in a cool place to rest for 24 hours, though it
improves if you leave it for longer, which is traditional.

Preheat the oven to 325°F. Do not use the fan setting.

When making a peperkoek with pearl sugar, toss the nibs all over the
surface just before baking, without pushing them into the batter: they will
stick, don't worry.

Bake the peperkoek in the middle of your oven for 1½ hours for the square
tin or 1 hour 45 minutes for the loaf tin. Check if a skewer comes out clean
after inserting it in the middle of the cake. If not, bake for 15 minutes more
and check again. Transfer the tin to a wire rack and let it cool in the tin.

Remove the cooled peperkoek and transfer to an airtight container. Set
aside to rest for at least 3 days, but 1 week or longer is better, as it will
improve the structure of the cake. Cut the sides away all around and (if you
used a square tin) cut the peperkoek in half. You now have 2 cakes that are
cut the traditional way. When using the loaf tins, you can cut away
a thin slice from the sides for a traditional feel.

The offcuts or kantkoek may be finely crumbled and used in the batter for
your next bake or as an ingredient for Oost Vlaamse Vlaai (see page 158)
or beef or venison stew. You can, of course, also eat them.

Eat slices of this peperkoek for breakfast or as a snack, spread generously
with butter. It also makes an excellent addition to a cheese platter.

Peper-koeckxkens

This is a recipe from *Het secreet-boek vol heerlijke konsten* (1600) by Carolus Battus, town physician of Antwerp, and later Dordrecht when he and other Protestants had to flee Antwerp. A Secreetboeck or *secreti*, after the Italian original, contains secrets of nature (how thunder works) and recipes for daily life. These could be medicines for humans and animals, but also advice on cleaning, pest control, paint, preserving wine, jam making, and beauty treatments.

These *peper-koeckxkens* appear in the confectionery chapter along with candying fruit, making marzipan, and clarifying sugar. The pepper in the name really does mean these are pepper cookies, as pepper is present as a very dominant flavor. In fact, I consider these cookies to be a pick-me-up, and it is very possible that this was their intended use. If you would like to taste a cookie that the well-to-do would have eaten in the 16th and 17th centuries, this is an experience for you. If you can't handle even a mild curry, stay away from these and make *speculaas* (see page 252).

Eat these cookies while they are still warm: when cold they firm up and become almost as hard as the *couque de Dinant*, which is a relation of this type of peperkoek. It might take a little while to source the grains of paradise – a relative of cardamom, only spicy and with a hint of fresh coconut – but you will usually be able to get them from specialist spice suppliers or online. For this recipe it is not worth omitting this spice because it is an essential part of the flavor and, most importantly, the experience. I have scaled the recipe down to reduce the ingredient cost for the spices.

For 45 cookies

½ cup (6 oz) runny honey

¾ cup (145 g) superfine sugar

1 ¼ cups (150 g) all-purpose flour

For the spice mix

1½ Tbsp ground cinnamon

1 Tbsp ground grains
 of paradise

1 Tbsp ground ginger

2 tsp ground nutmeg

1 tsp ground long pepper

Start a day ahead of baking.

In a large saucepan, warm the honey over low heat, making sure it doesn't boil. When the liquid just appears to move inward (not bubble) around the edges, remove from the heat. (If you have a sugar thermometer, it should be 175°F.) Boiling the honey gives it a bitter flavor.

Add the sugar and stir, then add the flour and spice mix and stir with a sturdy wooden spoon until well combined. When the mixture has cooled enough to handle, knead with one hand, using your knuckles to make the dough more workable. Then shape into hazelnut-sized balls and flatten slightly into an oval shape (see the small oval bite-sized cookies in the photograph on page 229, beside the honey pot).

Transfer to a baking sheet and cover, to rest overnight.

Preheat the oven to 400°F. Do not use the fan setting. Bake for 10 minutes.

Transfer to a wire rack and eat as soon as they are cool enough. When cold, you can eat them like candy, as they are very chewy. Store in an airtight container.

Hylickmaker

The recipe for *hylickmaker* (marriage maker), a honey cake, in *Volmaakte Grondbeginselen der Keukenkunde* from 1758, instructs to roll out the dough, which means it is a different kind of dough from the thick loaf *peperkoek* (page 226). The author also suggests making little balls with an adjustment of the recipe, which makes them into *pepernoten* (see page 211), or to shape into *theerandjes*. Imagine my delight to find out that today theerandjes are still known in Utrecht as a traybake peperkoek of only about a thumb's thickness, which is portioned into bars or rectangles. Theerandjes were, just like hylickmaker, given as a sign of affection.

The 18th-century recipe results in a dough that isn't workable, so I have reduced the flour content; however, it is still a tough dough, so you will need to use some elbow grease. It just goes to show how the focus of modern baking is with simple easy-to-handle dough. But after you've made the effort, the reward is a lovely chewy honey cake.

It's up to you how you shape it: neatly into a long flat loaf; as a traybake and portioned; to use as a marriage proposal (see page 223); or to keep all to yourself. This is the 18th-century recipe; the finished bake can be seen stacked and tied with ribbon in the photograph on page 229.

Makes 7 bars

1 ¼ cups (250 g) light brown sugar

½ cup (6 oz) honey

2 ¾ cups (330 g) rye flour or all-purpose flour

¼ tsp *each* of ground cloves, nutmeg and cinnamon

½ tsp baking soda

6 Tbsp (55 g) candied citron peel

6 Tbsp (55 g) candied orange peel

Milk, for smoothing the dough

For the glaze (optional)

¾ cup (100 g) confectioners' sugar

2½ Tbsp water

In a large saucepan, combine the sugar and honey. Warm over low heat, making sure it doesn't boil. When the liquid just appears to move inward (not bubble) around the edges, remove from the heat. (If you have a sugar thermometer, it should be 175°F.)

Tip in half of the flour and stir, then add the spices and stir, then the rest of the flour mixed with the baking soda. Use your elbow grease to mix the dough together, making sure no flour pockets remain. Finally knead in the candied peels.

Transfer the dough to a floured working surface and pat it out until it is just under the thickness of a pencil. I cut it into roughly 2 x 5½–inch bars, which yields 7 pieces. Smooth the surface using a tablespoon dipped in milk, which will give the top of the hylickmaker a nice sheen after baking.

Transfer to a baking sheet lined with parchment paper, cover, and set aside to rest for 24 hours, although you can also bake it immediately. It improves after resting for at least 1 hour.

When ready to bake, preheat the oven to 400°F. Do not use the fan setting. Bake in the middle of the oven for 20 minutes, then transfer the tin to a wire rack to cool.

Utrechtse theerandjes have a glaze added. If you want to use the glaze, dissolve the sugar in the water to make a paste and brush all over the warm hylickmaker.

Dikke speculaas

Dikke speculaas (thick or tray-baked speculaas), a traditional feast of Saint Nicholas and winter treat, is the type of speculaas that is most commonly baked in the home because it doesn't require a lot of technique. It has no airs as the dough is just pushed out on a baking sheet and baked as it is – no fancy shape using a speculaas mold. The result is a chewy speculaas with a thin crusty edge and soft inside. You can push in the middle and it will spring back a little. It should never be fully baked, as it becomes dry: 15–20 minutes is enough to leave the inner crumb still moist. When cold, this speculaas becomes more crisp, yet baked correctly it will not turn dry, as usually it is long gone before it has a chance to dry out. A lot of bakers used to sell it as well, and some old-fashioned ones still do.

This is a family recipe for homemade thick speculaas from a man who has been a custodian of one of the oldest remaining authentic Belgian cafés. I wrote about him and his café, De Kat, in my book about this fragile Belgian heritage: *Belgian Café Culture*. Ever since he gave me this recipe, I have made this speculaas often, and it has become a firm favorite with friends and family.

Makes 1 large speculaas loaf

1 cup (250 g) unsalted butter, softened

1 ⅔ cups (330 g) brown sugar

2 ½ Tbsp (20 g) ground cinnamon

¼ tsp ground cloves or allspice

3 medium eggs, whisked

4 cups (500 g) all-purpose flour

Preheat the oven to 400°F. Do not use the fan setting. Line a baking sheet with parchment paper.

Put the butter and sugar in a large bowl or the bowl of an electric mixer fitted with the dough hook and knead on low speed or use a spatula to rub the butter into the sugar. Add the spices and the eggs, bit by bit, until fully incorporated, then start adding the flour a scoop at a time, kneading until well combined.

Pat the dough into a block. It should not be so sticky that it sticks to your hands, but try to avoid adding flour. Better use a wooden spatula or chill the dough if it is too sticky.

Place the dough block onto the baking sheet, push it out to a ¾- to 1-inch thickness, and bake as one large sheet. Or do as I prefer – divide the dough in half and make 2 smaller ones, so there are more crusty edges for everyone to enjoy, or you have one to give away.

Bake for 20–25 minutes and then cool on a wire rack. The edges will be slightly darker than the rest and will have tiny cracks, while the middle should spring back when pushed with a finger.

This is best eaten lukewarm with a cup of milk, cut into random wedges according to how peckish you are.

Keep in an airtight container.

Hasseltse speculaas

Hasseltse speculaas is a free-form soft speculaas with mild flavor that comes from the town of Hasselt. It is sold in large flat loaves or speculaas the size of the palm of an adult hand. What is distinctive about this speculaas is that it has fissures in its surface created by the baking soda. It isn't a Hasseltse speculaas without them and you can obtain the right kind of cracks only by resting the dough.

The bakery around the corner from my high school had many old-fashioned types of bakes that were harder to find in other bakeries, which usually pursued French pâtisserie. That bakery had plump apple and cherry *stroedel*, *appelflappen*, bread pudding, and also Hasseltse speculaas. I often bought one, which I snacked on during the day. Because it is just flavored with cinnamon and a tiny bit of ground cloves, it appeals to many people, and children too.

There are many stories about the origin of this speculaas, none of them true and none of them spectacular.

Makes 14–22 speculaas

1 ⅔ cups (325 g) dark brown sugar

¾ cup (175 g) unsalted butter, softened

1 medium egg

4 tsp (10 g) ground cinnamon

¼ tsp ground cloves or allspice

⅛ tsp sea salt

4 cups (500 g) white rye or all-purpose flour

1 tsp baking soda

3½ Tbsp whole milk

Whisk the sugar and butter in a large bowl or the bowl of an electric mixer fitted with the whisk attachment until creamy, then add the egg, spices, and salt and mix until well absorbed. Combine the flour and the baking soda and add them scoop by scoop until the mixture is well blended.

Knead until you get a smooth dough, cover, and set aside to rest in a cool place for at least 24 hours and up to 1 week. You can bake your speculaas immediately too, but you will not get the characteristic cracks in the finished cake.

Preheat the oven to 450°F. Do not use the fan setting.

Measure out 2-oz (55-g) chunks and roll them into balls (for 22 pieces), or make bigger ones if you prefer. Flatten the balls slightly into ovals and place them, with ample space left between, on a baking sheet lined with parchment paper, as they will flatten out as they bake. You will either need more than one sheet, or you can keep part of the dough for the next day.

Bake for 15–18 minutes until slightly darker around the edges, then leave them on a wire rack to cool. When cooled, store in an airtight container. Stale speculaas can be used in stews or as a crumble, or you can use it for Oost Vlaamse Vlaai (see page 158).

Speculaas stuffed with almond

Speculaas and almond are great flavor friends, and in this version they really shine. This type of speculaas stuffed with an almond filling is available only in the shops around the feast of Saint Nicholas, and while I was never a fan because it is quite sweet, my mother absolutely adores it, so we always had it in December. Baking it for this book and distributing the test bakes among friends, my husband's colleagues, and family, I discovered it is a massive crowd-pleaser, even with children.

Another way to use the dough and filling is to cut out two squares of thinly rolled-out speculaas dough, place some of the almond filling in the middle, wet the dough all around with milk, and place the second square of dough on top, crimping it so it doesn't open while baking. These are usually also decorated with blanched almonds on top.

Makes one 9-inch cake

1 ⅔ cups (325 g) dark brown sugar

¾ cup (175 g) unsalted butter, softened

1 medium egg

3½ Tbsp whole milk

4 tsp (10 g) ground cinnamon

¼ tsp ground cloves or allspice

⅛ tsp sea salt

1 tsp baking soda

4 cups (500 g) white rye or all-purpose flour

1 beaten egg + 1 Tbsp milk, for egg wash

blanched almonds, for decorating

For the almond filling
Use the filling recipe for Banketletter on page 215.

Use a 9-inch square tin, greased and lined with parchment paper. You will need to begin the day before baking.

Whisk the sugar with the butter until creamy. Add the egg and milk and work it into the butter and sugar mixture. Add the spices and the salt.

Mix the baking soda with the flour and sift into the mixture, then stir until completely incorporated. Knead until the dough is smooth and transfer to an airtight container. Set aside to rest overnight.

Meanwhile, make the almond filling as in the recipe for Banketletter on page 215 and set aside to rest overnight.

The next day, measure two-thirds of the dough and roll it out to fit your prepared tin with 1½ inches up the sides. Spoon in the almond filling and smooth it out, then roll out the rest of the dough and lay it on top of the filling. Crimp the edges all around as neatly as you can manage.

Preheat the oven to 350°F. Do not use the fan setting.

Brush the top with the egg wash, gently press the blanched almonds into the top of the cake in a design of your choosing, then brush all over again with the egg wash.

Place the cake in the middle of the oven and bake for 30–35 minutes until a skewer inserted comes out clean. Transfer to a wire rack to cool in the tin.

You can cut the speculaas into cubes or rectangular loaves. You can then cut away the sides, leaving the filling visible all around, which is how they are packed and sold in Belgium. The offcuts you can eat as a well-earned snack!

PRINTING THE DOUGH

People have always striven to create attractive shapes for food, be it with gelatin to make shaped jellies, by freezing cream to create molded ice cream or, the oldest method, printing dough in a carved piece of clay or wood. In the 13th-century Baghdad cookery book *Kitāb Al-ṭabīkh* is a recipe for *"samak wa-aqras,"* a confection of honey boiled with sugar, ground almonds, and starch flavored with rosewater and musk (nutmeg). It is then pressed in wooden carved molds shaped like fish.

They are called *koekplank, speculaasplank,* or *koekprent* (after "printing") in Dutch *natiolects*; *Mézeskalács ütőfák* in Hungarian; *Lebkuchenform* or *Springerleform* in German; gingerbread mold in English: in fact, many northern and eastern European cultures, and Russia, have a history of shaping dough into a carved wooden board. Yet it was in the Low Countries, and especially the Netherlands, that they were the most plentiful, as we can judge by the surviving old wooden molds and the fact that their use is still common today.

The image is produced by reverse-carving, which in printing techniques is called intaglio. The baker usually carved his own molds, but traveling craftsmen could be commissioned, and a few examples exist of master carvers. One, Wennink, even had a book of models a customer could choose from, and was a royal purveyor. In Belgium there was Cluyts in Antwerp and Eug Limbor "Fabricateur de formes en bois" (maker of wooden forms) in Liège. They each had their distinctive style: Cluyts especially carved Brabantse figures like *Sintegreef* (see page 127).

Fruit wood and elm were the best choices due to their sleek nature and strength, while larger carvings were usually made out of beech. A mold could be one-sided or two-sided, but long planks with a variety of small carvings existed too; these were called *kleingoed* (small goods) or *strooigoed* (throwing goods) and made small *speculaas* cookies (see page 252).

The deepest carvings are for making honey cakes such as the *couque de Dinant* (see page 243), Lebkuchen (see page 246) and *taai-taai* (see page 251) – the old-style *peperkoek* – from before butter came into the equation. Around the outer edge of the carving these molds have a metal rim to help cut through the tough dough.

Honey cakes are one of the oldest bakes in the history of humankind. The earliest depiction of a molded honey cake appears in the *Landauer Hausbuch*, in which a friar called Hanns Buel is depicted in a painting with an oven and his printed Nuremberger Lebkuchen. The book dates to around 1520.

Not one wooden honey cake mold from before the 17th century survives. A 15th-century item usually found around the mid-Rhine area has similarities with the carved honey cake molds. This is called a "form model," made of clay, and it has all the looks of an item used to print either dough or wax.[24] It might depict biblical scenes like the Lamb of God, or Judith beheading Holofernes, and well-known folk characters such as the knight, the lady, the fool, or the reaper, which correspond to later honey-cake wood carvings of the *stadhouder* (stadtholder: magistrate or ruler), his lady, and the fool in the Low Countries.

Saint Nicholas, however important he was to Low Countries culture, did not appear in his ecclesiastical robes and mitre on honey cake molds until the Saint Nicholas feast was experiencing its revival in the 19th century (see pages 205–209). During the Reformation the veneration of saint figures had been banned and so were Saint Nicholas–shaped cakes. Jan Steen, with his 17th-century *The Feast of Saint Nicholas* painting (see page 207) depicting a honey-cake figurine in the background donning a mitre, was daring at that time. The saint figure was, however, not considered absent by people of that time, merely in disguise. He was recognized in the carvings of a horseman.

The most-often occurring figures are the stadhouder of the Dutch Republic and King of England, Willem II of Orange (1626–1650), and Mary Stewart, each carved into a side of one wooden plank. Their only child, Willem III, also stadhouder, also reigned as King of England and also married a Mary, the daughter of Charles I of England. The link with England prompted the discovery of a rare and exquisite example of a royal couple honey cake carving in England, now owned by food historian Ivan Day. He also mentioned the existence of an English royal carving dating to the 19th century depicting William IV and Queen Adelaide.

I have spotted the stadhouder figures on paintings and engravings showing Saint Nicholas markets and events. In an engraving titled *December Sinterklaasavond* created by Jan Caspar Philips (1690–1775), a child is holding a print of the Prince of Orange in her hand. In the left corner of *The Market Stall* (1730) by Willem Van Mieris (1662–1747), you can spot a stadhouder print too. Hanging above it is a honey cake printed in the shape of a deer. In another one of Van Mieris's paintings, we peep into a shop selling vegetables, fish, and, strangely, a shelf of glimmering honey cakes decorated with gold leaf; and there is a stadhouder, a rider on a horse – usually also depicting Willem II – a couple of ladies, and some block peperkoek. The practice of gilding honey cakes, and in England gingerbread, was a joyful pastime for families around midwinter.

The return of the saint
In the 19th century we see Saint Nicholas and heart prints in a bakery window in a painting by Jan Hendrik Van Grootvelt (1808–1855), *Admiring Candy for the Feast of Saint Nicholas* (1841). Here the saint is back out in the open in his bishop's robes. Children and adults surround the window, in the darkness of a winter evening, with the light shining from the bay window full of sweets as if it was heaven opening its gates. From that same era is a painting of a 17th-century Saint Nicholas market by Petrus Van Schendel (1806–1870). Under the cloak of darkness, the painting titled *The Gingerbread Seller* shows us glistening gilded honey cakes being weighed by candlelight, and at the far edge we can just make out the stadhouder as the largest figurine.

Honey cake carvings are always ambiguous. Willem and Mary honey cake carvings depicted the royal couple wearing a crown, but the crown evolved to feathers and hats until their royal pedigree got lost in time and they became known as "the lovers." In the 19th century these two figures were still often carved in the same 17th-century fashion, showing there was a practice of repetition, keeping familiar honey cake figurines alive. The stadhouder (see page 239) is now often confused with a hunter when he has a dog by his legs, or as a soldier when the dog isn't present but a weapon is.

Another popular couple was the farmer and his wife, also called *Jan Klaassen en Katrijn*. They are often confused with the *Sintegreef* or "*Graaf van Halfvasten*" (Earl of Laetare Sunday, see page 127), who is often accompanied by his wife on the flipside. They can be recognized by their distinctively large noses. Their figures are far less elegant than that of the lovers, oddly resembling Punch and Judy. Sintegreef is the forerunner of the Prince of Carnival: he appears in Ypres, Brabant, and specifically in Antwerp, where a koek mold carver specialized in these figures, and in Halle where the tradition continued the longest.

Colonialism and war, too, featured in the carving of ships and what appears to be a figure picking cacao. Politics and religion weren't missing from the printed honey cakes either, and so we see Judith with the severed head of Holofernes, a rare carving symbolizing the defeat of Protestant heresy. To whatever played in society, the honey cake carvings replied. Other carvings are less cryptic and show the motto "Viva Oranje" to celebrate victory over the French, while others say "Away with Napoleon," often in combination with a carving of a man on a horse.

Then there are the more lighthearted carvings of hearts and fruit, a windmill, a coach and horses symbolizing marriage. Animals such as pigs, cows, roosters, and cats were common, and so were swans and peacocks. Professions such as the butcher, streetlamp-lighter, fruit picker, and a spinner appear frequently together on small goods boards. Innovations too were made into honey cake molds: the first hot-air balloon, zeppelin, bicycle, and the first car.

The fashion worn by most good carvings is always 17th century in Low Country honey cake molds, while in Hungary the fashion is classical 18th-century Austrian with tall wigs.

The significance of the shapes in which honey cakes were molded was a means of spreading and holding on to ideas, ideals, and traditions. Like the print coming out of a printing press, these honey cakes, or *Printen* as they are also called in German, were a form and a means of communication.

Flour and honey
The early dough was simply made of flour and honey, creating a sturdy paste that could easily be molded and that would retain its shape and carving sharply while being baked. These cakes were rock-hard and far from a pleasurable eating experience, but they were sweet and pretty. I believe they were treated as confectionery: people broke pieces off the cakes to suck on like on hard-boiled sweets. Today in Wallonia in Belgium,

this ancient form of honey cake remains alive in the *couque de Dinant* (see page 243). Intricately carved molds are used to print the dough, depicting the town, mythical creatures, images of daily life (albeit from a few centuries ago), fruit, flowers, and animals. The honey cakes depicting the town, its name also carved into the fruit wood, tell us these honey cakes were not sold to eat and be done with it. They will never have been cheap. This was a cake to treasure, to keep as a souvenir of the occasion. Bakeries in Dinant today have clear signs saying not to bite into their honey cakes because you will break your teeth. Instead, they tell you to soak the hard cookie in tea, coffee, or milk to soften it.

When the price of sugar became more affordable, honey was replaced or partly replaced with sugar, and later butter was added to make the honey cake much less hard and easier to eat. Adding fat to the dough will make the print come out less sharply during baking, so while these honey cakes were originally prized for their appearance and edibility, the availability of sugar and butter as well as rising agents such as potash made the honey cake evolve, and the wooden mold become obsolete.

The decline of the printed peperkoek
Printed honey cakes were part of daily life: a young man could show his intentions to a girl by giving her a honey cake or peperkoek; a girl carried one at the *kermis* (fairground) to show she was spoken for. In some areas, girls went to sleep with a gingerbread man under their pillow after the first day of the village fair in the hope that they would find a husband that year. Queen Elizabeth I of England is said to have had a gingerbread man made of each of her suitors so she could bite off their heads, emasculating them symbolically. A cake shaped like a man is a powerful symbol, as were the animals – reminding us of pagan sacrifice.

With the industrial revolution, rural customs started to fade. Yet the ban of the Saint Nicholas markets and the printed honey cakes connected to them was opposed fiercely and loudly, and Calvinists didn't manage to destroy the custom. This is why today we still have printed speculaas and peperkoek or honey cake at Saint Nicholas or Sinterklaas time.

Wooden molds were handed down by generations of bakers. Naturally they sometimes broke, became too shallow from years of use, or got infested with woodworm. Others were made redundant when bakers wanted to modernize. They either stopped producing the honey cakes and bought them in from large bakeries, or they bought a speculaas machine with steel molds that wouldn't break or wear with age, and reduced production time considerably. Many old wooden molds disappeared in the fireplace, their owner ignorant of their social historic and folk art value. As a prominent baker once told me when I showed him my collection of molds: "That old crap, I chucked mine in the bin." This is how culture is lost, when people fail to see its value when it no longer has a place in modern day and age, until so much is lost that people search it out again. The most beautiful and oldest wooden speculaas molds now go for hundreds of euros or dollars in antique stores.

Now that most bakeries are modernized, we once again value old-fashioned bakery interiors that haven't changed for decades on end. Here the seasons in baking are still visible: from September onward the Saint Martin and Saint Nicholas–shaped *mantepeirden* and *klaaskoeken* breads appear, followed by printed speculaas, tall and small, at the end of November. Pastry filled with almond in the shape of letters or Christmas wreaths and bread shaped like babies or *cougnou, duivekater,* and *vollaard* from December on, along with thin New Year's waffles in multiple guises to bring luck for the new year. The Three Kings cake appears on 6 January, followed by sausage breads and baked apples for Lost Monday. Then there are pancakes for Candlemas, and *oliebollen* and waffles for Shrove Tuesday and Carnival. Lent begins the day after prune *vlaai* and ends with breads studded with raisins at Easter. From then on the fairs, or *kermis,* come to town, with a variety of waffles, oliebollen, and vlaai until the summer ends and Saint Martin and Saint Nicholas are waiting around the corner again.

Couque de Dinant

The legend of the *couque de Dinant* takes us to the attack on the Walloon town of Dinant during the Liège Wars in 1466. Charles the Bold sent troops to crush the rebellion; they burned down Dinant and murdered eight hundred civilians. The townsfolk, deprived of food and desperate, made a dough of flour and honey and created a rock-hard honey cake. They then threw them at the Burgundian army to force a retreat. It was then that the people of Dinant got the idea to print the couque in their famous Dinanderie copperware before wooden molds were used. The couque de Dinant was from then on baked out of pride for the time the people of Dinant defended their town, and often printed with city views for people to buy as a souvenir.

It is a great legend, but is there any truth to it? The history of the Aachener Lebkuchen tells us that after the destruction of Dinant in 1466 by Charles the Bold, many copper workers or *Kupfermeisters* moved to the Aachen area, taking their culture for copperwork and their favorite couque de Dinant with them. This prompted a culture in copper and couque in Aachen. Aachen at that time did have a peperkoek culture, but it was the printing of the harder peperkoek that is believed by the bakers of Aachen to come from Dinantaise migrants. This means that couque de Dinant was alive before the Liège wars, but it most likely achieved importance thanks to the legend of the Dinantaise using their rock-hard couques as projectiles.

Printing the couque is done using a cutter with a rough silhouette of the wood carving. The dough is then placed over the carving and pressed in. Kneading and rolling out this dough requires elbow grease, so I'd keep this recipe for when you are very angry about something and need to get that anger out of your system: this is the ultimate stress ball. Just don't bite into the baked cake, as it's as hard as stone!

Makes several couques depending on the size of the mold (the recipe can be halved)

1 ⅓ cups (1 lb) runny honey

5 cups (600 g) white rye or all-purpose flour

rice flour, for dusting

Please note: This couque is hard as rock; do not bite into it. Break it into pieces and suck it like hard candy, or soften it by dunking it in a hot beverage. I repeat, **do not bite into this couque** because you will break a tooth. This book is not responsible for any tooth damage! Also, do not throw it at annoying people.

In a saucepan, warm the honey over low heat. When the liquid just appears to move inward (not bubble) around the edges, remove from the heat (if you have a sugar thermometer, it should be 175°F). Do not boil. Put the flour in a large bowl and make a well in the center, then pour in the hot honey and stir with a sturdy wooden spoon. When the dough is cool enough to handle, knead into a supple yet sturdy dough. The mixture will appear crumbly but will eventually come together by kneading it some more.

Preheat the oven to 500°F, or as hot as your oven goes. Do not use the fan setting. Line a baking sheet with parchment paper.

Roll out until ½–¾ inch thick and, if using a wooden mold, cut out roughly the shape of the illustration or the wooden board (you can trim the dough afterward). If you are not using a mold, cut out shapes with your favorite cookie cutter.

Dust the mold with rice flour, lay the piece of dough on top, and press it in with the palm of your hand to work it into the carving. Now roll over with a rolling pin to even the top. Then use your fingertips to gently release the dough from the mold around the sides first, then gently releasing it completely from the carving. Lay the couque on a baking sheet. Brush all over with water.

Bake for 10 minutes until golden with a brown blush, not golden brown. Keep an eye on it!

When baked, the couque is still bendy, but it will firm up. Brush again with water as soon as it comes out of the oven.

Couque de Rins

The *couque de Rins* is a honey cake variation of the *couque de Dinant*, with the addition of sugar to make the couque soft instead of rock-hard. The result is a sweet, chewy cake full of honey flavor.

It was invented by *couquier* François Rins in the 19th century, by mistake. He added sugar instead of honey, then added honey and cinnamon, trying to cover it up. I can't tell you how many origin stories of bakes resulted from "mistakes"! Today both types of couque are sold in Dinant. The couque de Rins is usually sold in stacks, tied together with a ribbon. This recipe is based on one I found tucked into one of my old cookery books.

Makes 15 large couque

¾ cup + 2 Tbsp (300 g) runny honey

½ cup (100 g) demerara (coarse raw) sugar

2 ¼ cups (270 g) all-purpose flour

½ tsp (3 g) potassium carbonate powder*

1 tsp ground cinnamon

* Potassium carbonate is sometimes sold as crystals, but you can crush them to powder using a mortar and pestle.

Start a day ahead of baking.

Heat the honey and sugar in a medium saucepan over low heat and remove from the heat just before it starts to boil, at the moment when the honey starts to move inward. (Boiling the honey will give it a bitter flavor.)

Put the flour, potassium carbonate, and cinnamon into a large bowl and make a well in the center, then pour in the hot honey mixture and stir with a sturdy wooden spoon. The dough will seem too runny but will firm up after a night's rest. Set aside to rest overnight.

Preheat the oven to 400°F. Do not use the fan setting. Line a baking sheet with parchment paper.

Scrape the dough out of the bowl and knead on a floured work surface until it is no longer crumbly and sticky.

Roll out until ¼ inch thick and use a 3-inch-diameter cutter to cut out rounds. Lay them on the baking sheet with ample space between them, as they will spread to 4 inches in diameter.

Bake for 10 minutes until golden, not golden brown. Transfer to a wire rack to cool, then keep in an airtight container for up to 3 weeks.

Lebkuchen and Printen

Lebkuchen and *Printen* are the most common German words for *koek* or *peperkoek*. The etymology is hard to pinpoint, and there are many theories. "Lebkuchen" is the general term, while the term "Printen" is used in Aachen and Ostbelgien. The word "Lebkuchen" has been in use since the 13th century, while Printen came into existence after the continental blockade, when imported honey and sugar cane could no longer get to Europe and sugar derived from sugar beets became the sweetener in the Aachener Printen. Before that time, bakeries baked their Lebkuchen the traditional way, with honey and cane sugar.

The fashion for baking thin rather than thick loaf Lebkuchen and printing the dough with carved wooden molds traveled to Aachen with Walloon migrants from Dinant after the Liège wars destroyed much of the Meuse city in 1466. For the whole legend, accepted by the people of Aachen as well as Dinant, see page 243.

Although "Printen" comes from "printing the dough," these spiced cakes usually come in round or rectangular shapes and around Christmas also in heart shapes decorated with icing. On rare occasions, the shapes of a *Printenmann* with decorations in nuts and candied fruits still appear, but the custom for printing koek remains the strongest in Belgium and the Netherlands.

There are a few regional differences in Lebkuchen, the Nuremberg one being the most famous, but the main ones are the *Honigkuchen, Braune Lebkuchen,* and *Elisenlebkuchen.* The first is a loaf peperkoek, but is more popular in Belgium and the Netherlands. Braune Lebkuchen are made of the sturdiest dough and yield a more compact Lebkuchen. These are available in a hard or softer (*Weichprinten*) variety, made with a higher fat content. The hard one is the one used for *Lebkuchenherzen* (hearts) and is considered more traditional. They are either left plain, brushed with a thin sugar glaze, or decorated with nuts. *Oblatenlebkuchen* are Lebkuchen baked onto "Oblaten," which are communion hosts, showing the monastic history of these cakes. The highest grade of Lebkuchen are the Elisenlebkuchen: the composition is outlined in the *Deutschen Lebensmittelbuchs*, saying they need

to consist of 25 percent almonds, hazelnuts, or walnuts and a maximum of 10 percent flour or 7.5 percent starch. Their composition, adding nut flour, makes these Lebkuchen much softer.

Unique to Lebkuchen is that they are also made covered in chocolate, which is something unseen in Belgium and the Netherlands, apart from chocolate-covered *kruidnoten* cookies. Decoration is rather muted these days, with nuts or candied fruits, but up until twenty years ago *Oblatenbild* were beautiful paper pictures that were stuck to the Lebkuchen in a fashion similar to the *patacons* baked into the *vollaard* (see page 67). Saint Nicholas was a popular figure for the plates, but so was the devilish Krampus (see the photograph above, bottom left corner). Secular images included Hansel and Gretel and greetings.

Ever since I was a little girl we traveled to Aachen for the Christmas fair each year. Without the scent and spiced flavor of dark chocolate–covered Printen in December, Christmas just doesn't feel like Christmas to me.

Makes 2 large and 12–24 smaller Printen

4 oz (100 g) rock candy (brown *kandij* sugar crystals; optional)

1 cup + 2 Tbsp (360 g) runny honey, sugar beet syrup, or glucose syrup

2 ½ cups (300 g) white rye flour

¾ cup (100 g) all-purpose flour

1 cup (100 g) almond flour

⅓ cup + 2 Tbsp (85 g) soft light brown sugar

¼ cup (35 g) candied citrus peel, finely chopped

1 tsp baking soda

1 tsp (5 g) potassium carbonate powder*

5 Tbsp (28 g) Lebkuchen Spice Mix (see below)

rice flour, for dusting

2 Tbsp milk, for brushing

* Potassium carbonate is sometimes sold as crystals, but you can crush them to powder using a mortar and pestle.

Lebkuchen Spice Mix
(You can make more than you need and store in an airtight container: this makes about 5 Tbsp/28 g in total.)

3 ½ tsp (10 g) ground aniseed

2 ½ tsp *each* of ground coriander and cinnamon

1 tsp *each* of ground cloves, allspice, cardamom, and nutmeg

You will need to make the dough 3 days before baking.

If using rock candy, crush the crystals in a mortar and pestle and set aside. You need to do this otherwise you will break a tooth. You can easily omit this ingredient and it will still be just as good, but it is traditionally used in this bake.

In a large saucepan, warm the honey or syrup over low heat, making sure it doesn't boil. When the liquid just appears to move inward (not bubble) around the edges, remove from the heat. (If you have a sugar thermometer, it should be 175°F/80°F.) Boiling the honey will give it a bitter flavor.

Add the flours, brown sugar, crushed candy (if using), candied peel, bicarbonate of soda, potassium, and spices and combine with a sturdy wooden spatula, then knead until you get a smooth yet sticky dough. When cold it will toughen up.

Let the dough rest in an airtight container for at least 3 days and up to a month to mature. Time will improve its flavor and texture and will also darken the dough (see the photograph on page 248 for a printed, unbaked piece of dough that has rested for a month).

Preheat the oven to 350°F. Do not use the fan setting. Line a baking sheet with parchment paper.

Knead the dough briefly to make it supple. Roll out the dough ¼–½ inch thick. Use the rice flour to flour the wooden mold if you have one. Turn it over and tap the back to remove the excess flour. Cut the dough approximately to the size of the picture carved into the mold; if the dough is sticky, flour it and then press it into the wooden mold. Roll over it with a rolling pin to smooth the surface. Now use the tips of your fingers to loosen the dough from the carving and lay it on the baking sheet. Trim off excess dough if needed. Alternatively, if you do not have a mold, cut out rectangles or other shapes and lay them on the baking sheet. The carving will not be super visible after baking, as that is only possible with doughs like couque de Dinant that use no leavening and, less so, taai-taai.

Brush the Lebkuchen all over with the milk for a nice sheen. Bake in the middle of the oven for 15–18 minutes. Rest on the sheet for a few minutes to firm up, then cool on a wire rack. When just baked they are quite hard, but they will become softer after a few days. These Lebkuchen can be kept for weeks in an airtight container.

Ideas to finish Lebkuchen or Printen, the German way

• Whole or halved blanched almonds completely covering the surface, or placed in a pattern.

• Candied cherries, or a mixture of candied cherries and almonds.

• Dark chocolate, or a combination with roasted hazelnuts.

• A thin coating of icing so they appear frozen.

Taai-taai

Taai-taai translates as "tough-tough" or "chewy-chewy," as these honey cakes are incredibly tough, though not as rock-hard as *couque de Dinant* (see page 243). A bakery manual from the 1950s has five recipes, all with different ratios of honey, sugar, and light and dark syrup. The dough is made in the traditional way, beginning with a mother dough of honey and rye flour, which is left to rest. The next day, or even weeks later, all the other ingredients – more flour, honey, syrup, leavening agent, and spices – have to be kneaded into the mother dough. This is very hard to do by hand: bakeries used to have kneaders that were operated by horsepower and later industrial kneaders. I've not had any good results making a mother dough at home because you cannot blend the dough well after it has rested and you don't want to break your electric mixer. That is why this recipe is made in one day, and then the whole dough is left to mature for a few days to weeks. There were bakers who started their dough as soon as the new harvest came in, leaving it to rest until Saint Nicholas, when these cakes are traditionally eaten and given as gifts.

Because the dough is so tough, these honey cakes are perfect for printing. In fact, wooden molds were fitted with a steel cutter surrounding the carving so the tough dough could be cut more easily.

Today taai-taai is mostly found in the Netherlands, though I have found that molds with metal rims were made by a company in Liège, showing we did bake them in recent times, but have come to favor *speculaas* instead. In Dinant, of course, the couque de Dinant lives on.

For several taai-taai, depending on the size of the mold

⅔ cup (225 g) runny honey

½ cup (100 g) light brown sugar

1 tsp ground aniseed

2 ⅓ cups (280 g) white rye flour

2 tsp baking soda

pinch of salt

rice flour, for dusting

1 egg, whisked, or milk for brushing

You will need to make the dough 3 days before baking.

In a saucepan, warm the honey, sugar, and aniseed over low heat. When the liquid just appears to move inward (not bubble) around the edges, remove from the heat (if you have a sugar thermometer, it should be 175°F.) Put the flour, baking soda, and salt in a large bowl and mix well. Make a well in the center, pour in the hot mixture, and stir with a sturdy wooden spoon. When the dough is cool enough to handle, knead into a supple yet sturdy dough. The mixture will appear crumbly at first but will eventually come together. Let the dough rest, covered, in a cool place for a minimum of 3 days.

On the day of baking.
Preheat the oven to 400°F. Do not use the fan setting. Line a baking sheet with parchment paper.

Knead the dough to make it supple, then roll it out ½–¾ inch thick and, if using a wooden mold, cut out roughly the shape of the illustration or the wooden board (you can trim the dough later).

Flour the mold with rice flour, lay the piece of dough on top, and press it in with the palm of your hand to work it into the carving. Now roll over with a rolling pin to even the top. Then use your fingertips to gently release the dough from the mold around the sides first, then gently releasing it completely from the carving. Trim off excess dough, if necessary.

If you are not using a mold, cut out shapes with your favorite cookie cutter, or use a piece of lace placed over your floured dough, pressing the design into the dough using a rolling pin.

Place on a baking sheet and brush all over with the egg or milk. Bake for 12 minutes until golden with a brown blush, not golden brown. Keep an eye on it! Let cool on a wire rack.

Speculaas cookies

Once butter came into the mix and sugar replaced honey, tough *peperkoek* and honey cakes like the *couque de Dinant*, *Lebkuchen*, *Printen* and *taai-taai* got a new sibling in *speculaas* or *speculatie* (*Spekulatius* in German). The origin of the name is unclear, but etymologists have two theories. One is that it comes from "speculum," being Latin for mirror-image, because the finished printed *koek* is the mirror image of the carved mold, which of course makes sense and explains why the word appears not just in Dutch but also in German texts. The other theory is that it comes from "speculator," an old word for bishop, referencing the fact that speculaas is a popular Saint Nicholas treat.

Speculaas or speculoos

Famous for speculaas at home and abroad, bakery Maison Dandoy was started in 1829, and they used a variation of the word speculatie or speculaas – *speculoos* – as in French. A century later another famous bakery, Lotus, launched their Speculoos, the first company to pack cookies individually for distribution in coffee houses and on airplanes. Today when speaking of speculaas, the cookie will contain spices that are more robust, but when speaking of Speculoos, we mean the Lotus cookie, which contains only cinnamon, getting its warm flavor from caramelizing sugar. The latter has taken over the world in recent years, rebranded as Biscoff, which created public outcry in Belgium where everyone had grown up with Lotus Speculoos.

The recipe here makes spiced speculaas, not speculoos. It is the closest I could get to my memory of the large printed speculaas we were given each year in school around Saint Nicholas time, usually after a trip to the Antwerp youth theater. I'd be the only child to take my whole speculaas home to show my parents, display it for a few days on the sideboard, and share it with them. The other children all ate theirs on the walk back to school. I was always terribly upset if mine broke before I got home. It felt like bad luck when that happened.

The more buttery and sugary a dough gets, the more satisfying it becomes to eat, but the more the print of a honey-cake mold fades. I have given you butter quantities that will result in a sharp imprint from the mold, but also for the more delicate variation and for a whole-grain speculaas.

Without a wooden mold

If you don't have a wooden speculaas or gingerbread mold, you can still make these cookies. Just use your favorite cookie cutter – hearts are always good – or a cookie stamp.

Variation: more butter, more delicate

When not using a mold or stamp, you can increase the amount of butter, which creates a more delicate speculaas, but one that won't keep an imprint well because it spreads out during baking. This type of speculaas is perfect for sandwiching between two slices of buttered bread, often dipped in coffee first, which is a tradition for breakfast in Belgium and also gave rise to Biscoff Speculoos spread.

Whole-grain speculaas

In Belgium a whole-grain speculaas is also available. Simply replace ¾ cup (100 g) of the all-purpose flour in the recipe with whole-grain rye, spelt, or wheat flour. If the flour is dry, you might need to add a splash of milk, if the dough really doesn't come together.

Makes 56 small speculaas using a 1½ x 2½-inch cutter, wooden mold, or stamp

11 Tbsp (160 g) unsalted butter, softened (when using a mold); or use 14 Tbsp (190 g) butter (when not using a mold) for more delicate speculaas

1 ¼ cups (250 g) dark brown sugar

½ tsp sea salt

2 Tbsp Speculaas Spice Mix (see below)

3 Tbsp whole milk

2 ⅔ cups (320 g) all-purpose flour or white rye flour

7 Tbsp (50 g) cornstarch

½ cup (50 g) almond meal

1 tsp baking soda

almond slivers (optional)

rice flour, for dusting a wooden mold, if using

Speculaas Spice Mix
(Makes more than you need, but keeps very well in a jar.)

2 Tbsp ground cinnamon

½ tsp ground cloves

¼ tsp *each* of ground ginger, nutmeg, coriander, allspice, mace, cardamom, long pepper (or the pepper you have)

Cream the butter with the brown sugar. Creaming cuts little air pockets into the fat, which is why this step is important and best achieved with an electric mixer. The mixture has to appear lighter in color than when you first started to beat it, and it will also become creamier as you go. People often don't take creaming far enough, but please do: you will be amazed if you wait a little and see how different the mixture looks.

Add the salt, speculaas spice mix, and the milk and combine well. Blend the flour with the cornstarch, almond meal, and baking soda and add it to the butter and sugar mixture bit by bit. Knead until well combined, which can take a while, and don't be alarmed if the dough seems dry and crumbly; it will come together into a smooth yet sturdy dough by kneading with your hands. You can use a mixer for the butter and sugar, but for the rest you need elbow grease. Wrap in plastic wrap and set aside in a cold place overnight or in the fridge for an hour (or up to 3 days if you have time).

Preheat the oven to 325°F. Do not use the fan setting. To give the cookies a nutty almond base, scatter almond slivers all over a baking sheet lined with parchment paper. This will also prevent the dough from spreading out, so it will keep its shape and imprint better.

Knead the rested dough to make it supple: if it is crumbly or dry, this means your sugar or flour were very dry, but just knead and it will come together.

Flour the mold with rice flour, lay a small piece of dough on top, and press it in with the palm of your hand to work it into the carving. Now roll over with a rolling pin to even the top. Then use your fingertips to gently release the dough from the mold around the sides first, then gently releasing it completely from the carving. Trim off any excess dough. Lay it on the baking sheet and repeat the process until you run out of dough.

If using a cookie cutter, roll out the dough to around ⅜ inch thick on a lightly floured work surface and cut out as many cookies as you can, gathering the offcuts and kneading them back together. Or use a piece of lace placed over your floured dough, then use a rolling pin to press the design into it. Rest the speculaas in the fridge for an hour: this will help them keep their shape.

Bake in the middle of the oven. Bake small speculaas for about 20 minutes and large for 20–25 minutes. As the dough is brown, it's hard to give a cue, but I find that they are best when the cookies are a darker brown around the edges.

The speculaas are bendy and soft when freshly baked but will quickly firm up. Small ones can be transferred to a wire rack immediately, but leave larger ones, especially figures, on the sheet to rest until firm to avoid decapitation or severing an arm.

When stored in an airtight cookie tin, speculaas keep for 3 weeks, so it makes sense to make loads and reap the benefits for many tea breaks to come.

A MEMORY OF FLAVOR AND SCENT

My mother always says that when I recall memories of my childhood they are always connected to food. I was three when I first tasted strawberries in Switzerland. I tasted them, then looked out of the window, and my dad was there, backlit; behind him a sea view and a large steamship that was passing on the horizon. The flavor memory encapsulated the memory of the view.

I was four when I absorbed the scent of paprika in a Hungarian village, where it was hung drying in strands on every white-painted house. That same scent I recognized in the *gulash* in the Czech Republic when I was five. That very year I had freshly fried thick-cut potato chips, heavily salted, in a pointy paper bag from a food cart by the Donau river in Budapest. My first encounter with chips.

My first nectarine came out of a brown-paper bag after a long walk on a summer day. I remember smelling the warm skin of the fruit, investigating the texture, and I can recall the bitterness of the magenta red stone as I was trying to get the last of the flesh from it.

Germany to me means an overload of thick cream and cherries in a choux pastry – a *Windbeutel* – in a tearoom where we took refuge after a snowstorm and what seemed like hours of walking across a frozen lake.

Christmas is the spiced scent and flavor of Lebkuchen, a tiny sip of *Glühwein*, cinnamon, greasy *Reibekuchen* and a red candy apple at the annual Christmas fair in Aachen or Cologne. And then there was England with its welcoming traditional food, the first time I had sweet baked tiny tomatoes on the vine, my first taste of fragrant Indian-inspired pub food, the wonders of a popadum, and the joys of handheld Cornish pasties after a swim in the Cornish sea.

I sought out these flavor memories. I asked my parents about places in Hungary or the Czech Republic we had visited before so I could taste what I remembered. Reliving a memory of flavor and scents felt deeply emotional, a bit like time travel, like your whole body can understand and recognize the memory of this flavor. There is also a soothing feeling that comes with flavors that stay the same, flavors you thought were lost

but are found again. A bakery that doesn't change its recipe gives you a piece of your childhood back with every sniff of the paper bag that holds the same sliced raisin loaf you had when you were a child, a teenager, a student, and now a grown woman wondering where time has gone.

I moved back to Antwerp and now I line up again in front of that same bakery I left behind, along with the city, sixteen years before.

We often take these scents and flavors for granted, and they are usually missed when they are gone. I didn't travel back to Hungary or the Czech Republic for more than twenty years; I moved away from the town with the bakery that bakes the best raisin bread. But recently when I visited Hungary I found the scent again in a jar of freshly ground paprika. It brought back those sandy roads and the hay cart that drove in front of us. The relentless heat of 1989, the apple my mother cut for me in the car with my grandmother's knife to provide refreshment. I remember its pearly white flesh, crisp red skin, and the strawberry-like flavor and scent.

Waffles

When I was growing up in Antwerp, there were distinctive scents in the air that defined the smell of the city for me. The first and most dominant was the scent of caramelizing sugar and a whiff of cinnamon from the waffle irons that turned out Liège waffles all day, every day. When exiting our majestic central station, onto the "Champs Élysées" of Antwerp, you would be greeted with this sweet scent, and by the time it had worn off and you reached the large Meir shopping street, the smell of the next waffle baker would greet you. The Meir is about six hundred yards long and used to house three or four waffle bakers. Their little shabby makeshift shops squeezed into small spaces that could just fit one human, a waffle iron, and a fridge to keep the waffle batter. These waffle shops were not at all nostalgic or authentic, but they were there for my formative years.

Every week in winter, autumn, and on chillier spring days I would go to town with my mother and we would buy ourselves a freshly baked Liège waffle: thick, yeasty, crisp on the outside, dotted with caramelized sugar nuggets and bits of bitter burnt caramel, and still doughy on the inside. This waffle was lunch, it was substantial, it was not a quick snack, you had to have an appetite to finish a whole one.

Somewhere in the mid-1990s my favorite waffle shop opened on the corner of the street that led to the Wild Sea area in town. They had room for at least twenty irons, some for Liège waffles, but also for *lacquemant* waffles, butter waffles, and Brussels waffles. Their dough was the best in the city, their caramelization ratio perfect, and it was an utter joy to bite into their waffle because they always hit the spot just right. Sadly, today the scent of Liège waffles has disappeared from Antwerp.

Koekestad

My parents are of an older generation and they remember the scent of Antwerp differently. My hometown is and was called the *koekestad*, or "cookie city," because the city wasn't only home to two large cookie factories, but also because the first scent that hit your nostrils when you got out of the train in Antwerp was the smell of freshly baked cookies.

Cookie factory De Beukelaer, founded in 1885 because they were fascinated by the English biscuit phenomenon, was situated next to the Central Station. The smell was distinctive enough in the area for my mum and dad to remember it vividly.

Cookie factory Cordemans, later Parein, occupied a dominant part of Antwerp South. For someone traveling to Antwerp at the time, the cookie factory with its tall chimneys must have seemed as imposing on the skyline as the cathedral. There used to be a beautiful Antwerp South Station near the cookie factory, so when people got off the train at South, they too would have been welcomed with the inviting scent of cookies.

Another sweet smell in Antwerp was the smell of chocolate. The first chocolate factory in Belgium opened in 1845 on the Dam, next to the train station. It is as if a marketing strategist carefully thought about the location of these cookie and chocolate factories so that visitors would be greeted with the smell of sweetness as soon as they arrived in Antwerp.

It appears that Antwerp always carried a sweet scent in the air. But as sugar refineries, cookie factories, and waffle trends left the city center, koekestad became the definition of the town.

PRACTICAL INFORMATION

GUIDE TO INGREDIENTS

The higher the protein content of your flour, the more elasticity your dough will have. Flour with a high protein content is therefore good for bread and other pastries that are supposed to be light or would benefit from a little elasticity. A flour with a lower protein content, like all-purpose flour, is good for cakes and cookies. Unlike white flour, whole-grain flour is brown because it is made from the entire grain and still contains bran. Cake flour and self-rising flour are never used in these recipes. Bleached flour should be avoided.

All-purpose flour – has around 10 g of protein per 100 g of flour (10%).

Bread flour – has around 12.5 g of protein per 100 g of flour (12–13%).

Rye flour – white rye flour has the brain and germ removed, while whole-grain, or dark, rye flour is milled from whole brown rye kernels, or berries.

Rye groats – are the whole, brown rye kernel. In this book broken groats are used, which is the kernel broken into smaller bits. They require scalding and soaking.

Rye bran – the hard outer layers of the cereal grain that are removed before grinding to create white flour but left intact for whole-grain flour. Bran looks like small flakes.

Buckwheat flour – a flour made from the grains of the buckwheat plant. It is not a wheat or cereal, and buckwheat contains no gluten.

Yeast – I prefer dry yeast because you can keep this handy in your larder, and I therefore also use instant dry yeast in the recipes in this book. If you prefer to use fresh yeast, use double the quantity of the dry yeast.

Water – the quantity of water given is for fresh flour; older flour might need a splash more water, while flour kept in a humid space will need less. Teach yourself to judge the dough and always wait before adding the last splash of water to see how the dough behaves.

Butter – always unsalted unless otherwise indicated, minimum 80% fat content.

Eggs – always medium, about 1¾ oz (50 g) weighed without shells (US large egg). If you can only get larger or smaller eggs, just use the equivalent weight instead.

Milk – always whole milk, organic preferable.

Cream – the recipes in this book were mainly tested with double cream, a British name for heavy cream with a fat content of at least 38%. In many countries heavy cream has a fat content of between 33% and 35%. Look carefully on the packaging, choose the fattiest, and stay away from light versions.

Brown sugar – in Belgium, this is sugar derived from sugar beets. It is heated and cooled until crystals appear, then those brown crystals are ground into brown sugar we call *kandij*. You can use any good-quality brown sugar, or seek out beet sugar from well-stocked markets or online.

Glucose syrup – can be bought from baking shops or online. You can substitute honey, though this will cost more, which is why bakeries use glucose.

Appelstroop – also known as apple butter or apple spread.

Apricot kernels – in the past, bitter almonds were used instead of almond flavoring. These almonds contain a toxin that can be harmful if you eat too many of them. Apricot kernels contain the same toxin, but to a much lesser extent, making them a good alternative. **Adhere strictly to the quantities in this book and do not eat the kernels without incorporating them into the bake. Do not eat the kernels like regular nuts. Label the jar and keep them out of the reach of small children and housemates who are looking for something to nibble.**

GUIDE TO MEASURING

In Europe, dry ingredients are measured by weight rather than by volume, as is customary in America. My original metric weights for dry ingredients are preserved in these recipes, alongside the cup or spoon measures, and a basic kitchen scale will let you measure out your ingredients more accurately, for better results. When using cup measures, be sure to use nesting cups for dry ingredients and level off with a knife. Do the same for spoon measures.

WAFFLE IRONS

While it would be great to use antique waffle irons, not everyone is an avid collector like me who owns these curiosities, and not everyone has the muscle to handle them. Here is a guide if you are excited to use the right waffle plate for the correct waffle. In Belgium having a waffle iron with more than one waffle plate is very common because, let's be honest, this is waffle country. Waffles are part of our identity.

The Brussels (or Flemish) waffle is made in a very deep waffle iron plate today, which can only really be used for this waffle. It can be made in a more shallow plate and be just as delicious, and that shallow plate then also works for other waffles, which means you can try out more recipes, so it is a good all-rounder.

It goes without saying that super-thin cookie-like waffles such as *lukken* and *oublies* cannot be made in a deep iron. You can use an ice-cream cone iron for these, or invest in one of the two irons listed here that allow you to swap the plates. They cost a little more (though not as much as professional ones), but are also much more versatile and you only need one machine.

I want to mention that none of the waffle iron brands have sponsored or contributed to the making of this book. I just want you to know what the best gear for home baking is, in my experience, so that your waffle iron will give you (and maybe your children) a lifetime of joy...and waffles.

FriFri waffle irons with interchangeable waffle plates are the 21st-century version of the Nova Electro waffle irons our parents and grandparents used in Belgium. The following plates have been used with the waffle iron FriFri WA102A - BMC2000.

Waffle plate 4x6 FriFri M001:
Deep iron, for thick Vlaamse, Brusselse, and Liukse waffles.

Waffle plate 4x7 FriFri M002 and 6x10 FriFri M003: Plain iron, creates a waffle with ½-inch thickness, for 16th- and 17th-century waffles, savory waffles, Regula's waffles; will also work for thinner Liukse, Vlaamse and Brusselse waffles.

Waffle plate thin FriFri M004:
Shallow iron for lukken, *Nieuwjaarsrolletjes*; will also work for *oublies, gaufres de Tournai, lacquemants.*

Waffle plate FriFri M007 (thinner than M004): Shallow iron for oublies, lacquemants.

Lagrange waffle irons with interchangeable waffle plates are a French brand that has been made since the 1950s. Today the iron still has quite a retro look. The following plates have been used with the Lagrange Waffle iron 039425.

Waffle plate 5x8 030122:
Plain iron, for 16th- and 17th-century waffles, savory waffles, Regula's waffles; will also work for thinner Liukse, Vlaamse, and Brusselse waffles.

Gaufrettes iron 030222:
Shallow iron for gaufres de Tournai (with a fantasy imprint as seen on page 57), lukken, and lacquemant.

And...
For historical-looking oublies: Nordicware Krumkaka iron (stovetop, not electric).

For wide-imprint lacquemant waffles, have a look for an inexpensive ice-cream cone iron; this will also work for the gaufre de Tournai, lukken, and lacquemant.

NOTES ABOUT DUTCH WORDS

A plural is generally formed by the addition of "-en" to a word, as in *krakeling* (one pretzel) or *krakelingen* (many pretzels); or *vlaai* (pie) and *vlaaien* (many pies). The suffix "-je" usually indicates a diminutive, as "-ette" would in French or English, e.g., *Nieuwjaarsrolletjes* (New Year's rollettes). Sometimes we also add "-ke" to a word as in *vlaai* (one large tart) or *vlaaikes* (small tartlets). To indicate that a recipe belongs to a particular town or place, we use the suffix "-se," in place of "-ese" or "-ian," as in *Diestse* (from Diest) or *Brugse* (from Bruges).

PEPERKOEK MOLDS

I know, I know, my collection of wooden *peperkoek* (or *speculaas*/Lebkuchen) molds is rather impressive. But just like for my antique waffle iron obsession, I am not expecting you to go and spend all your birthday cash on antique molds. However, if you search online, you can find many affordable simple wooden molds that will give you the satisfaction of printing dough. In fact, modern carved molds will yield a much better result as they are made for modern dough.

That said, it is absolutely not a requirement to buy a wooden peperkoek mold. You can just use a cookie cutter instead and make fun shapes. I am partial to hearts, as this is still very much a historical shape (though dinosaur-shaped speculaas will go down a treat with children). I want you to enjoy the recipes in this book. And while for some people this means the joy of adding to their collection of kitchen tools to play with, to others this is not as important and that is totally fine.

TABLEWARE USED IN THIS BOOK

As in my other books where I exclusively used British pottery, I wanted for this book to use only Belgian and Dutch pottery. I want to thank two iconic pottery manufacturers, Heinen Delfts Blauw from the Netherlands and Royal Boch from Belgium, for helping me achieve that. Furthermore, the immensely talented ceramicist Janah Van Cleven completely understood my vision and created many beautiful pieces that help tell the story in the book, combining the traditional Dutch and Belgian style with new techniques.

Heinen Delfts Blauw: *heinendelftsblauw.com*
Royal Boch: *royalboch.com*
Janah Van Cleven: *lovebirdceramics.com*

AN IMPORTANT WORD ON OVEN USE

Most updated domestic ovens these days have, as well as conventional top and bottom heat, a fan-assisted or convection function. I cannot stress this enough: avoid using the fan setting for baking. (If your oven is only fan, then reduce the temperature by 25°–50°F and reduce the cooking time by 5–8 minutes.)

My experience has taught me that baking on the fan setting is usually when home bakers get disappointing results. Even though I mentioned this in my earlier books, people continue to use the fan and then send me pictures of collapsed cakes and cakes with a burnt top and pale bottom. Fan-assisted or convection function creates an aggressive heat, which does wonderful things for the top of your mac 'n' cheese but terrible things for your cake or pie. I've decided to put "do not use the fan setting" in every instruction because many people don't read this practical information at the back of the book, or have read it and forgotten, which is understandable.

Another important thing to note: never take your oven's word for it when it comes to temperature. Buy an oven thermometer and be amazed about how variable the temperature of your oven can be. This is no big deal for mac 'n' cheese, but can mean the difference between a burnt or a perfect bake (mine is off by 20–40 degrees, often more, and that matters!).

I get many pictures of bakes with a burnt top because bakers have placed their bakes too high in the oven. It is important, it really is, to think about where your baking sheet goes. When a bake should go in the middle of your oven, this means the sheet goes lower. The top racks are for that mac 'n' cheese, not for your beautifully egg-washed loaf of bread or tart.

Remember, always keep an eye on the bake, and happy baking!

ACKNOWLEDGMENTS

A book like this cannot be made without the help and advice of several people. On a personal level, my thanks go to my husband, Bruno Vergauwen, for his endless support and the beautiful illustrations in this book and on the cover.

A big thank you also goes out to everyone at Murdoch Books, my main publisher since my debut book in 2016.

Then there are people I thank for their advice and expertise and sometimes even unique access. Thank you Liesbeth De Belie from KMSK Brussels and Frédéric Jonckheere from KMSK Antwerp for allowing me in the catacombs of the museum to study some of the important works of art in this book. To Erfgoed Bibliotheek Hendrik Conscience Antwerp, in particular Peter Rogiest. Thank you Andre Delcart for bringing me into contact with *patacon* artist Marie-Christine Meire, and Marie-Christine for sharing your knowledge.

Thank you Jack Knapen from Bakery Knapen for your advice and stories, and for teaching me how to dry pears the traditional way. To Jakob Druwé from bakery Broodhuis for teaching me to make *Geraardsbergse mattentaart*. Sylvie from pâtisserie Defossez in Dinant for showing me how to make *flamiche*. The brotherhoods of the Walloon tarts for allowing me to use their recipes to create my own: Confrérie du Lothier and Confrérie du Stofé de Wavre. To Gina Guth for teaching me US Belgian pies. To bakery De Duivekater for baking perfect Kroes *duivekaters* for the photos.

Thank you to Yohan Hautekeur from Firma Abel and Robert De Roover from Booms Frituur for their advice and stories about *oliebollen*, waffles, and other *kermis* sweets. Thank you to Pieter from Geutelingen De Koekelaere for the stories and advice on my recipe.

Thank you Chris Van Hese at Candico for showing me the sugar-refining process of *kandij* sugar.

Thanks to Belgian ceramic artist Janah Van Cleven for her pottery genius in creating some key pieces for the book that help tell the story. To Heinen Delfts Blauw and Royal Boch for sending me a few sets to play with, to truly make this a book with pottery exclusively from the region.

Thanks to Celia at Omnivore Books in San Francisco; Jorien and Richard at Luddites in Antwerp, and Cookbookbake in Brighton for their advice and support.

Finally, thank you to historian Dr Annie Gray for her general awesomeness, continual support, and her foreword.

WITH THANKS TO THE FOLLOWING ORGANIZATIONS FOR PERMITTING THE REPRODUCTION OF PAINTINGS FROM THEIR COLLECTIONS

Getty Images
Page 195 Still life with pastry crust, chicken, a pitcher, olives and bread, *Clara Peeters (1594–1657)*

KBC Antwerpen, Snijders & Rockoxhuis, Antwerpen
Pages 144–145 Spreekwoorden, *Pieter Bruegel II (the younger)*

KMSK Koninklijke Musea voor Schone Kunsten Antwerpen
Page 69 Aquarius, *Peter Snijers (1681–1752)*, (Inv.no. 5103), Collection KMSKA – Flemish Community

KMSKB Koninklijke Musea voor Schone Kunsten Brussels
Page 12 Het gevecht tussen Carnaval en Vasten, *Pieter Bruegel II (the younger)* (repro inv. 12045)
Page 66 Winterstilleven met pannenkoeken, wafels en duivekater, *Hans Francken* (repro inv. 3825) J. Geleyns – Art Photography

National Gallery of Art Washington
Page 197 Dishes with Oysters, Fruit, and Wine, *Osias Beert (1580–1624)* Open Access Policy

Rijksmuseum Amsterdam
Page 23 Het Kranenhoofd aan de Schelde te Antwerpen, *Sebastiaen Vrancx*
Page 112 Bakker Arent Oostwaard en zijn vrouw Catharina Keizerswaard, *Jan Havicksz. Steen*
Page 207 Het Sint-Nicolaasfeest, *Jan Havicksz. Steen*

SOURCES AND REFERENCES

SOURCES

1 Van Keymeulen, Jacques, *Het 'Vlaams', een taal of een misverstand?*, UGent Biblio, biblio.ugent.be/publication/6979123/ file/7102703.pdf

2 Gerlache Alain, in Plan B, episode 13, *Walen "Untermenschen"?*, 20/12/2019

3 Kockartz, Andreas, in Plan B, episode 9, *De Laatste Belgen*, 22/11/2019

4 Thijs, Alfons K L, *De geschiedenis van de suikernijverheid te Antwerpen (16de–19de eeuw) : een terreinverkenning, in Bijdragen tot de geschiedenis*, 1979

5 Van der Wee, Herman, *The growth of the Antwerp market and the European Economy (fourteenth-sixteenth centuries)*, Vol II, 1963

6 Derycke, Ivan (ed), in *Antwerpen Bierstad - acht eeuwen biercultuur*, 2011

7 Goldstein, Claudia, *Pieter Bruegel and the Culture of the Early Modern Dinner Party*, 2013

8 Poelwijk, Arjan, *"In diensten vant Suyckerbacken" De Antwerpse suikernijverheid en haar ondernemers 1580–1630*, 2003: quoted from Von Lippman, E O, from *Geschichte des Zuckers seit dem ältesten zeiten...*, 1970 (original 1929)

9 Ramsay, George Daniel, *The Queen's Merchants and the Revolt of the Netherlands: The End of the Antwerp Mart*, Volume 2, Manchester University Press, 1986

10 National Geographic, *New York World's Fair*, April 1965

11 Thiele, Ernst, *Waffeleisen und Waffelgebäcke in Mitteleuropa*, 1959

12 Anon, *Cockbouck*, EHC B 79834, c. 1580, and transcription in: *Een Antwerps kookboek voor Leckertonghen*, Braekman, Willy, 1995

13 Anon, Ordinances concerning Duivekater, Amsterdam City Archive: A06903000086, A06903000087, A14782000051, A14786000111, A14786000132

14 Anon, *Ordinance no. 119*, 22 December 1698, City Archives Namur, Belgium, as mentioned in, Brouwers P-P (ed.), *Cartulaire de la commune de Namur, Part 6: 1692–1792*, 1924

15 Bert, Louis, *Rond den Heerd*, Brugge, 1879

16 Van Vaernewyck Marcus, *De historie van België*, 1829

17 Van Waesberghe, Ioannis, *Gerardi Montium sive altera imperialis Flandriae metropolis eiusque Castellanian*, Brussels, 1627

18 De Leeuw, B, De Wilde, P, en Verbeke, K, o.l.v. Deprez, A, *De briefwisseling van Guido Gezelle met de Engelsen 1854–1899*, KANTL, 3 delen, Gent, 1991

19 Kouwenhoven, John, A, *The Columbia Historical Portrait of New York*, 1953: quoted in: ACG 52, 1995, Rose, Peter G, *Dutch Colonial foodways*

20 *Brabantsche Mattentaarten*, De Volksstem, Kookkunst, 8 August 1896

21 Hennepin, Nicholas, *A New Discovery of a Vast Country in America, Extending Above Four Thousand Miles, Between New France and New Mexico*, London, 1699

22 Van der Ven, Dirk Jan, *Feestbrood in midwinter*, Libellon serie n° 204, 1936

23 Anon, *Compendium medicinale*, Reyner Oesterhusen, Doctor of Deventer, Holland, c. 1500, British Library, MS SLOANE 345

24 Weiner, Piroska, *Carved Honeycake Molds*, 1981

REFERENCES

Academie voor de Streekgebonden Gastro-nomie (ASG) no. 50–51, Sept 1995; no. 2, April 1996

Aerts, Erik, Daeleman, Paul, de Keukeleire, Denis, *Antwerpen Bierstad, acht eeuwen biercultuur*, 2011

al Tabikh, Kitâb & b.al-Hasan b, Muhammad & b.al-Karîm, Muhammad, Perry, Charles, (tr.) *A Baghdad Cookery Book, al-Baghdadi*, 2005, original: *MS Ayasofya 3710* in the Süleymaniye Library

Anon, *Brabants kookboek*, EHC 744810, c. 1651–1700, and transcription in *Brusselse recepten uit Antwerpen*: Ferro, R N (ed), Terroir: mededelingsblad en verzamelde opstellen / ASG jg. 30, no. 4, 2014-2015

Anon, *De Amsterdamsche banket-bakker*, Volume 1, 1866

Anon, *De hoofsche pasteybacker*, In: *De verstandige huyshouder*, Amsterdam 1669. Transcription by: Willebrands, Marleen

Anon, *De mey-blom of de zomer-spruyt*, Amsterdam, ca 1734: digital at dbnl.org

Anon, *De Verstandige Kok ofte sorghvuldighe Huys-houdster*, Antwerpen, 1668, 1671 & 1805

Anon, *De volmaakte Hollandsche keuken-meid*, Amsterdam, 1772, 1746 & 1838

Anon, *Den verstandigen hovenier*, Den verstandigen kock, Antwerpen 1685

Anon, *Den verstandigen kok*, Gent, 1781

Anon, *Den volmaecten cocke: keukenboeck der oud vermaerde abdije van Affligem bij Aelst...*, c. 1700–1800, Ockeley, Jaak (ed. & tr.) in no. 32 'Ascania-Bibliotheek', 1975

Anon, *Derden placcaet-boeck van Vlaenderen, inhoudende de placcaeten, ordonnancien, reglementen, tractaeten, alliancien, ende andere...*, Volume 2, 1685

Anon, *Een notabel boecxken van cokeryen*, 1510, plus new edition edited by R Jansen-Sieben, Marleen Willebrands, De Kan, 1994

Anon, *Handboekje voor koek- en banketbakkers, benevens konfituriers, als ook koks en keukenmeiden*, 1840

Anon, *Koock en geback boeck*, c. 1704 in *Dit te saamen lustig geklopt*, 2011

Anon, *Le Ménagier de Paris*, and translation in: *The Good Wife's Guide: A Medieval Household Book*, Greco, Gina L. (tr), Rose, Christine, M. (tr), and recipe translation by Dr. Annie Gray in *Food for Thought*, Macmillan 2020

Anon, *Lodge's Wit's Miserie, or the World's Madnesse*, 1596

Anon, St. Bartholomew, from the *Hours of Catherine of Cleves*, Utrecht, The Netherlands, c. 1440. Morgan Library, New York: MS M.917/945, pp. 228–229

Anon, *Schatkamer, der nederduytische en francoysche tale begrypende*, Rotterdam, 1654

Anon, *Selected receipts of a Van Rensselaer Family*, 1785-1835, Historic Cherry Hill, 1976

Ansion, Frédéric, *Binche au fil de l'Histoire*, Editions Luc Pire, 2014

Athenaeus, *The Deipnosophists. Or Banquet Of The Learned Of Athenaeus*, London,1854

Baedeker, K, *Belgique et Hollande*, 1888, 1891

Baillien, Marie-Sophie, *Perceptie van België door jonge Walen (NLM1 en ALM1) en Vlamingen (FLM1) in 2020: Stereotypen, identiteitsgevoel, nationalisme en toekomstbeeld*, Université de Liège (Tom Lanoye quote)

Barella, Madame, *Manuel de Cuisine et de Pâtisserie*, Bruxelles, 1903

Barnes, Donna R, and Rose, Peter G, *Matters of Taste: Food and Drink in Seventeenth-century Dutch Art and Life*, 2002

Barneveld, D, *De oude banketbakkerij*, 1968

Battus, Carolus, *Medecynboek & coc-boeck*, 1593, *Het secreet-boek vol heerlijke konsten*, 1609 & 1694, and transcriptions of Christianne Muusers en Marleen Willebrands in *Het excellente kookboek van doctor Carolus Battus uit 1593*, 2020, and ASG 9, no. 37, 1991

Bellens, Tim, *Antwerpen: een archeologische kijk op het ontstaan van de stad*, 2020

Berends, R, en Werkgroep Deventer OVT: *Tijd van steden en staten: 1000-1500*, 2005.

Berends, René, *De geschiedenis van Deventer Koekbakkers*, Het gilde der koekbakkers, 2013

Bicker-Raye, Jacob, *Het dagboek van Jacob Bicker Raye 1732-1772* (eds. F Beijerinck en M G de Boer). H J Paris, Amsterdam, 1935

Blankaart, Steven, *De Borgerlyke Tafel, Om Lang Gesond Sonder Ziekten te Leven*, 1683

Borella, S P, & Harris, H G, *All About Pastries*, 1900

Braekman, Willy, *Een Antwerps kookboek voor 'Leckertonghen'*, 1995

Braekman, Willy, *Medische en technische middelnederlandse recepten*, Gent: KANTL, 1975

Braekman, Willy, *Een nieuw Zuidnederlands kookboek uit de vijftiende eeuw*, Brussels: 1986, and online transcription: Muusers, Christiane, *The convolute Ghent KANTL 15*, coquinaria.nl/

Brantegem, Herman, *Doods, Begrafenis- en Rouwgebruiken te Okegem*, Tijdschrift Hobonia, November 25, 2020

Bruylant, Emile, *Biographie Nationale de Belgique*, Tome 21ème, Brussel, 1911

Burema, Dr L, *De voeding in Nederland van de Middeleeuwen tot de twintigste eeuw*, Assen 1953

Caesar, Julius, *De Bello Gallico*, Book I

Cauderlier Philippe Edouard, *Het Spaarzame Keukenboek*, 1930

Cauderlier Philippe Edouard, *Gebak en confituren*, 1905

Chomel, M Noel, *Huishoudelyk woordboek*, 1743

Chong, Alan & Kloek, Wouter, *Still-life Paintings from the Netherlands 1550–1720*, 1999

Colinette, Tante, *Le Guide de la Ménagèrie*, 1917

Crowen, T J, *Mrs. Crowen's American Lady's Cookery Book*, New York 1847, *American Lady's System of Cookery*, New York, 1860,

Davelaar, R, *Schriftelijke opleiding van*

H H broodbakkers in de banketbakkerij, c. 1927

Davidson, Alan, *Oxford Companion to Food*, 1999

d'Huyvetter C, de Longie, B and Eeman, M, met medewerking van Linters, A, *Inventaris van het cultuurbezit in België*, 1978

de Boerin, *Maandschrift van den Belgischen Boerinnenbond*, 1929

de Boerinnenbond, *Ons Kookboek*, 1954

de Brune, Johan, *Emblemata of zinne-werck ...*, Amsterdam, 1624

de Casteau, Master Lancelot, *Ouverture de Cuisine*, translation based on transcription by Thomas Gloning, 2011, 2012 Daniel Myers

de Gouy, Jan *De burgerskeuken en pasteibakkerij in ieders bereik*, 1924

de Longé, G, *Coutumes de la ville d'Anvers*, vol 3, as mentioned in Goldstein, Claudia, *Pieter Bruegel and the Culture of the Early Modern Dinner Party*, 2013

de Puydt, Hendrik, *Den wonderbaren leeraar en uitlegger van den bakkersstiel*, Gent, 1898

de Telegraaf, *Amsterdamse Koeketers*, 4 april 1937

de Volksstem, 1895, 1 maart 1895

de Volksstem, 1900, 1 september 1900

de Volksstem, 4 juni 1898

de Vries, Marleen, *De Boekenwereld*, Jaargang 31, 2015

Deutsches Lebensmittelbuch, bmel.de

Devriend, K.L. (INL.) - *Naar hoger melkverbruik. Een keuze van recepten voor melkdranken, keukengerechten en gebak bereid met melk en zuivelprodukten.*

Dodoens, Rembert, *Cruydeboeck*, Antwerp, 1554

Ehlert, Trude, *Küchenmeisterei: Edition, Übersetzung und Kommentar...*, 2010, first published 1485

Erasmus, Desiderius, *The Colloquies of Erasmus*, Volume 1 & 2, London, 1878

Evelyn, John, *The Diary of John Evelyn*, E S de Beer (ed), 1959

Fagel, R, *The Origins of the Spanish Fury at Antwerp (1576): A Battle Within City Walls. Early Modern Low Countries*, 4, 2020

Ferro, R.N. (ed.), *De recepten van Bakkerij Soecker Alkmaar 1782*, ACG, Terroir no. 135, 2019

Gessler, J (ed), *De bouc vanden ambachten*, 1371, as published in: *Het Brugsche Livre des mestiers en zijn navolgelingen*, Brugge 1931

Grimbergen, E M, *De volmaakte Hollandsche keukenmeid*, 1931, & *De volmaakte Vlaamsche keukenmeid*, 1931

Grimm, Jacob and Wilhelm, *German dictionary*, Leipzig 1854–1961, Volume 12, Col. 467, sv 'Lebkuchen'

Guicciardini, Lodovico, Petrus Montanus (ed), *Beschrijvinghe van alle de Neder-landen*, Cornelis Kiliaan (tr), 1979, facsimile from 1612

Haagsche Post, 5 April 1924, *Amsterdamse Koeketers*

Hamer-Uitgave voor de Volksche Werkgemeenschap, December 1940

Hemminga, *Koock ende huyshoudt boeck : receptenboek van Hemminga*, Ferro, R N (ed), ASG 47, no. 3, November 1995

Henderson, George and Dele, Olasiji, Thompson, *Migrants, Immigrants, and Slaves: Racial and Ethnic Groups in America*, 1995

Het Liers Vlaaikesboek, Stadsmuseum Lier, 2018

Hochstrasser, Julie Berger, *Still life and trade in the Dutch Golden Age*, 2007

Huis van Alijn, *Sinterklaasintrede, bavikhove*, 1949, object VI-0007-0001

Irving, Washington, *The History of Old New York*, 1809

Jansen, H P H, *Lexicon Geschiedenis der Lage Landen*, 1983

Jansen-Sieben, Ria and van Winter, Johanna Maria, *HS 476 UB Gent* in *De keuken van de late middeleeuwen. Een kookboek uit de lage landen*, 1989

Janssens, Paul; Zeischka, Siger, *La noblesse à table: des Ducs de Bourgogne aux rois des Belges (The dining nobility : from the Burgundian Dukes to the Belgian royalty)*, 2008

Kalm, Pehr, *Travels Into North America: Containing Its Natural History*, Volume 2, T Lowndes, 1771

Keijser, Paula, *Suikerriet, suikerverdriet: slavernij in enkele 18e-eeuwse teksten*, 1985

Kiliaan, Cornelis, *Etymologicum Teutonicae Linguae*, Antwerpen, 1599 (1ste druk)

Kittelberger, Karl F, *Lebkuchen und Aachener Printen. Geschichte eines höchst sonderbaren Gebäcks*, 1988

Klingshirn, William E, *Caesarius of Arles: The Making of a Christian Community in Late Antique Gaul*, 1994

Knight, Christine, *Deep-frying the nation:*

Communicating about Scottish food and nutrition, Food and Communication: Proceedings of the Oxford Symposium on Food, 2015

Kreis, Soest, *Mitteilung der schule Eineckerholsen*, 1949, quoted in, Thiele, Ernst, *Waffeleisen und Waffelgebäcke in Mitteleuropa*, 1959

Lambrecht, Joos, *Nederlandsche Spellijnghe*, Gent, 1550, facsimmile by Heremans, Jacob and van der Haeghen, Ferdinand, 1882

Le Dictionnaire de l'Académie françoise dedié au Roy (1st edition), Paris, 1694

Le Graive, Emile, *Le Patissier Royal Belge*, 1912

Leslie, Eliza, *Seventy-Five Receipts for Pastry, Cakes, and Sweetmeats By A Lady of Philadelphia*, Boston, 1828

Leufkens, H, *Mooi Zuid-Limburg I en II*, 1937

Löhr, J. A. Christian, *Voorvallen en merkwaardigheden uit het leven den kleinen Andries*, Amsterdam, 1821

Loofft, Marcus, *Niedersächsisches Koch-buch*, 1766

Magirus Antonius, *Koocboec oft familieren Keukenboec*, 1612, in Sels, Hilde and Willebrands, Marleen: *Lieve schat, wat vind je lekker?*, 2007

Magirus, Antonius, *Koock-Boeck ofte familieren Keuken-Boeck*, Leuven, c. 1612

Manden, A.C., *Recepten van de Haagsche kookschool*, 1896

Mariani, John F, *Encyclopedia of American Food and Drink*, New York, 1999

Marks, Gil, *Encyclopedia of Jewish Food*, 2010

Martino, Maestro, *Libro de Arte Coquinaria* (The Art of Cooking) ca.1465, Scans at Washington Library of Congress

Martino, Maestro, *The art of cooking : the first modern cookery book, composed by The Eminent Maestro Martino of Como*; Luigi Ballerini (ed), Jeremy Parzen (trans), 2005

Monaghan, Tom, *Renaissance, Reformation and the Age of Discovery, 1450–1700*, 2002

Moore, Clement Clarke, *Twas the night before Christmas*, 1823

Nannings, J H, *Brooden gebakvormen en hunne Beteekenis in de Folklore*, 1932

Niermeyer, A, *Verhandeling over het Booze wezen in het bijgeloof onzer natie*, 1840

Nieuwland, Petrus, *De bespookte waereld ontspookt*, 's-Gravenhage, 1766

Nuremberg City Library, Solg.Ms. 25.2°, f. 12r

Ortelius, Abraham, *Theatre oft Toonneel des aerdt-bodems...*, Antwerp, 1571–1584

Perckmans, Frans, *Sinte Mette*, 1949

Pohl, Hans, *Die Portugiesen in Antwerpen (1567–1648): zur Geschichte einer Minderheit*, 1977

Pohl, Hans, *Die Zuckereinfuhr nach Antwerpen durch Portugiesische Kaufleute während des 80jährigen Krieges*, in *Jahrbuch fur die Geschichte von Staat, Wirtshaft und Gesellschaft Lateinamerikas IV*, 1967

Reisig, J H, *De suikerraffinadeur; of Volledige beschrijving van het suiker, deszelfs aankweking, bereiding en verzending*, Dordrecht, 1793

Rodríguez, Domingos, *Arte De Cozinha*, 1680

Rose, Peter G, *Food, Drink and Celebrations of the Hudson Valley Dutch*, 2009

Rowley, Anthony, *Une histoire mondiale de la table: Stratégies de bouche*, 2009

Sceperus, Jacobus, *Geschenk, op geseijde [zogenaamde] St. Nicolaes Avont*, Gouda, 1658

Schilstra, J. J, *Prenten in hout. Speculaas, taai- en dragantvormen in Nederland*, 1985

Scholliers, Peter, *Buitenshuis eten in de Lage landen sinds 1800*, 2002

Scully, Terence, *The Viandier of Taillevent*, 1988

Serrure, C A, *Keukenboek, uitgegeven naar een handschrift der vijftiende eeuw*, Maatsch. Der Vlaemsche Bibliophilen, Gent, 1872

Sharpe's London Magazine, Volume 1, 1846,

Sleeckx Domien, *Kronyken der straten van Antwerpen*, Deel 2, 1843

Spillemans, Adriaen, *Beschrijving van Cornelis van Zele*, Stadsarchief Antwerpen (SAA), T1317, fol. 32

Stroobants, Aimé, *Patacons uit het Dendermonde*, 1992

Sweers, Erik, *Van Sunderum tot klozum: sinterklaas op de wadden*, historien.nl

Sys Annelien, Segers, *De geheimen van de mattentaart*, Centrum Agrarische Geschiedenis (CAG)

Ter Gouw, Jan, *De volksvermaken*, 1871

Teyras, J B, *De Hollandsche banketbakker, of De kunst van banketbakker, likeurstoker en...*, 's-Gravenhage, 1830

The Bredasche Courant, 28 September 1917

Thijm, Jozef Alberdingk, *St Niklaasgoed*, 1850

Tijdschrift voor Nederlandse Taalen Letterkunde, Jaargang 101(1985)

Van den Bergh, Laurens Philippe Charles, *Nederlandsche volksoverleveringen en godenleer*, 1839

Van Berkhey, J le Francq, *Natuurlyke historie van Holland*. Deel 3, 1772-1776

Van den Brenk, Gerrit, *'t Zaamenspraaken tusschen een mevrouw, en een banket-bakker en Confiturier., banket-bakker en Confiturier te Amsterdam*, 1758

Van der Donck, Adriaen, *Descriptions of the New Netherlands*, 1655, 2008

Van der Ven, Dirk Jan, *Ons eigen volk in het feestelijk jaar*, 1942; *Friese volksgebruiken weerspiegeld in Europese folklore*, 1972

Van Loon, Gerard, *Antwerpsch chronykje, in het welk zeer veele en elders te vergeefsch gezogte geschiedenissen sedert den jare 1500 tot het jaar 1574 zoo in die toen vermaarde koopstad als de andere steden van Nederland*, 1743

Van Poolsum, Jacob, *Groot placaatboek vervattende alle de placaten, ordonnantien en edicten, der...Staten's lands van Utrecht*, Vol III, 1729

Verbeke, Eleonora, *Winckelboeck HS*, Sint-Janshospitaal, Brugge,1751

Verhaegen, George H M J, *Rationeele broodvoorziening in Nederland*, 1942

Volkskunde, jr no. 120, Jan–April, 2019 photo *Sinterklaasintrede c. 1900*, J. C van Nuenen Nationaal Archief, Collectie Spaarnestad

Vorselman, Gheeraert, *Eenen nyeuwen coock boeck*, 1560, facs. 1971, Cockx-Indestege, Elly (ed)

Wannée, C J, and Baere-Rovers, A G, *Kookboek van de Amsterdamsche Huishoudschool*

Wiesner, Merry E, *Working Women in Renaissance Germany*, 1986

Wolthuis, J, Vragen van den dag; Maandschrift voor Nederland en koloniën,..., *Amsterdamsche woorden*, 1919

Wyts, Margareta, *De recepten van Margareta Wyts (1575/6–1615) kookkunst uit de tachtigjarige oorlog*, ACG, Terroir, 2013, vol. 118

INDEX

weldon**owen**

an imprint of Insight Editions
800 A Street, San Rafael, CA 94901
www.weldonowen.com

First published in English by Murdoch Books
Copyright © Murdoch Books, an imprint of Allen & Unwin 2022

Text, design, styling and photography copyright © Regula Ysewijn, 2022
Illustrations and cover copyright © Bruno Vergauwen

ISBN: 978 1 68188 854 5

Library of Congress Cataloging-in-Publication data is available.

Printed and bound in China by C&C Printing Ltd.

The paper in this book is FSC® certified.
FSC® promotes environmentally responsible,
socially beneficial and economically viable
management of the world's forests.

Every reasonable effort has been made to trace the owners of copyright
materials in this book, but in some instances this has proven impossible.
The author(s) and publisher will be glad to receive information leading to
more complete acknowledgments in subsequent printings of the book and
in the meantime extend their apologies for any omissions.

*The publishers acknowledge that they meet and work on the traditional lands
of the Cammeraygal people of the Eora Nation and pay their respects to their
elders past, present and future.*

**Typeset in Garamond, a late Renaissance font designed by Claude
Garamond which was hugely influential in the Low Countries and
used by Antwerpian Christoffel Plantin in the 16th century.**